X-MEN

WITH GREAT POWER

It's been a long, hard road for the X-Men of late, having fought a number of big battles, most recently repelling an all-out attack from legions of vampires led by Dracula's son, Xarus. Cyclops was forced to take drastic measures, including resurrecting Dracula from the dead to help fight Xarus and temporarily dampening Wolverine's healing power without his knowledge, allowing him to be turned into a vampire and then returned to health at a strategic moment in battle. With Xarus now defeated, a shaky truce made with Dracula and Wolverine recovered from his bout of vampirism, Cyclops turns his eyes to the future to determine the next step for the X-Men.

WRITER
VICTOR GISCHLER

PENCILERS
CHRIS BACHALO (ISSUES #7-10) WITH PACO MEDINA (ISSUE #10) AND **AL BARRIONUEVO** (ISSUE #11)

INKERS
TIM TOWNSEND, WAYNE FAUCHER, JAIME MENDOZA, AL VEY & JUAN VLASCO (ISSUES #7-10) AND **MICHEL LACOMBE** (ISSUE #11)

COLORISTS
CHRIS BACHALO (ISSUES #7-9), **ANTONIO FABELA** WITH **JIM CHARALAMPIDIS** (ISSUE #10) AND **RAIN BEREDO** (ISSUE #11)

LETTERER
VC'S JOE CARAMAGNA

COVER ART
TERRY DODSON & RACHEL DODSON (ISSUES #7-10) AND **DAVID YARDIN** (ISSUE #11)

ASSOCIATE EDITOR
DANIEL KETCHUM

EDITOR

COLLECTION EDITOR: JENNIFER GRÜNWALD • EDITORIAL ASSISTANTS: JAMES EMMETT & JOE HO … SON RIBEIRO
EDITOR, SPECIAL PROJECTS: MARK D. BEAZLEY • SENIOR EDITOR, SPECIAL PROJECTS: JEFF Y… GABRIEL
SVP OF BRAND PANNING & COMMUNICATIONS: MICHAEL PASCIU…
EDITOR IN CHIEF: AXEL ALONSO • CHIEF CREATIVE OFFICER: JOE QUESADA • PUBLISH… EXECUTIVE PRODUCER: ALAN FINE

-MEN: WITH GREAT POWER. Contains material originally published in magazine form as X-MEN #7-11. First printing 2011. Hardcover ISBN# 978-0-7851-4848-7. Softcover ISBN# 978-0-7851-4849-4. Published by ARVEL WORLDWIDE, INC., a subsidiary of MARVEL ENTERTAINMENT, LLC. OFFICE OF PUBLICATION: 135 West 50th Street, New York, NY 10020.

Printed in the U.S.A. ALAN FINE, EVP - Office of the President, Marvel Worldwide, Inc. and EVP & CMO Marvel Characters V.; DAN BUCKLEY, Publisher & President - Print, Animation & Digital Divisions; JOE QUESADA, Chief Creative Officer; JIM SOKOLOWSKI, Chief Operating Officer; DAVID BOGART, SVP of Business Affairs & Talent Management; TOM BREVOORT, SVP of Publishing; C.B. CEBULSKI, SVP of Creator & Content Development; DAVID GABRIEL, SVP of Publishing Sales & Circulation; MICHAEL PASCIULLO, SVP of Brand Planning & Communications; JIM KEEFE, VP of Operations & Logistics; DAN CARR, Executive Director of Publishing Technology; JUSTIN F. GABRIE, Director of Publishing & Editorial Operations; SUSAN CRESPI, Editorial Operations Manager; ALEX MORALES, ublishing Operations Manager; STAN LEE, Chairman Emeritus. For information regarding advertising in Marvel Comics or on Marvel.com, please contact John Dokes, SVP Integrated Sales and Marketing, at jdokes@marvel.om. For Marvel subscription inquiries, please call 800-217-9158. **Manufactured between 5/9/2011 and 6/6/2011 (hardcover), and 5/9/2011 and 11/21/2011 (softcover), by R.R. DONNELLEY, INC., SALEM, VA, USA.**

0 9 8 7 6 5 4 3 2 1

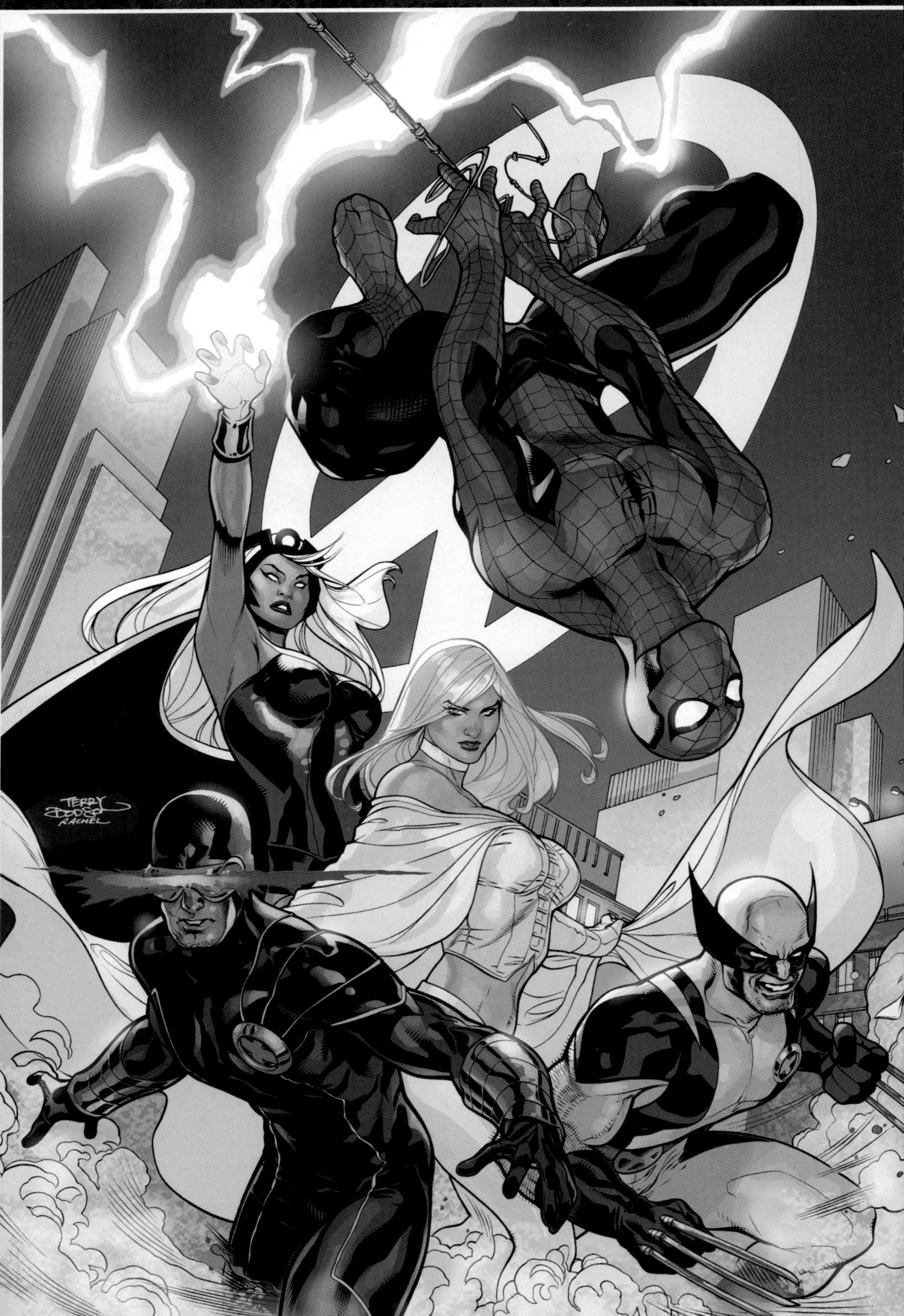
TERRY DODSON
RACHEL

SEVEN

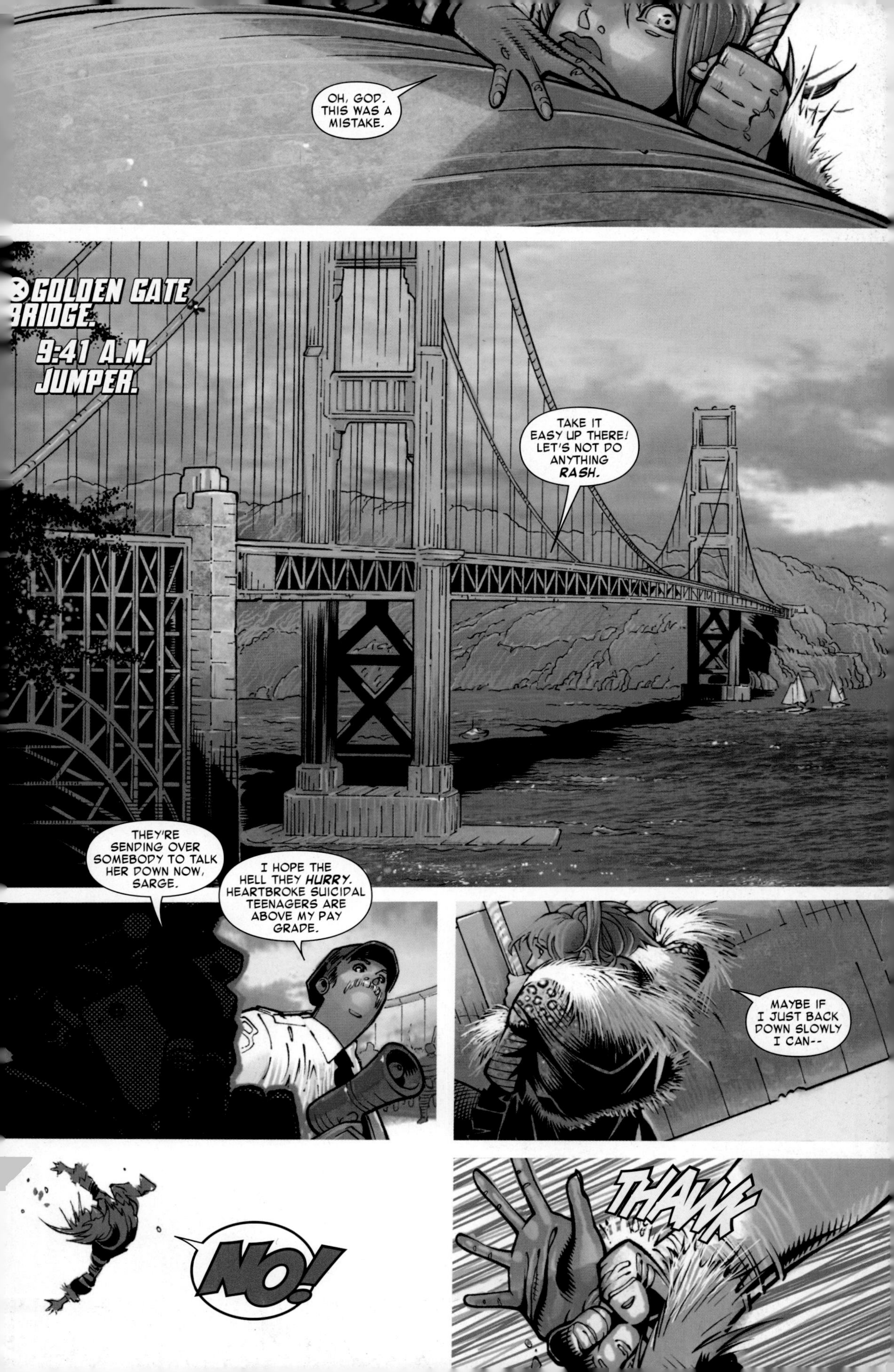
OH, GOD. THIS WAS A MISTAKE.
GOLDEN GATE BRIDGE.
9:41 A.M. JUMPER.
TAKE IT EASY UP THERE! LET'S NOT DO ANYTHING RASH.
THEY'RE SENDING OVER SOMEBODY TO TALK HER DOWN NOW, SARGE.
I HOPE THE HELL THEY HURRY. HEARTBROKE SUICIDAL TEENAGERS ARE ABOVE MY PAY GRADE.
MAYBE IF I JUST BACK DOWN SLOWLY I CAN--
NO!
THWAK

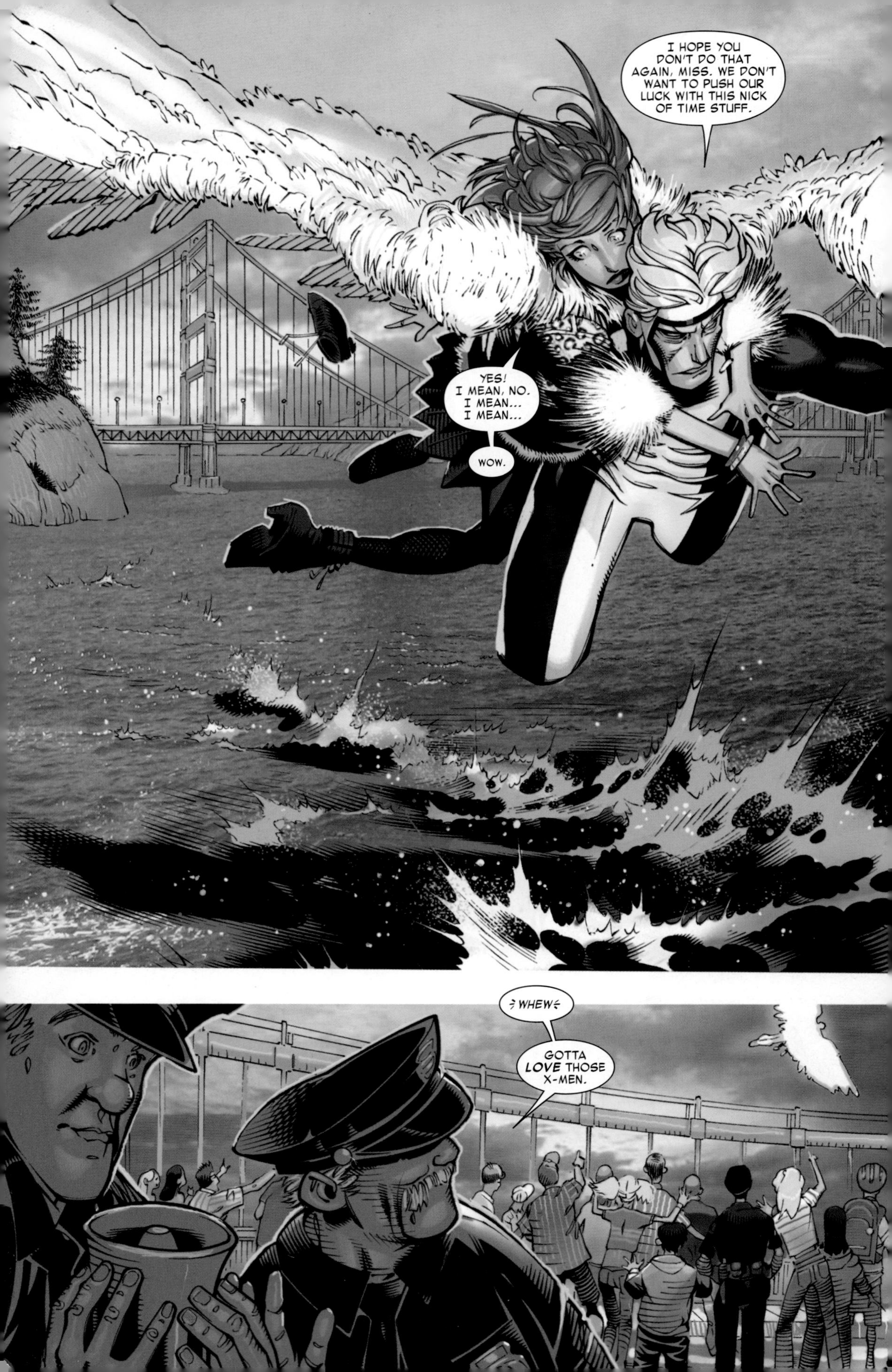
I HOPE YOU DON'T DO THAT AGAIN, MISS. WE DON'T WANT TO PUSH OUR LUCK WITH THIS NICK OF TIME STUFF.
YES! I MEAN, NO. I MEAN... I MEAN...
WOW.
WHEW
GOTTA LOVE THOSE X-MEN.

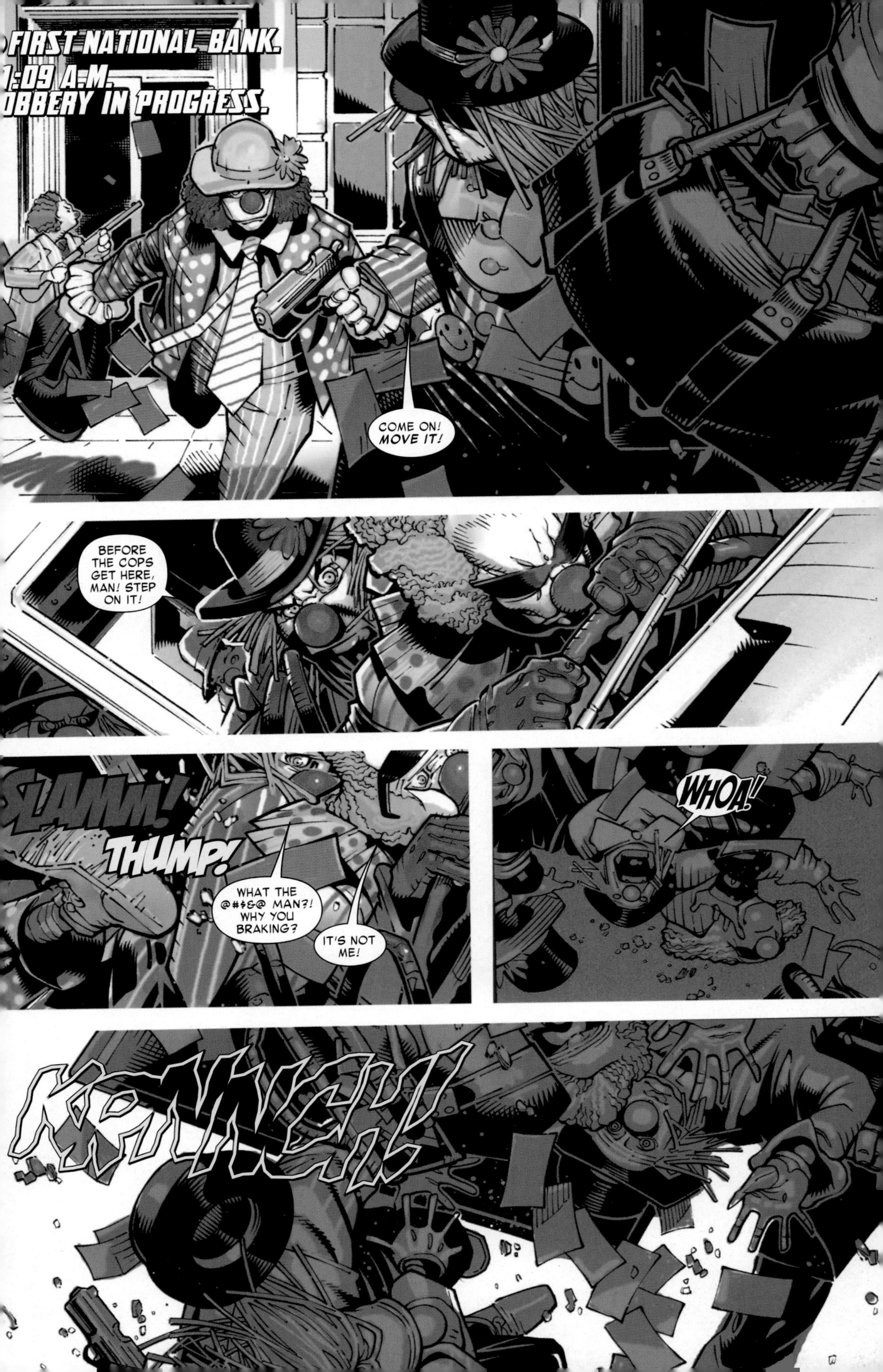
FIRST NATIONAL BANK.
1:09 A.M.
OBBERY IN PROGRESS.
COME ON! MOVE IT!
BEFORE THE COPS GET HERE, MAN! STEP ON IT!
SLAMM!
THUMP!
WHAT THE @#$&@ MAN?! WHY YOU BRAKING?
IT'S NOT ME!
WHOA!

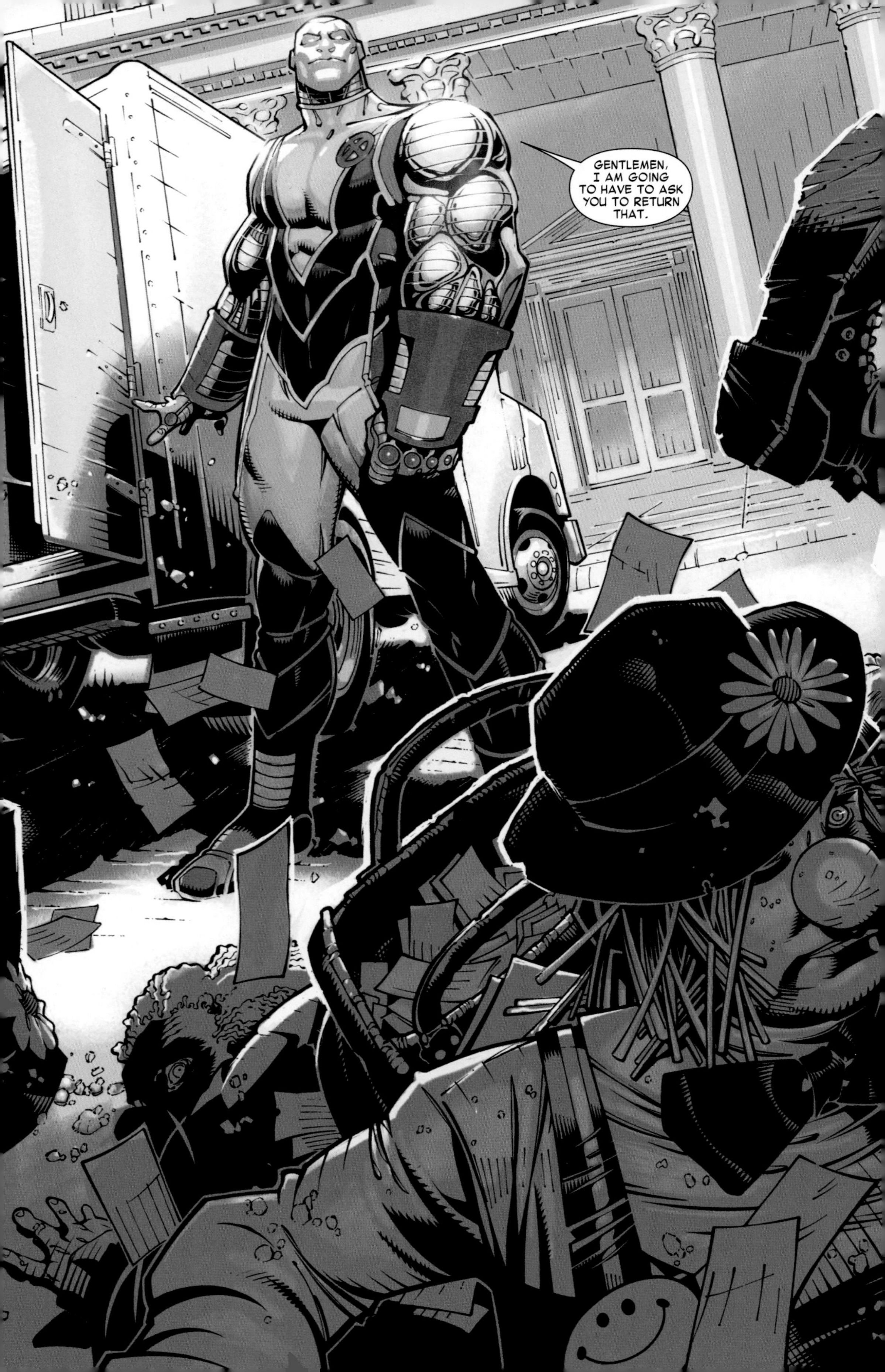
GENTLEMEN, I AM GOING TO HAVE TO ASK YOU TO RETURN THAT.

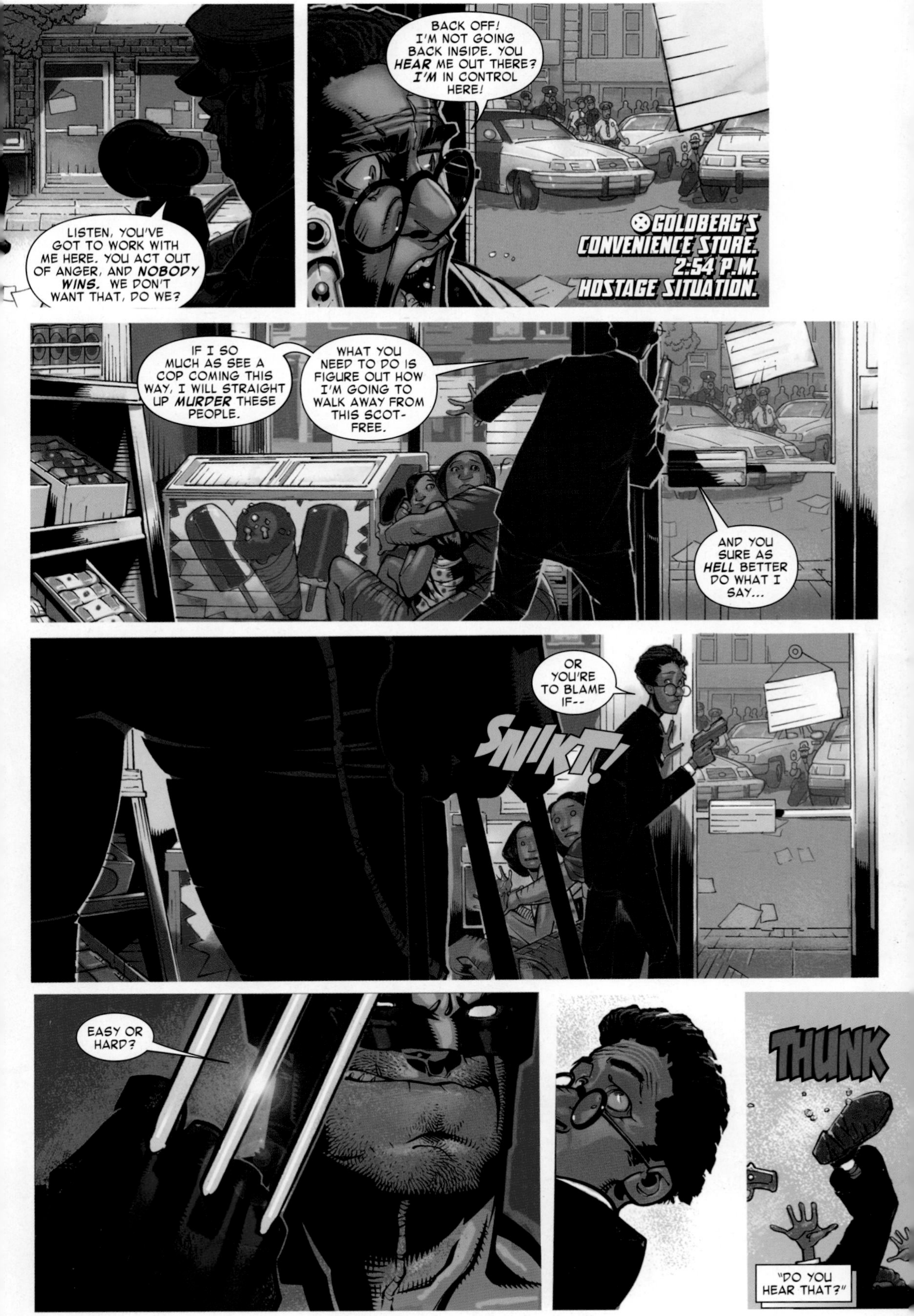

LISTEN, YOU'VE GOT TO WORK WITH ME HERE. YOU ACT OUT OF ANGER, AND NOBODY WINS. WE DON'T WANT THAT, DO WE?
BACK OFF! I'M NOT GOING BACK INSIDE. YOU HEAR ME OUT THERE? I'M IN CONTROL HERE!
GOLDBERG'S CONVENIENCE STORE. 2:54 P.M. HOSTAGE SITUATION.
IF I SO MUCH AS SEE A COP COMING THIS WAY, I WILL STRAIGHT UP MURDER THESE PEOPLE.
WHAT YOU NEED TO DO IS FIGURE OUT HOW I'M GOING TO WALK AWAY FROM THIS SCOT-FREE.
AND YOU SURE AS HELL BETTER DO WHAT I SAY...
OR YOU'RE TO BLAME IF--
SNIKT!
EASY OR HARD?
THUNK
"DO YOU HEAR THAT?"

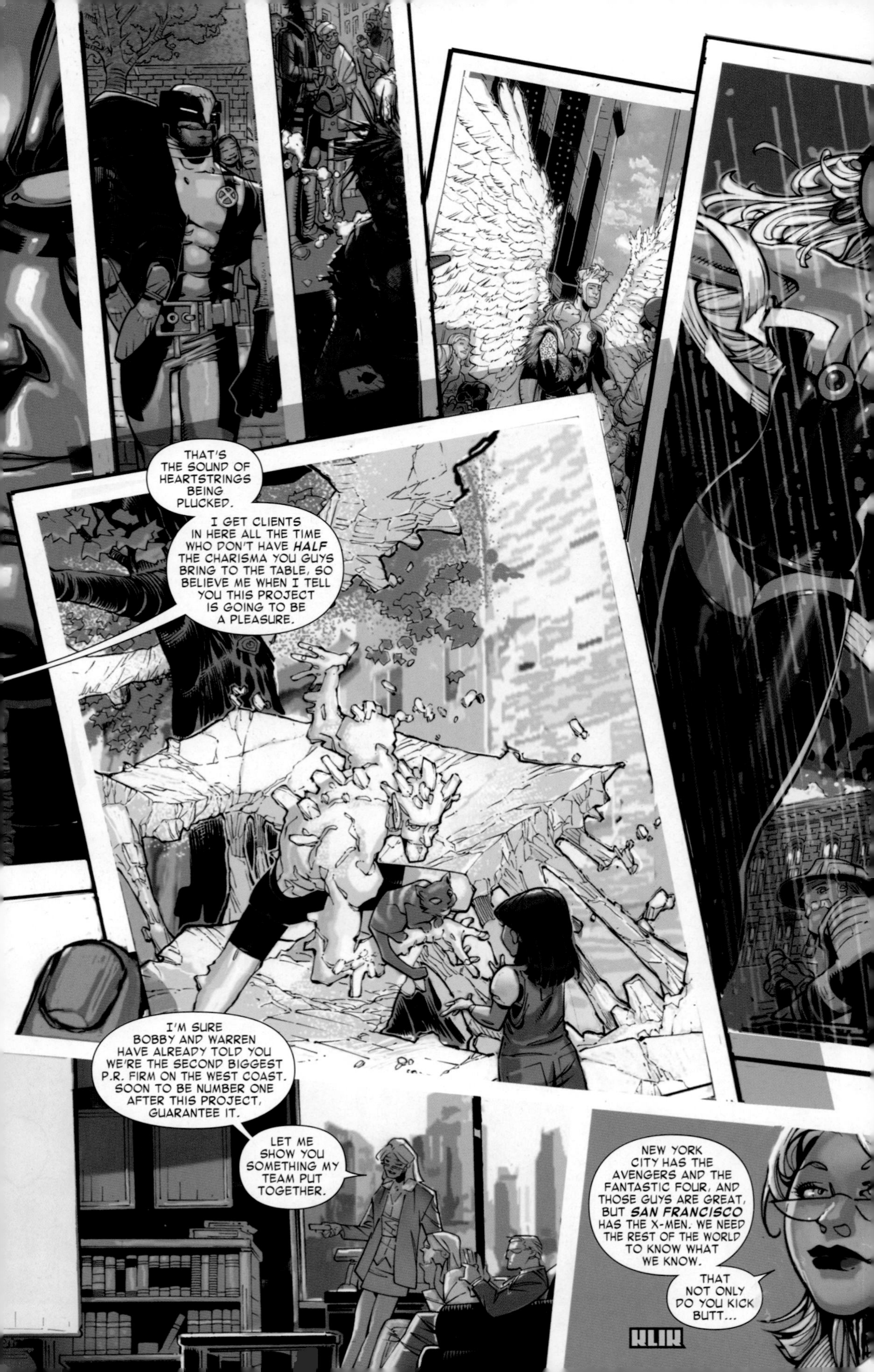

THAT'S THE SOUND OF HEARTSTRINGS BEING PLUCKED.
I GET CLIENTS IN HERE ALL THE TIME WHO DON'T HAVE HALF THE CHARISMA YOU GUYS BRING TO THE TABLE, SO BELIEVE ME WHEN I TELL YOU THIS PROJECT IS GOING TO BE A PLEASURE.
I'M SURE BOBBY AND WARREN HAVE ALREADY TOLD YOU WE'RE THE SECOND BIGGEST P.R. FIRM ON THE WEST COAST. SOON TO BE NUMBER ONE AFTER THIS PROJECT, GUARANTEE IT.
LET ME SHOW YOU SOMETHING MY TEAM PUT TOGETHER.
NEW YORK CITY HAS THE AVENGERS AND THE FANTASTIC FOUR, AND THOSE GUYS ARE GREAT, BUT SAN FRANCISCO HAS THE X-MEN. WE NEED THE REST OF THE WORLD TO KNOW WHAT WE KNOW.
THAT NOT ONLY DO YOU KICK BUTT...
KLIK

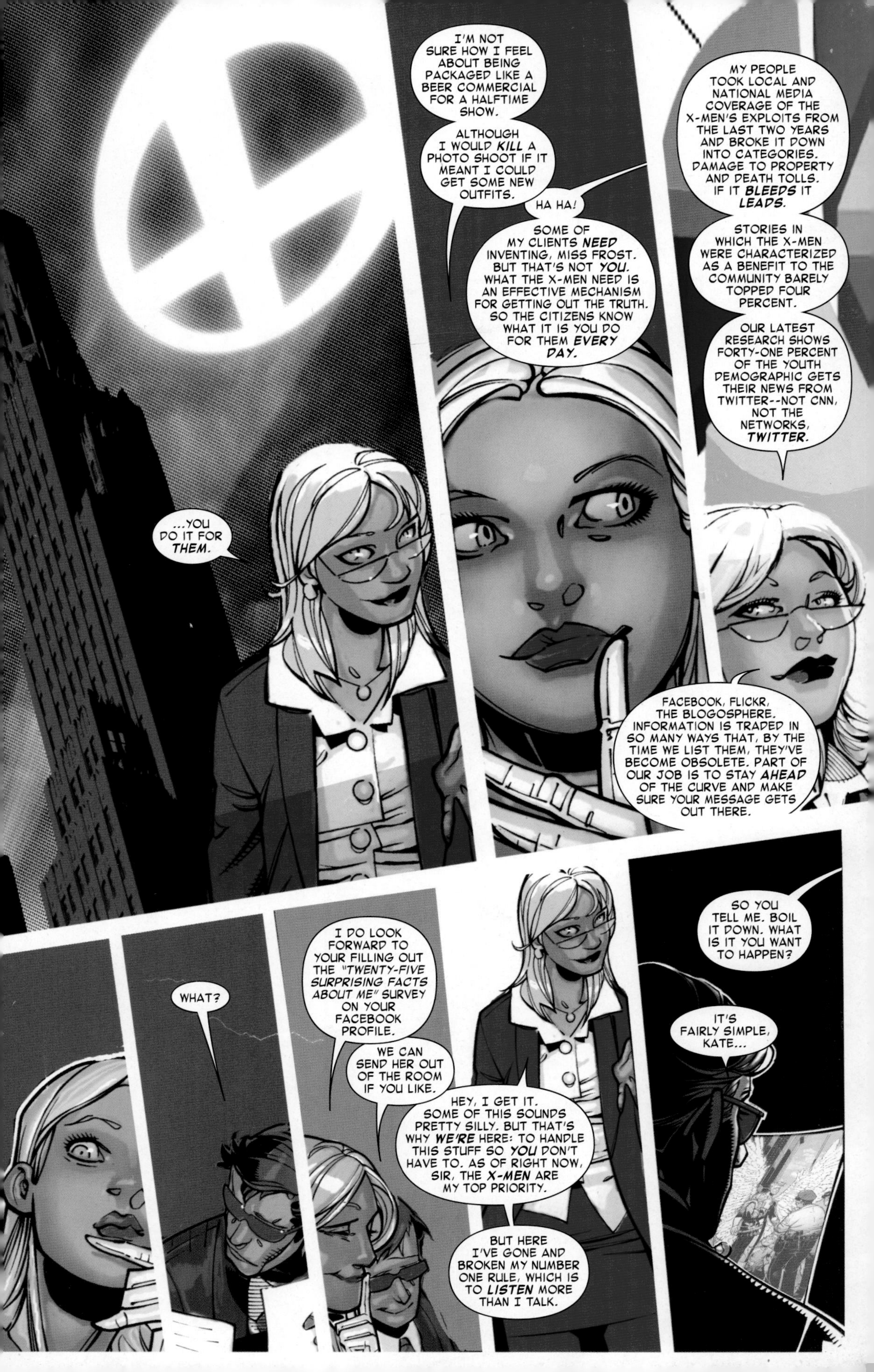
I'M NOT SURE HOW I FEEL ABOUT BEING PACKAGED LIKE A BEER COMMERCIAL FOR A HALFTIME SHOW.
ALTHOUGH I WOULD KILL A PHOTO SHOOT IF IT MEANT I COULD GET SOME NEW OUTFITS.
HA HA!
SOME OF MY CLIENTS NEED INVENTING, MISS FROST. BUT THAT'S NOT YOU. WHAT THE X-MEN NEED IS AN EFFECTIVE MECHANISM FOR GETTING OUT THE TRUTH. SO THE CITIZENS KNOW WHAT IT IS YOU DO FOR THEM EVERY DAY.
...YOU DO IT FOR THEM.
MY PEOPLE TOOK LOCAL AND NATIONAL MEDIA COVERAGE OF THE X-MEN'S EXPLOITS FROM THE LAST TWO YEARS AND BROKE IT DOWN INTO CATEGORIES. DAMAGE TO PROPERTY AND DEATH TOLLS. IF IT BLEEDS IT LEADS.
STORIES IN WHICH THE X-MEN WERE CHARACTERIZED AS A BENEFIT TO THE COMMUNITY BARELY TOPPED FOUR PERCENT.
OUR LATEST RESEARCH SHOWS FORTY-ONE PERCENT OF THE YOUTH DEMOGRAPHIC GETS THEIR NEWS FROM TWITTER--NOT CNN, NOT THE NETWORKS, TWITTER.
FACEBOOK, FLICKR, THE BLOGOSPHERE. INFORMATION IS TRADED IN SO MANY WAYS THAT, BY THE TIME WE LIST THEM, THEY'VE BECOME OBSOLETE. PART OF OUR JOB IS TO STAY AHEAD OF THE CURVE AND MAKE SURE YOUR MESSAGE GETS OUT THERE.
WHAT?
I DO LOOK FORWARD TO YOUR FILLING OUT THE "TWENTY-FIVE SURPRISING FACTS ABOUT ME" SURVEY ON YOUR FACEBOOK PROFILE.
WE CAN SEND HER OUT OF THE ROOM IF YOU LIKE.
HEY, I GET IT. SOME OF THIS SOUNDS PRETTY SILLY. BUT THAT'S WHY WE'RE HERE: TO HANDLE THIS STUFF SO YOU DON'T HAVE TO. AS OF RIGHT NOW, SIR, THE X-MEN ARE MY TOP PRIORITY.
BUT HERE I'VE GONE AND BROKEN MY NUMBER ONE RULE, WHICH IS TO LISTEN MORE THAN I TALK.
SO YOU TELL ME. BOIL IT DOWN. WHAT IS IT YOU WANT TO HAPPEN?
IT'S FAIRLY SIMPLE, KATE...

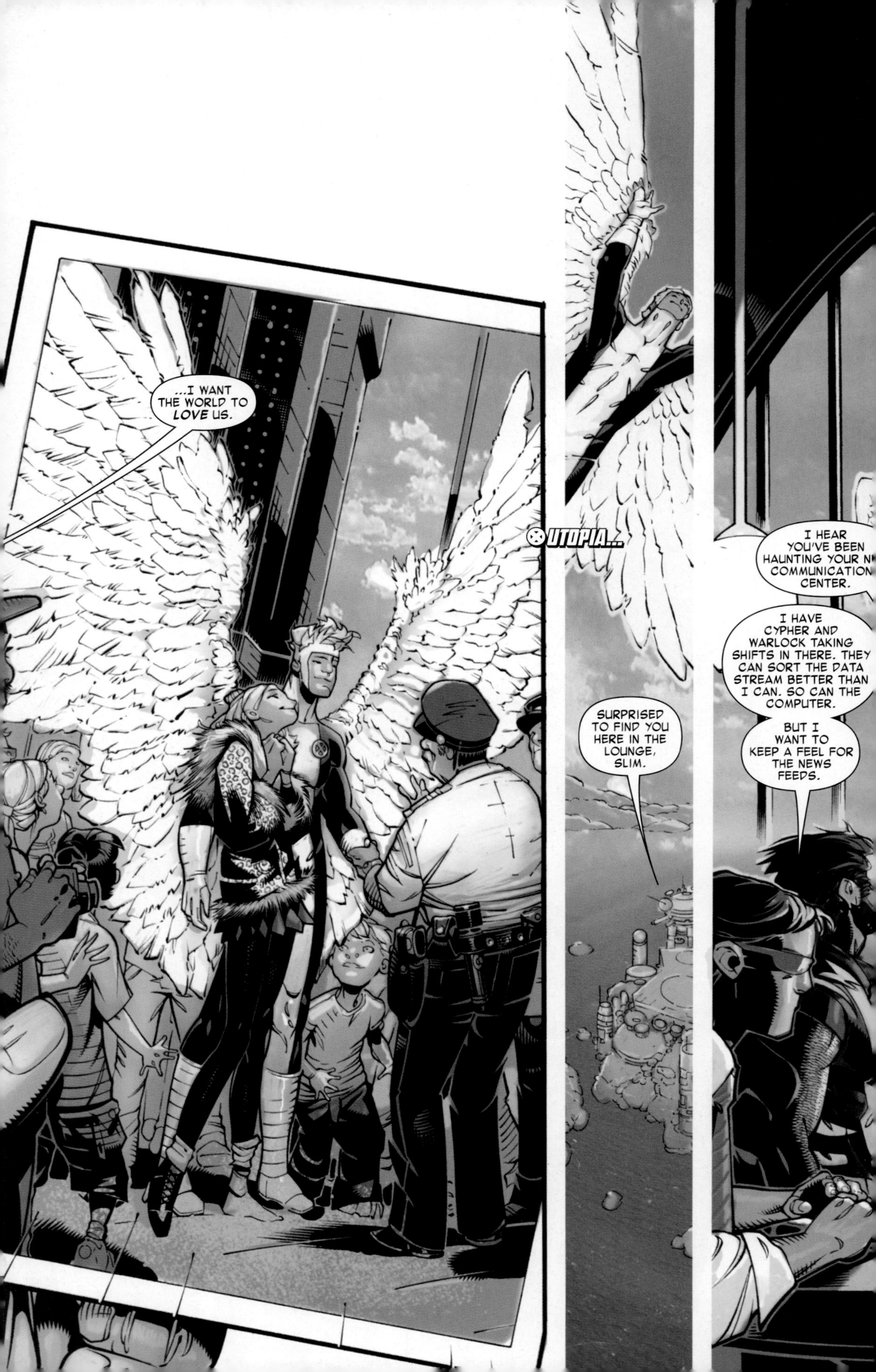
...I WANT THE WORLD TO LOVE US.
UTOPIA...
SURPRISED TO FIND YOU HERE IN THE LOUNGE, SLIM.
I HEAR YOU'VE BEEN HAUNTING YOUR N COMMUNICATION CENTER.
I HAVE CYPHER AND WARLOCK TAKING SHIFTS IN THERE. THEY CAN SORT THE DATA STREAM BETTER THAN I CAN. SO CAN THE COMPUTER.
BUT I WANT TO KEEP A FEEL FOR THE NEWS FEEDS.

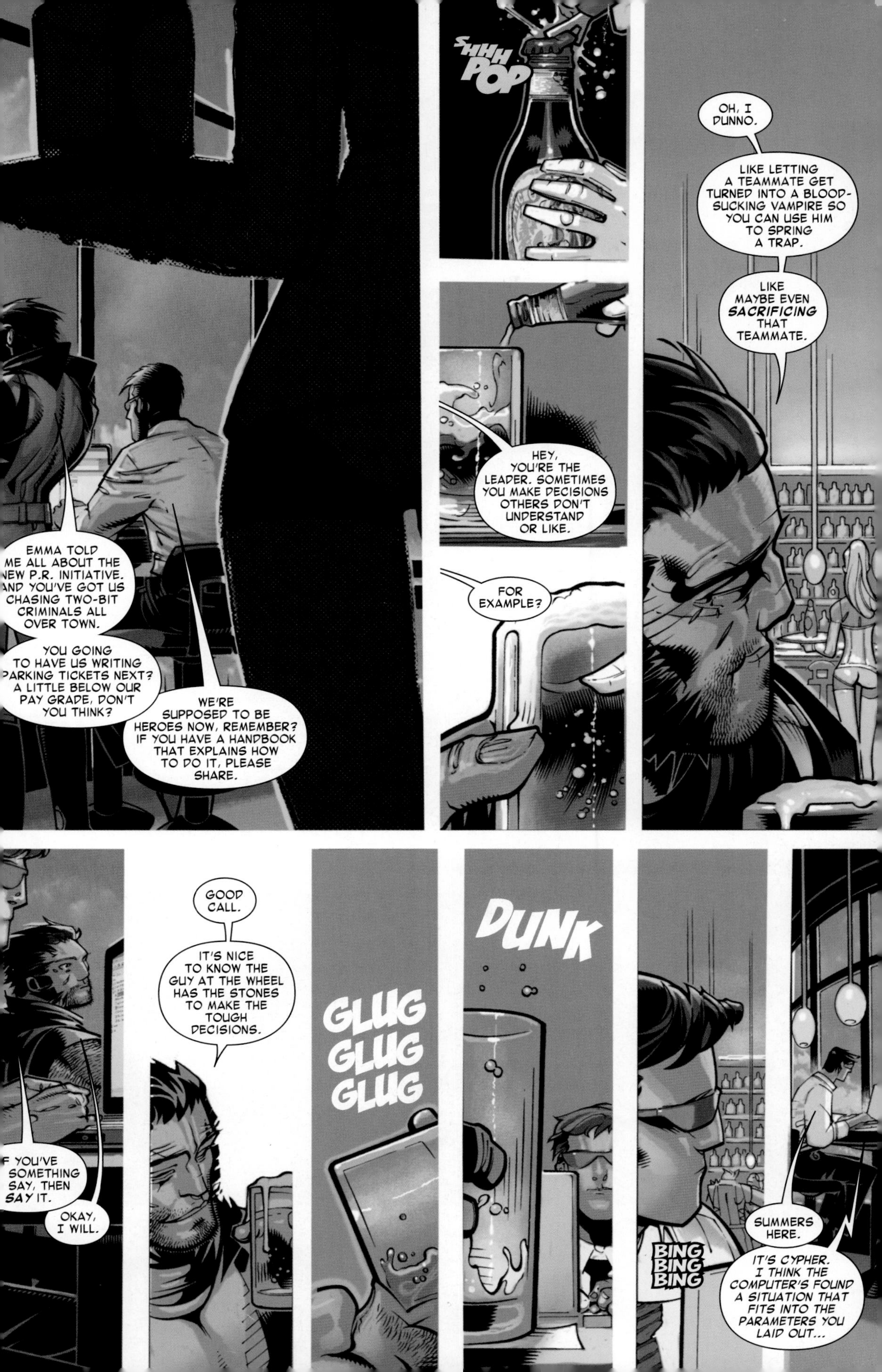

EMMA TOLD ME ALL ABOUT THE NEW P.R. INITIATIVE. AND YOU'VE GOT US CHASING TWO-BIT CRIMINALS ALL OVER TOWN.
YOU GOING TO HAVE US WRITING PARKING TICKETS NEXT? A LITTLE BELOW OUR PAY GRADE, DON'T YOU THINK?
WE'RE SUPPOSED TO BE HEROES NOW, REMEMBER? IF YOU HAVE A HANDBOOK THAT EXPLAINS HOW TO DO IT, PLEASE SHARE.
SHHH POP
HEY, YOU'RE THE LEADER. SOMETIMES YOU MAKE DECISIONS OTHERS DON'T UNDERSTAND OR LIKE.
FOR EXAMPLE?
OH, I DUNNO.
LIKE LETTING A TEAMMATE GET TURNED INTO A BLOOD-SUCKING VAMPIRE SO YOU CAN USE HIM TO SPRING A TRAP.
LIKE MAYBE EVEN SACRIFICING THAT TEAMMATE.
F YOU'VE SOMETHING SAY, THEN SAY IT.
OKAY, I WILL.
GOOD CALL.
IT'S NICE TO KNOW THE GUY AT THE WHEEL HAS THE STONES TO MAKE THE TOUGH DECISIONS.
GLUG GLUG GLUG
DUNK
BING BING BING
SUMMERS HERE.
IT'S CYPHER. I THINK THE COMPUTER'S FOUND A SITUATION THAT FITS INTO THE PARAMETERS YOU LAID OUT...

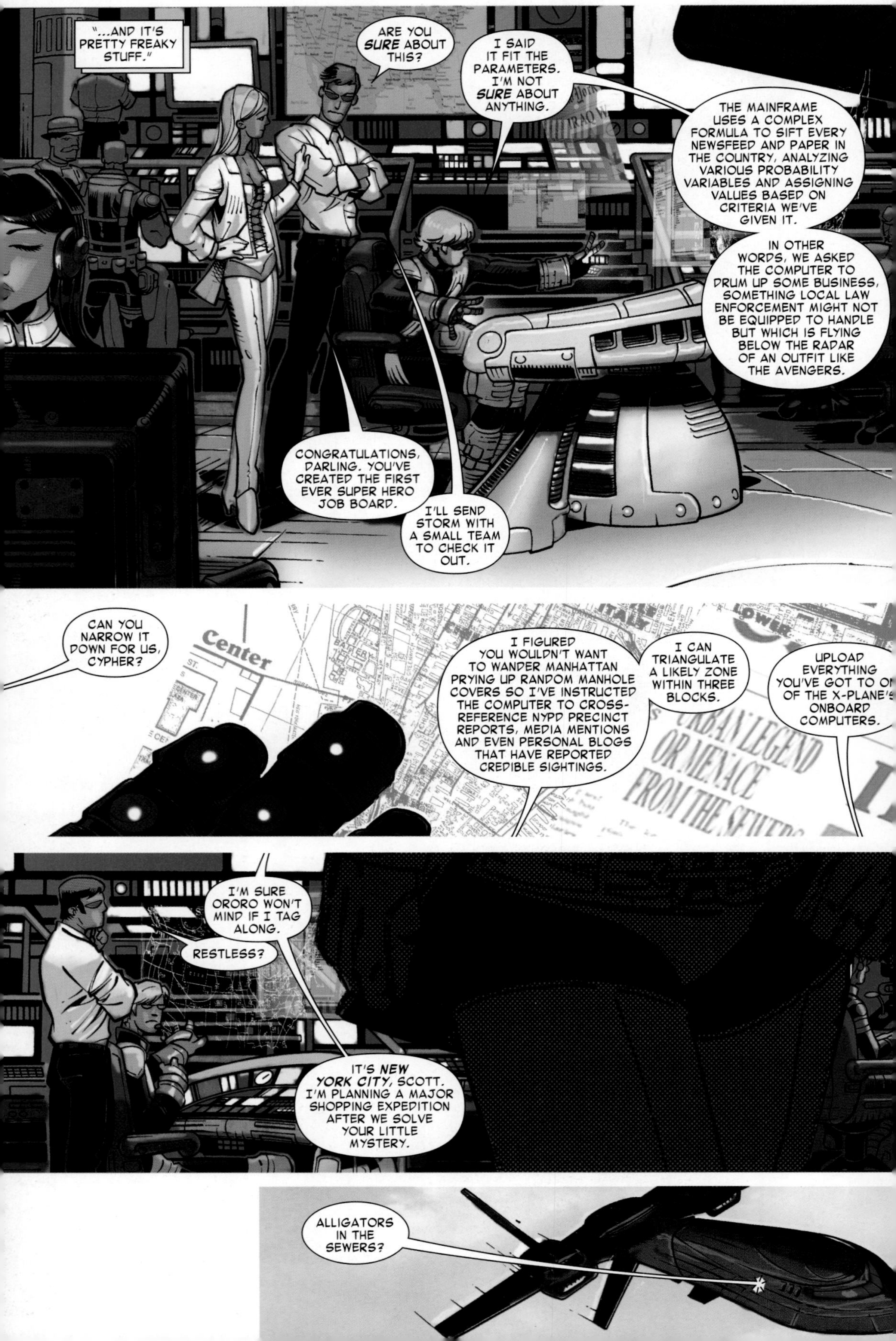
"...AND IT'S PRETTY FREAKY STUFF."
ARE YOU SURE ABOUT THIS?
I SAID IT FIT THE PARAMETERS. I'M NOT SURE ABOUT ANYTHING.
THE MAINFRAME USES A COMPLEX FORMULA TO SIFT EVERY NEWSFEED AND PAPER IN THE COUNTRY, ANALYZING VARIOUS PROBABILITY VARIABLES AND ASSIGNING VALUES BASED ON CRITERIA WE'VE GIVEN IT.
IN OTHER WORDS, WE ASKED THE COMPUTER TO DRUM UP SOME BUSINESS, SOMETHING LOCAL LAW ENFORCEMENT MIGHT NOT BE EQUIPPED TO HANDLE BUT WHICH IS FLYING BELOW THE RADAR OF AN OUTFIT LIKE THE AVENGERS.
CONGRATULATIONS, DARLING. YOU'VE CREATED THE FIRST EVER SUPER HERO JOB BOARD.
I'LL SEND STORM WITH A SMALL TEAM TO CHECK IT OUT.
CAN YOU NARROW IT DOWN FOR US, CYPHER?
I FIGURED YOU WOULDN'T WANT TO WANDER MANHATTAN PRYING UP RANDOM MANHOLE COVERS SO I'VE INSTRUCTED THE COMPUTER TO CROSS-REFERENCE NYPD PRECINCT REPORTS, MEDIA MENTIONS AND EVEN PERSONAL BLOGS THAT HAVE REPORTED CREDIBLE SIGHTINGS.
I CAN TRIANGULATE A LIKELY ZONE WITHIN THREE BLOCKS.
UPLOAD EVERYTHING YOU'VE GOT TO ON OF THE X-PLANE'S ONBOARD COMPUTERS.
URBAN LEGEND OR MENACE FROM THE SEWERS
I'M SURE ORORO WON'T MIND IF I TAG ALONG.
RESTLESS?
IT'S NEW YORK CITY, SCOTT. I'M PLANNING A MAJOR SHOPPING EXPEDITION AFTER WE SOLVE YOUR LITTLE MYSTERY.
ALLIGATORS IN THE SEWERS?

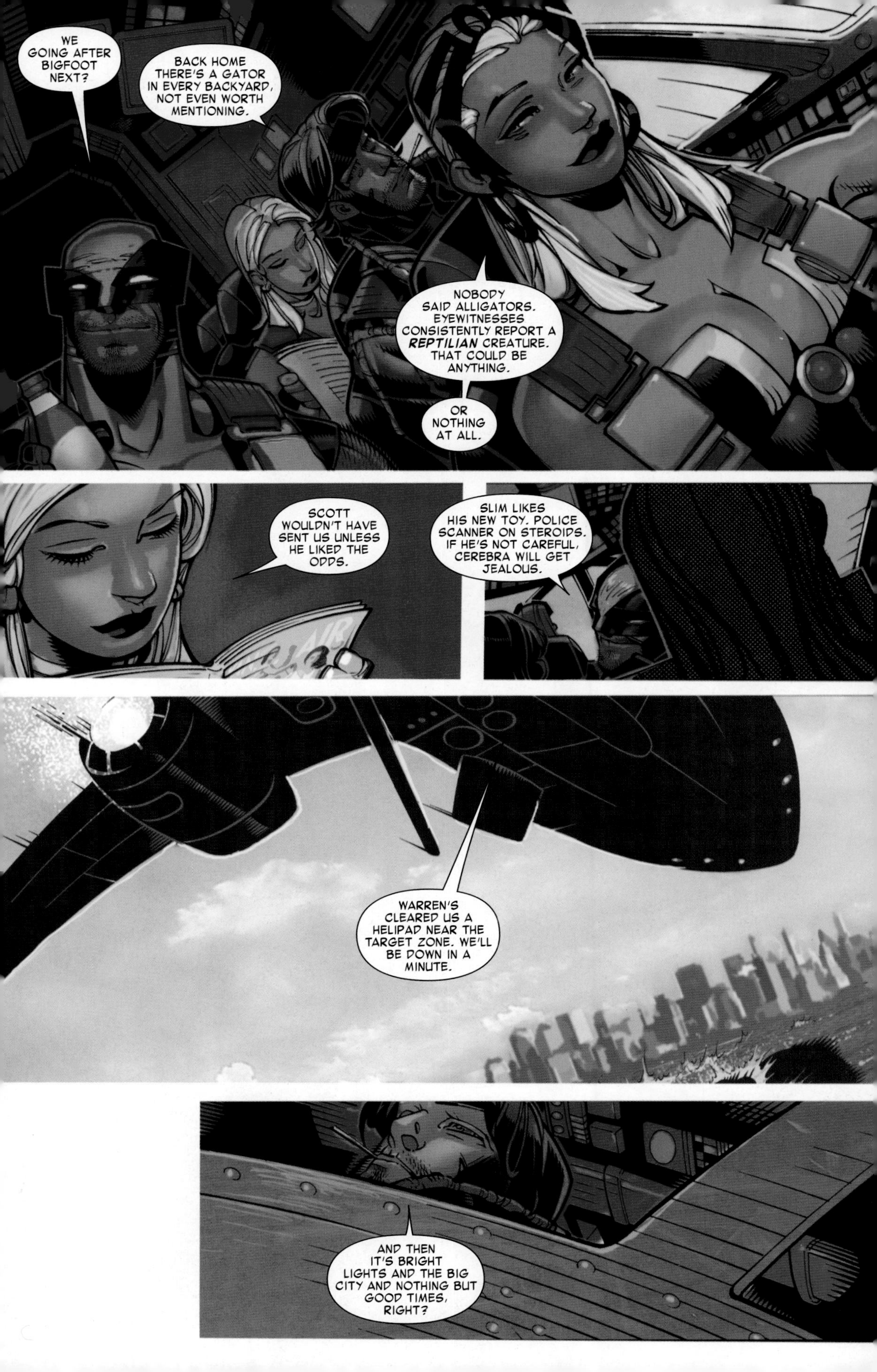
WE GOING AFTER BIGFOOT NEXT?
BACK HOME THERE'S A GATOR IN EVERY BACKYARD, NOT EVEN WORTH MENTIONING.
NOBODY SAID ALLIGATORS. EYEWITNESSES CONSISTENTLY REPORT A *REPTILIAN* CREATURE. THAT COULD BE ANYTHING.
OR NOTHING AT ALL.
SCOTT WOULDN'T HAVE SENT US UNLESS HE LIKED THE ODDS.
SLIM LIKES HIS NEW TOY. POLICE SCANNER ON STEROIDS. IF HE'S NOT CAREFUL, CEREBRA WILL GET JEALOUS.
WARREN'S CLEARED US A HELIPAD NEAR THE TARGET ZONE. WE'LL BE DOWN IN A MINUTE.
AND THEN IT'S BRIGHT LIGHTS AND THE BIG CITY AND NOTHING BUT GOOD TIMES, RIGHT?

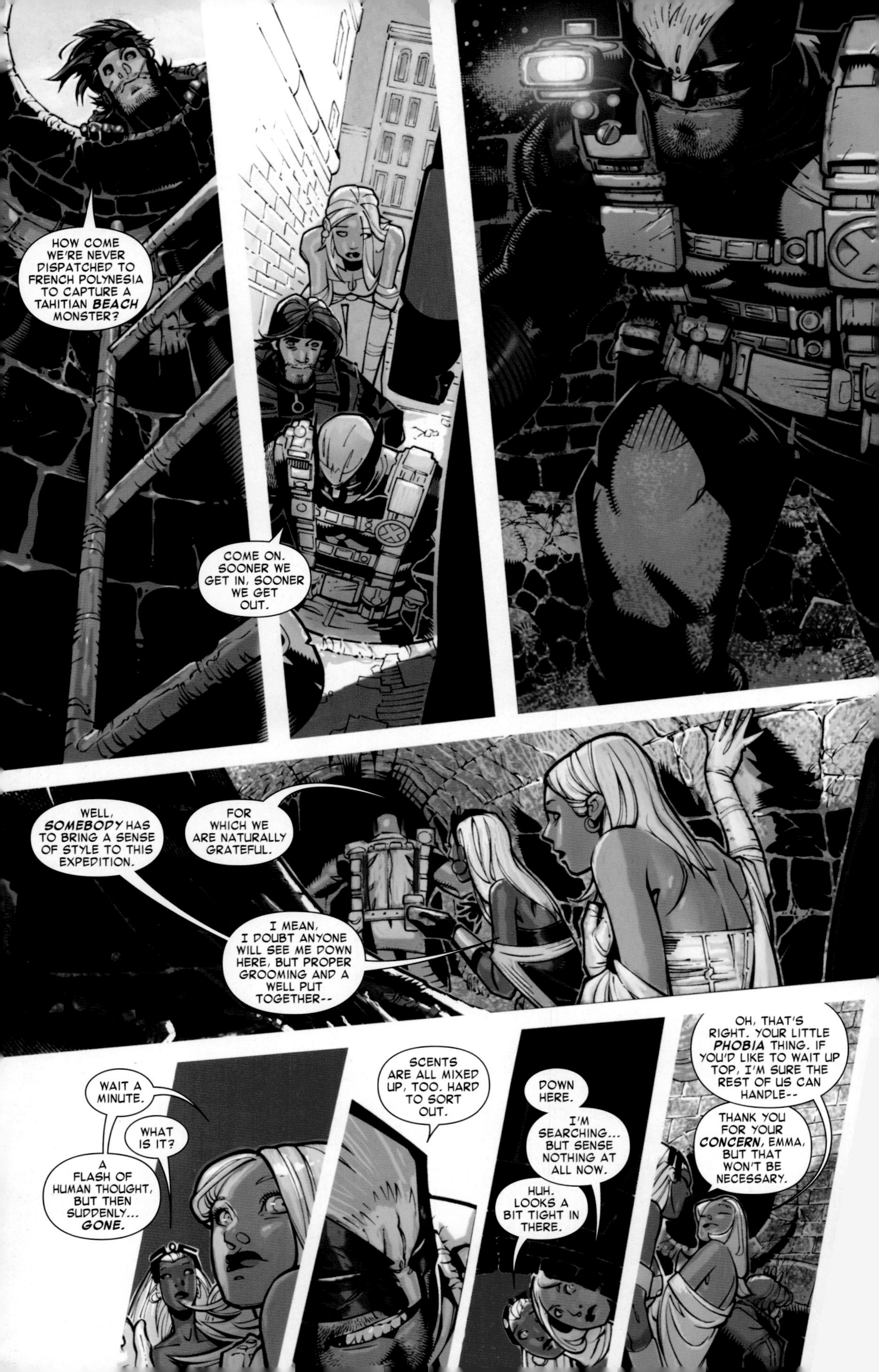
HOW COME WE'RE NEVER DISPATCHED TO FRENCH POLYNESIA TO CAPTURE A TAHITIAN *BEACH* MONSTER?
COME ON. SOONER WE GET IN, SOONER WE GET OUT.
WELL, *SOMEBODY* HAS TO BRING A SENSE OF STYLE TO THIS EXPEDITION.
FOR WHICH WE ARE NATURALLY GRATEFUL.
I MEAN, I DOUBT ANYONE WILL SEE ME DOWN HERE, BUT PROPER GROOMING AND A WELL PUT TOGETHER--
WAIT A MINUTE.
WHAT IS IT?
A FLASH OF HUMAN THOUGHT, BUT THEN SUDDENLY... *GONE.*
SCENTS ARE ALL MIXED UP, TOO. HARD TO SORT OUT.
DOWN HERE.
I'M SEARCHING... BUT SENSE NOTHING AT ALL NOW.
HUH. LOOKS A BIT TIGHT IN THERE.
OH, THAT'S RIGHT. YOUR LITTLE *PHOBIA* THING. IF YOU'D LIKE TO WAIT UP TOP, I'M SURE THE REST OF US CAN HANDLE--
THANK YOU FOR YOUR *CONCERN,* EMMA, BUT THAT WON'T BE NECESSARY.

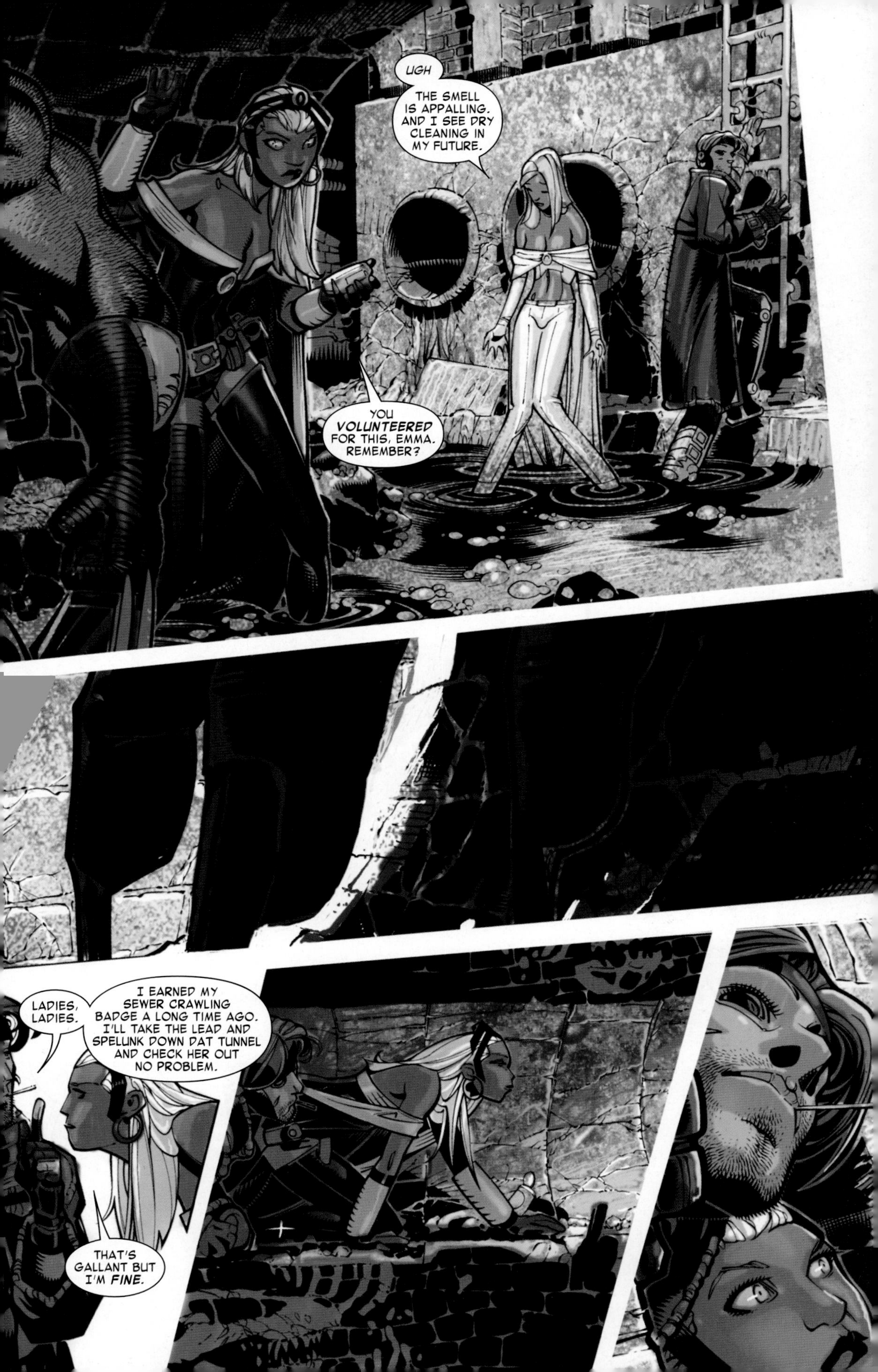
UGH
THE SMELL IS APPALLING. AND I SEE DRY CLEANING IN MY FUTURE.
YOU VOLUNTEERED FOR THIS, EMMA. REMEMBER?
LADIES, LADIES.
I EARNED MY SEWER CRAWLING BADGE A LONG TIME AGO. I'LL TAKE THE LEAD AND SPELUNK DOWN DAT TUNNEL AND CHECK HER OUT NO PROBLEM.
THAT'S GALLANT BUT I'M FINE.

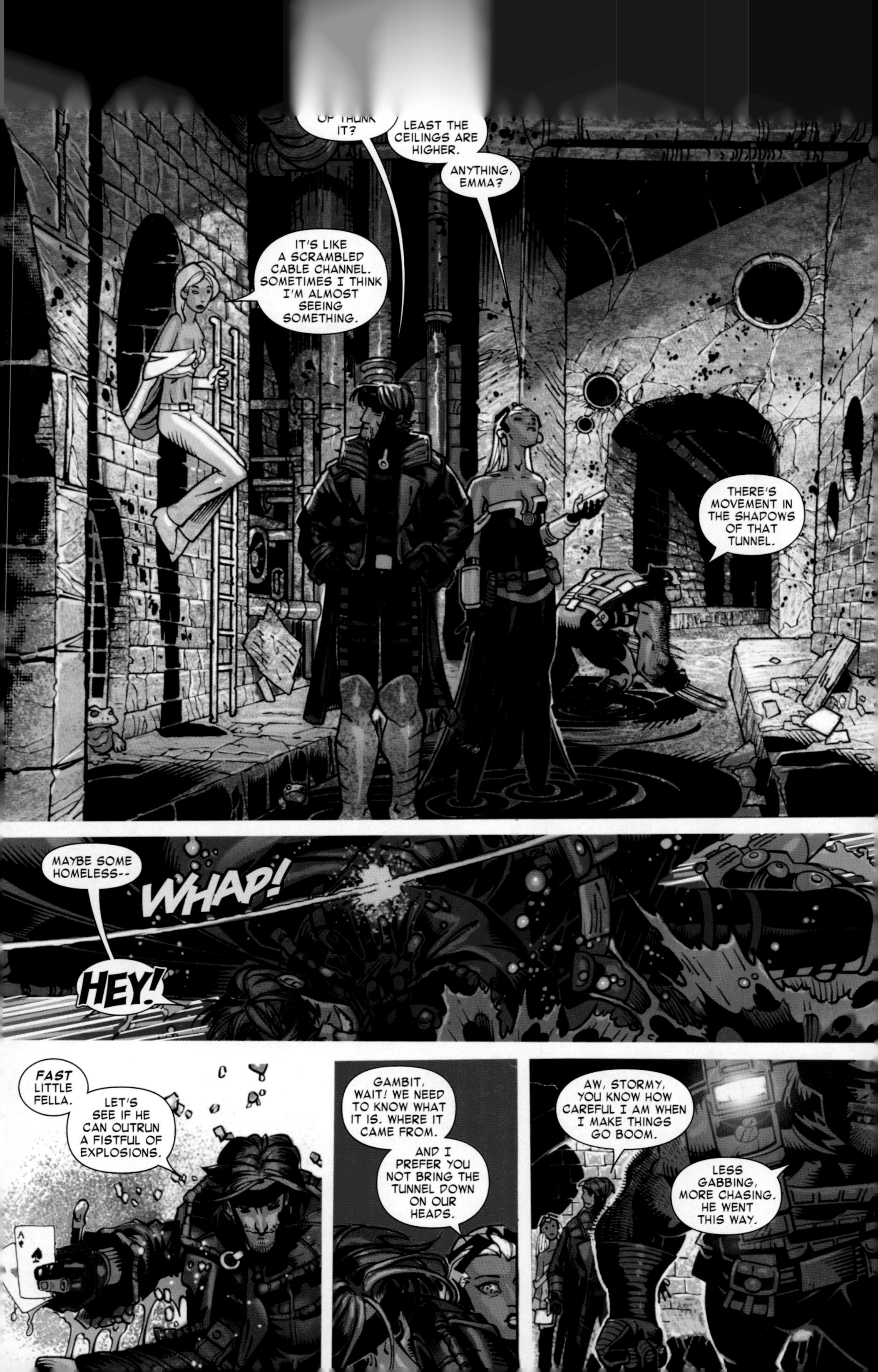
OF THUNK IT?
LEAST THE CEILINGS ARE HIGHER.
ANYTHING, EMMA?
IT'S LIKE A SCRAMBLED CABLE CHANNEL. SOMETIMES I THINK I'M ALMOST SEEING SOMETHING.
THERE'S MOVEMENT IN THE SHADOWS OF THAT TUNNEL.
MAYBE SOME HOMELESS--
WHAP!
HEY!
FAST LITTLE FELLA.
LET'S SEE IF HE CAN OUTRUN A FISTFUL OF EXPLOSIONS.
GAMBIT, WAIT! WE NEED TO KNOW WHAT IT IS. WHERE IT CAME FROM.
AND I PREFER YOU NOT BRING THE TUNNEL DOWN ON OUR HEADS.
AW, STORMY, YOU KNOW HOW CAREFUL I AM WHEN I MAKE THINGS GO BOOM.
LESS GABBING, MORE CHASING. HE WENT THIS WAY.

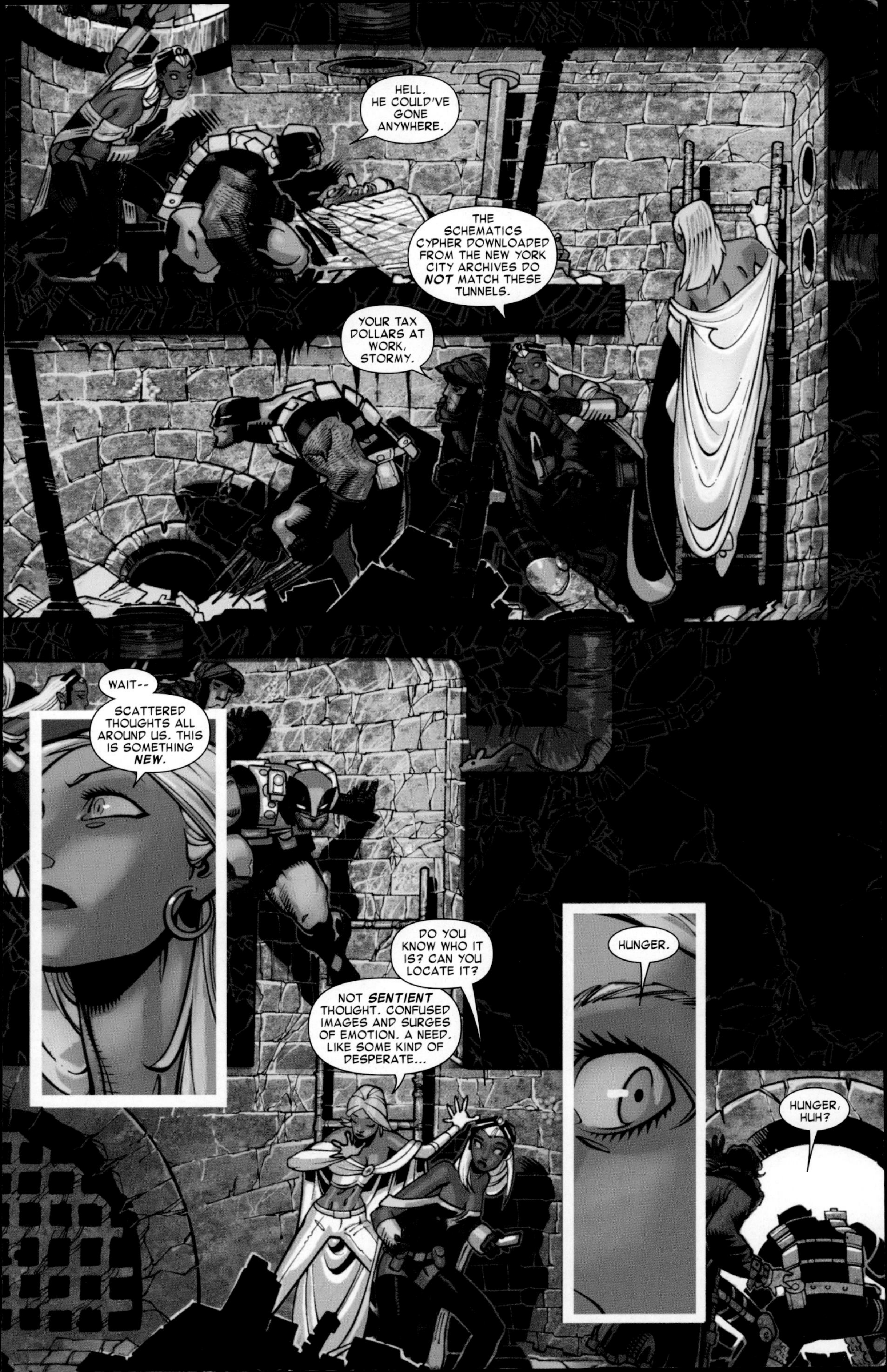

HELL. HE COULD'VE GONE ANYWHERE.
THE SCHEMATICS CYPHER DOWNLOADED FROM THE NEW YORK CITY ARCHIVES DO NOT MATCH THESE TUNNELS.
YOUR TAX DOLLARS AT WORK, STORMY.
WAIT--
SCATTERED THOUGHTS ALL AROUND US. THIS IS SOMETHING NEW.
DO YOU KNOW WHO IT IS? CAN YOU LOCATE IT?
NOT SENTIENT THOUGHT. CONFUSED IMAGES AND SURGES OF EMOTION. A NEED. LIKE SOME KIND OF DESPERATE...
HUNGER.
HUNGER, HUH?

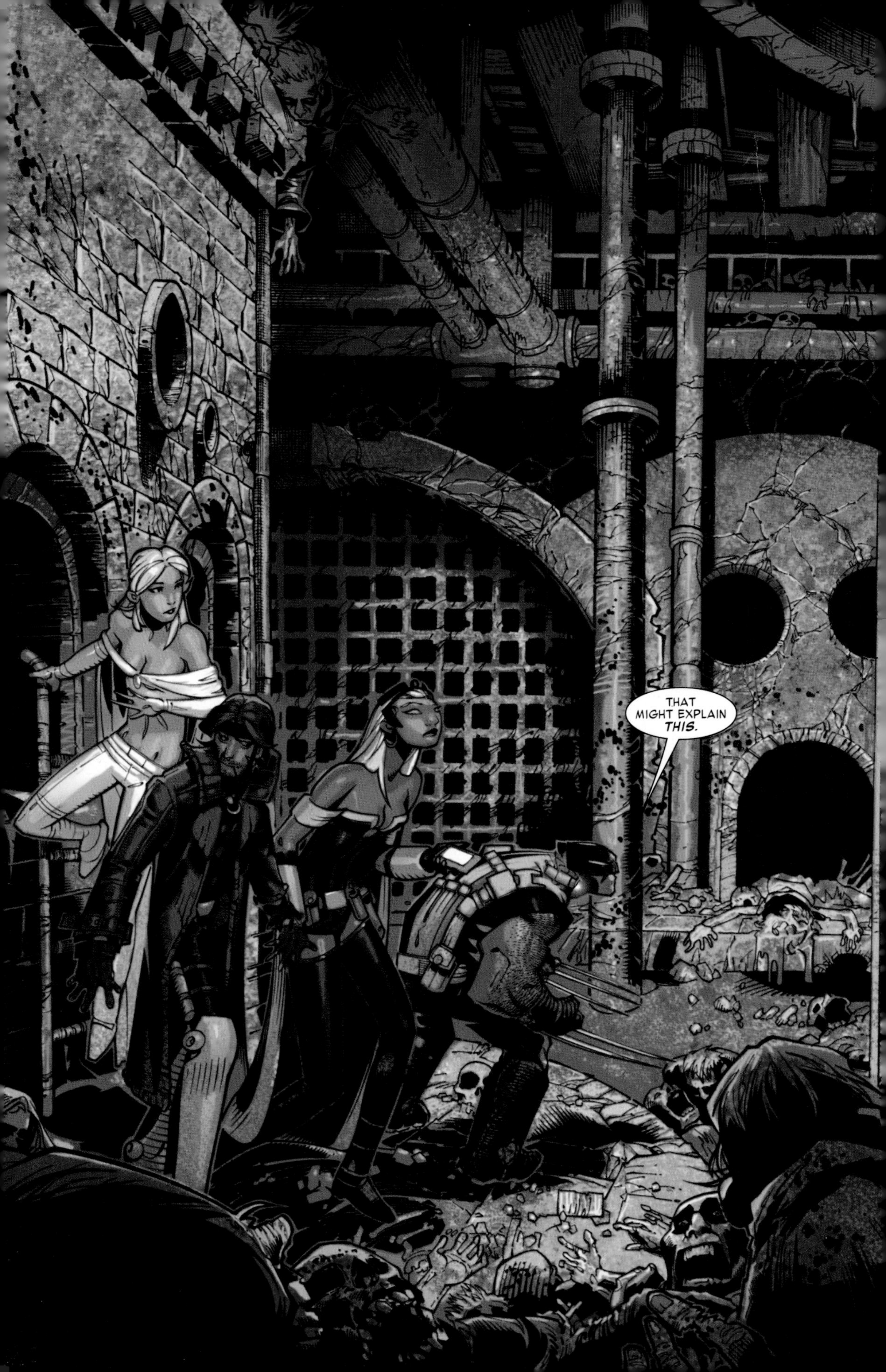
THAT MIGHT EXPLAIN THIS.

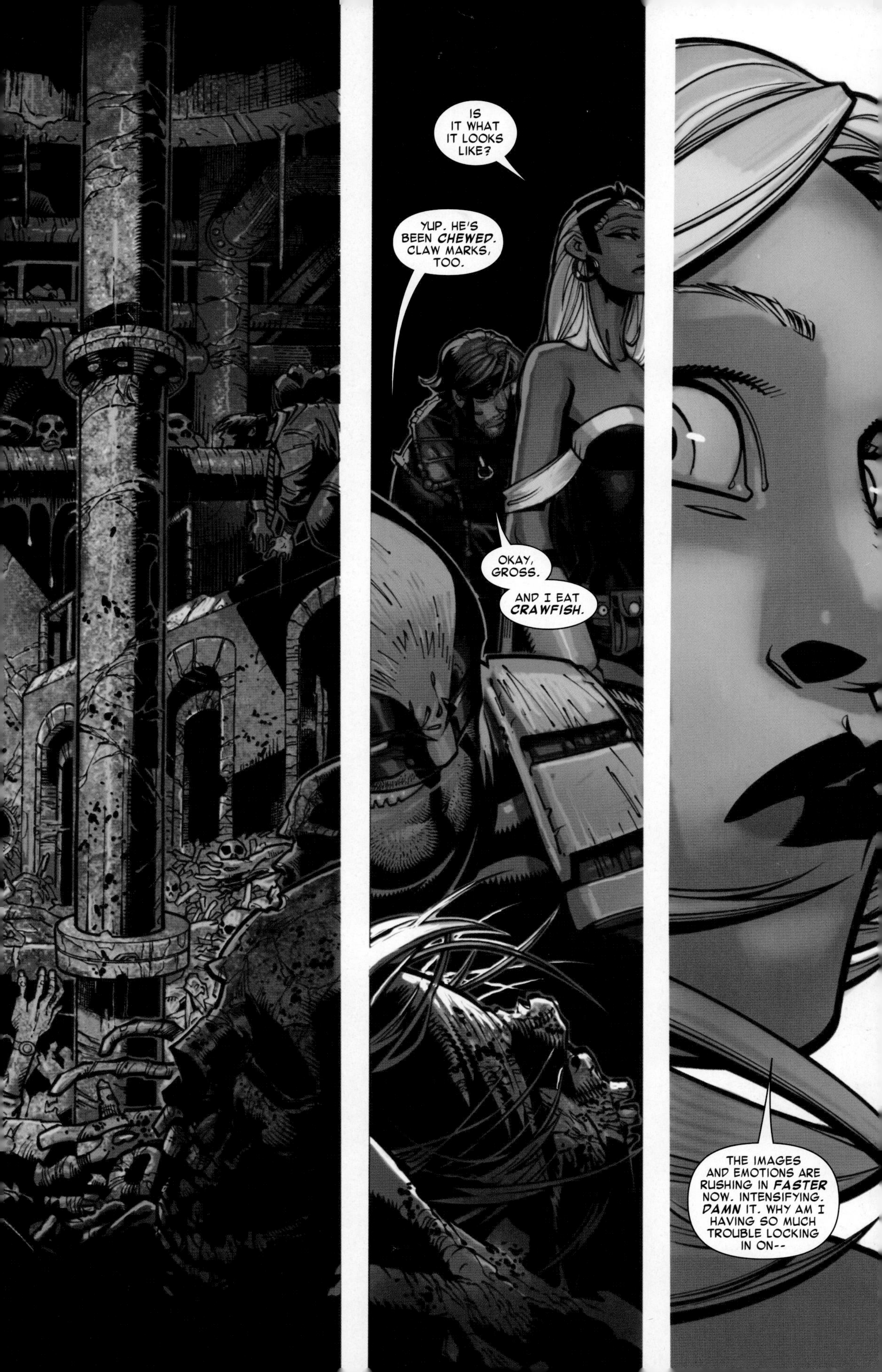
IS IT WHAT IT LOOKS LIKE?
YUP. HE'S BEEN CHEWED. CLAW MARKS, TOO.
OKAY, GROSS.
AND I EAT CRAWFISH.
THE IMAGES AND EMOTIONS ARE RUSHING IN FASTER NOW. INTENSIFYING. DAMN IT. WHY AM I HAVING SO MUCH TROUBLE LOCKING IN ON--

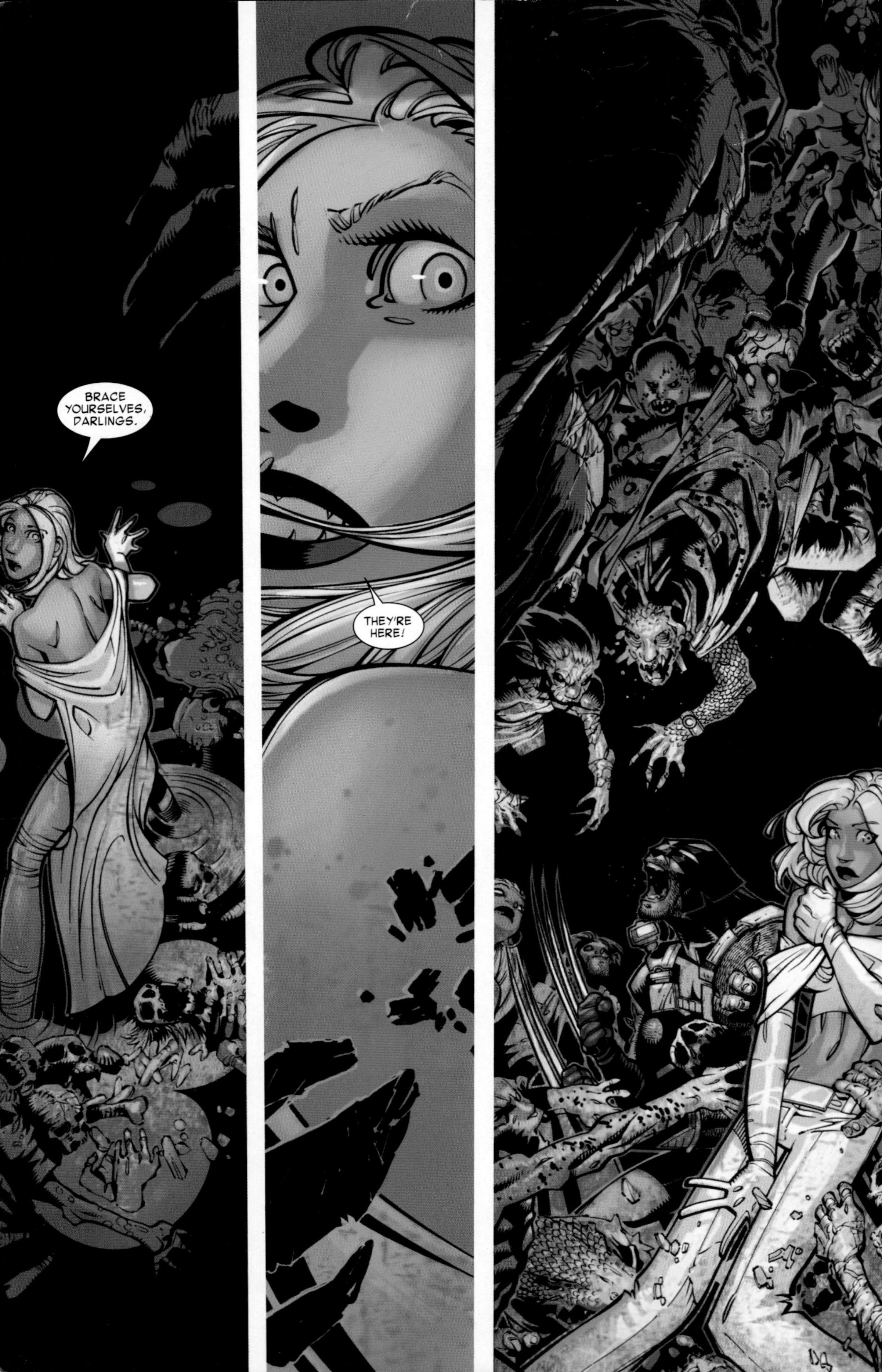
BRACE YOURSELVES, DARLINGS.
THEY'RE HERE!

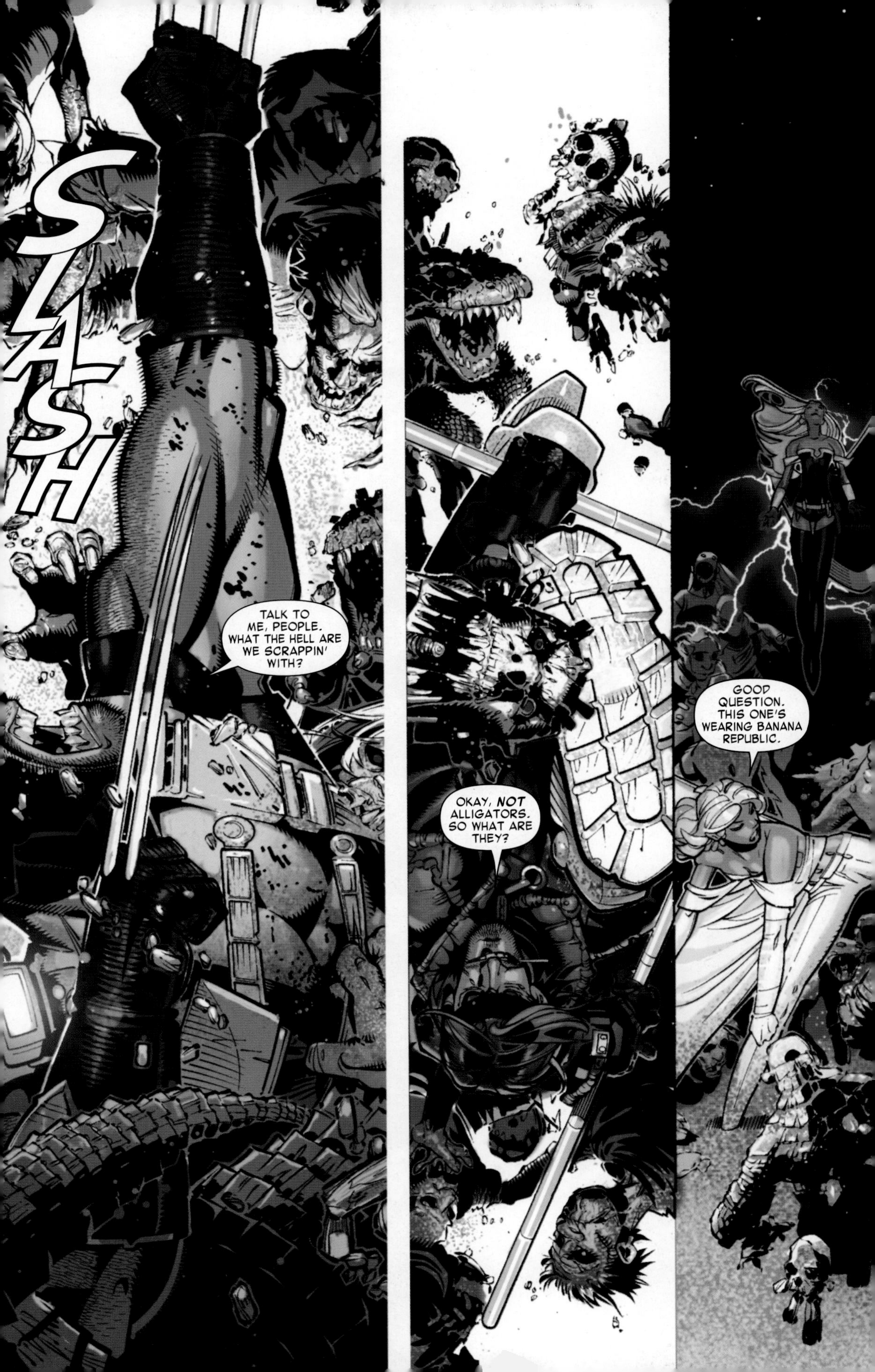
SLASH
TALK TO ME, PEOPLE. WHAT THE HELL ARE WE SCRAPPIN' WITH?
OKAY, NOT ALLIGATORS. SO WHAT ARE THEY?
GOOD QUESTION. THIS ONE'S WEARING BANANA REPUBLIC.

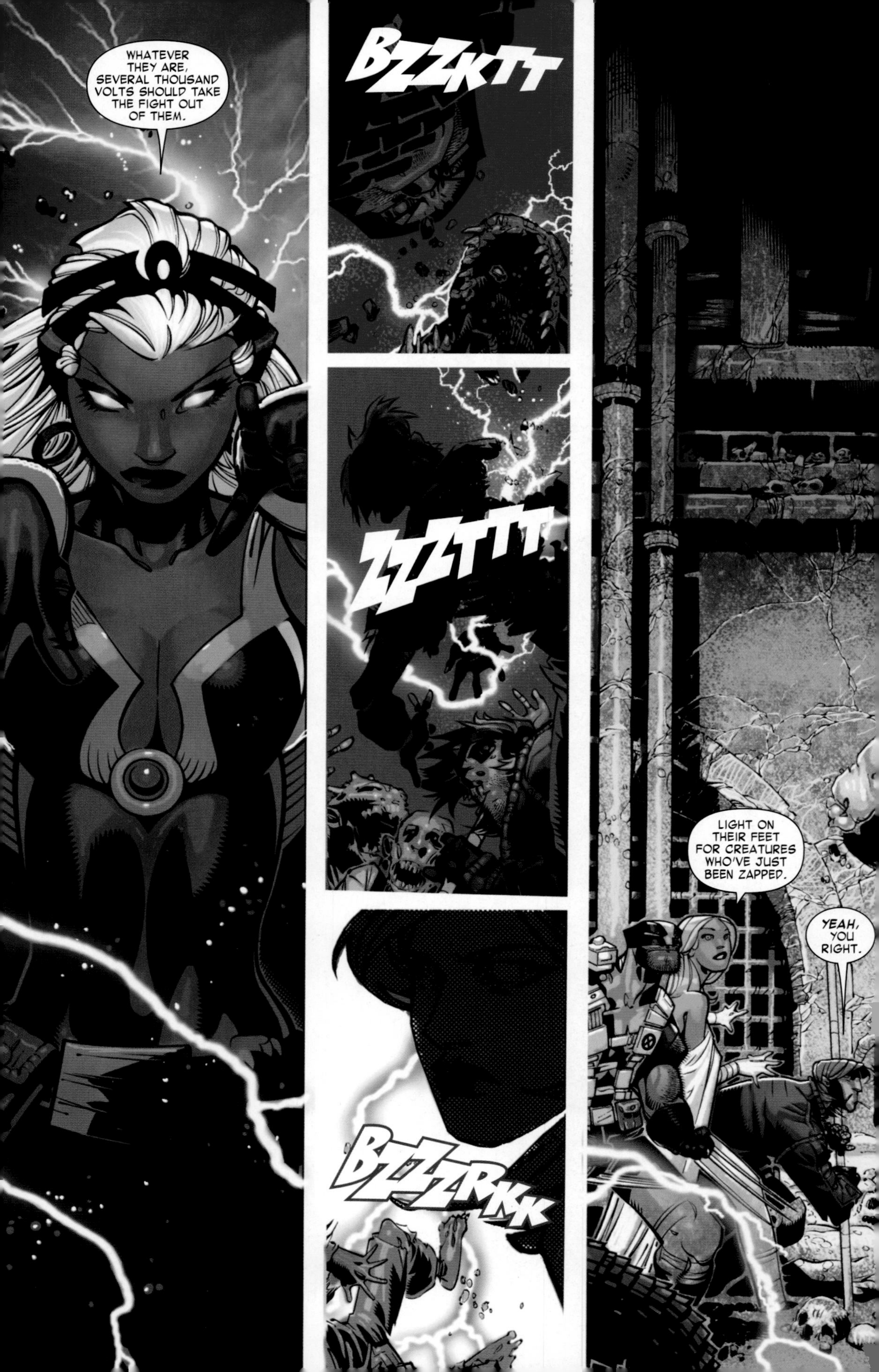
WHATEVER THEY ARE, SEVERAL THOUSAND VOLTS SHOULD TAKE THE FIGHT OUT OF THEM.
BZZKTT
ZZZTTT
BZZZRKK
LIGHT ON THEIR FEET FOR CREATURES WHO'VE JUST BEEN ZAPPED.
YEAH, YOU RIGHT.

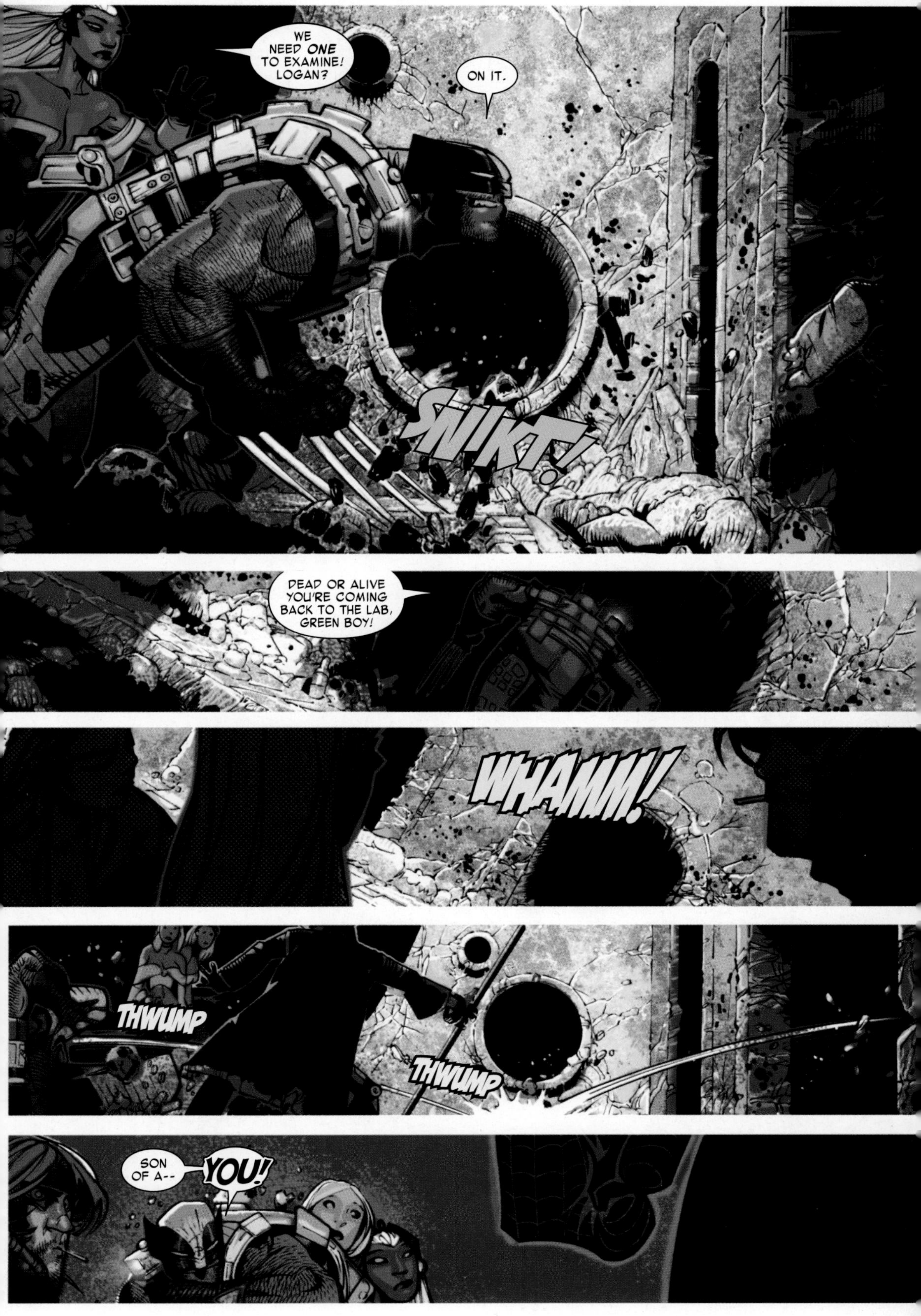

WE NEED ONE TO EXAMINE! LOGAN?
ON IT.
SNIKT!
DEAD OR ALIVE YOU'RE COMING BACK TO THE LAB, GREEN BOY!
WHAMM!
THWUMP
THWUMP
SON OF A--
YOU!

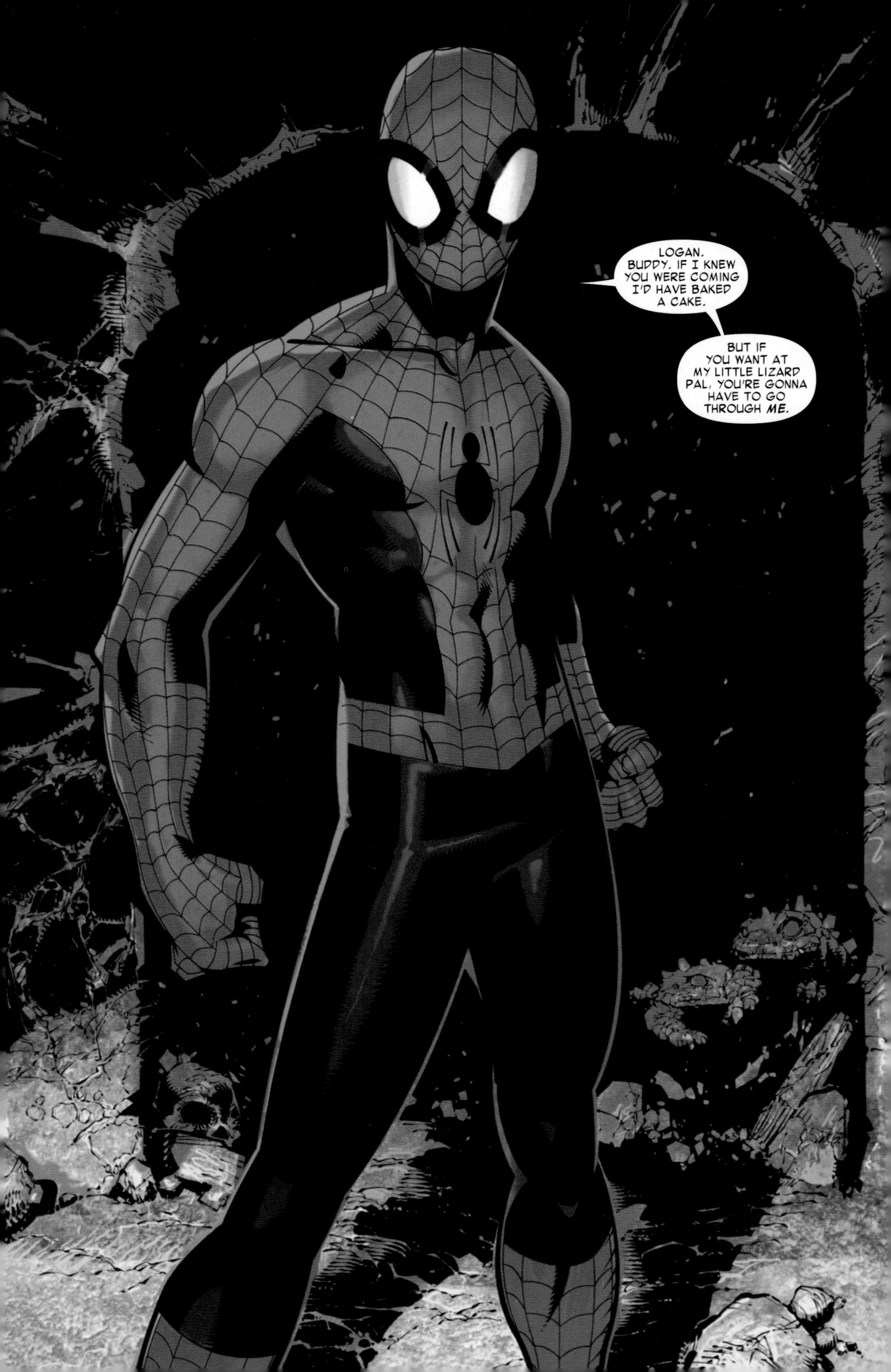
LOGAN. BUDDY. IF I KNEW YOU WERE COMING I'D HAVE BAKED A CAKE.
BUT IF YOU WANT AT MY LITTLE LIZARD PAL, YOU'RE GONNA HAVE TO GO THROUGH *ME.*

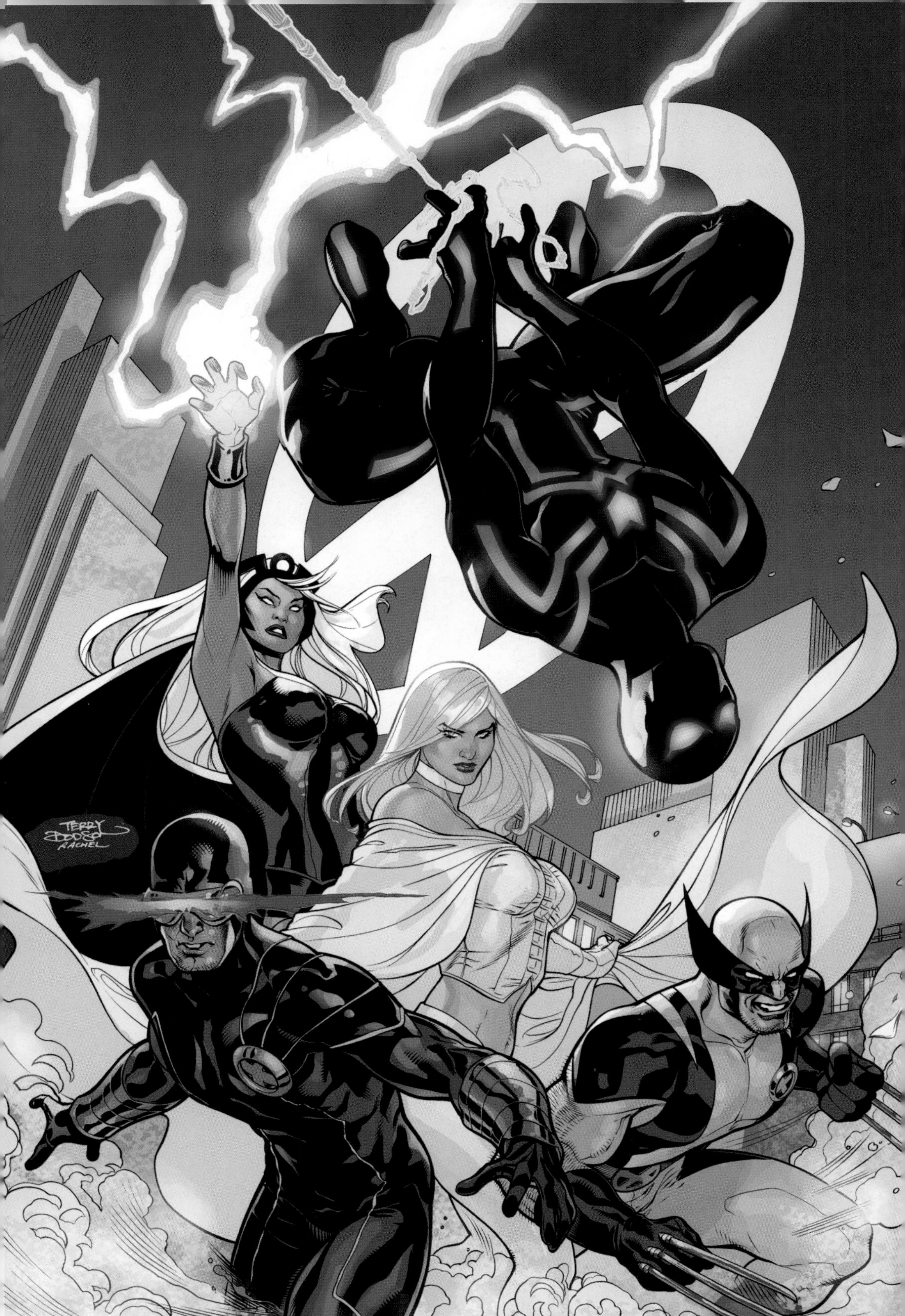
TERRY
DODSON
RACHEL

#7 VARIANT BY TERRY DODSON & RACHEL DODSON

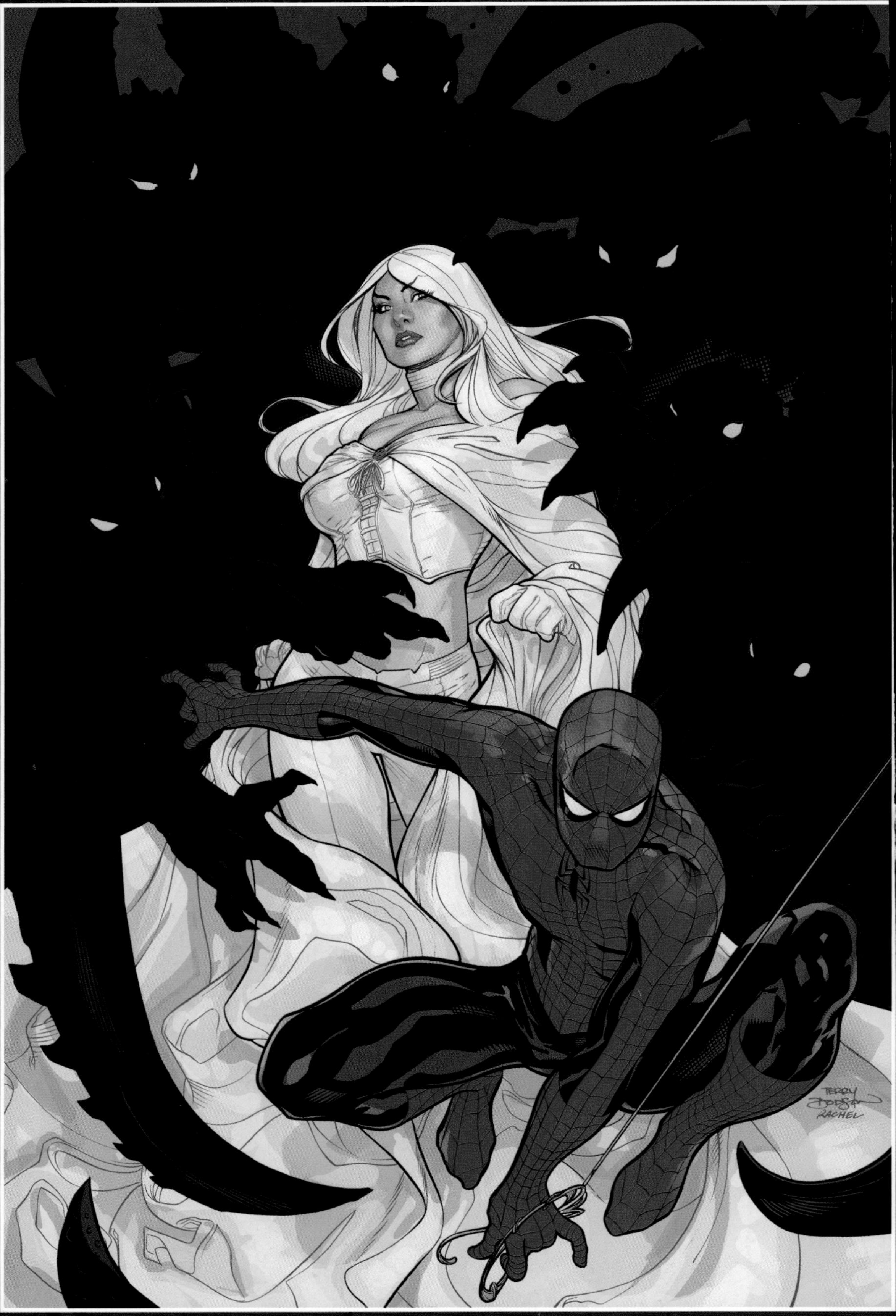
TERRY DODSON RACHEL

EIGHT

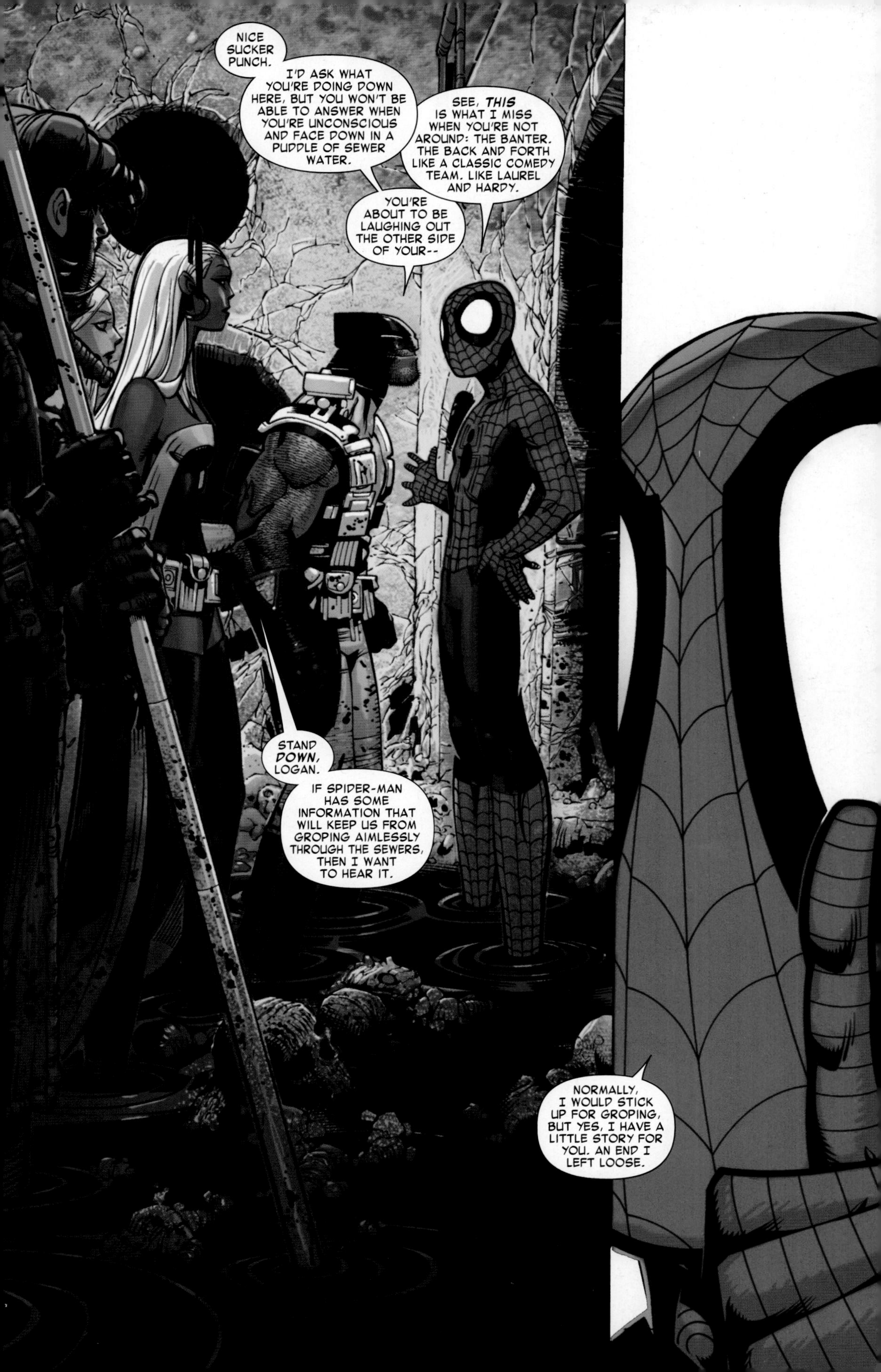
NICE SUCKER PUNCH.
I'D ASK WHAT YOU'RE DOING DOWN HERE, BUT YOU WON'T BE ABLE TO ANSWER WHEN YOU'RE UNCONSCIOUS AND FACE DOWN IN A PUDDLE OF SEWER WATER.
SEE, THIS IS WHAT I MISS WHEN YOU'RE NOT AROUND: THE BANTER. THE BACK AND FORTH LIKE A CLASSIC COMEDY TEAM. LIKE LAUREL AND HARDY.
YOU'RE ABOUT TO BE LAUGHING OUT THE OTHER SIDE OF YOUR--
STAND DOWN, LOGAN.
IF SPIDER-MAN HAS SOME INFORMATION THAT WILL KEEP US FROM GROPING AIMLESSLY THROUGH THE SEWERS, THEN I WANT TO HEAR IT.
NORMALLY, I WOULD STICK UP FOR GROPING, BUT YES, I HAVE A LITTLE STORY FOR YOU. AN END I LEFT LOOSE.

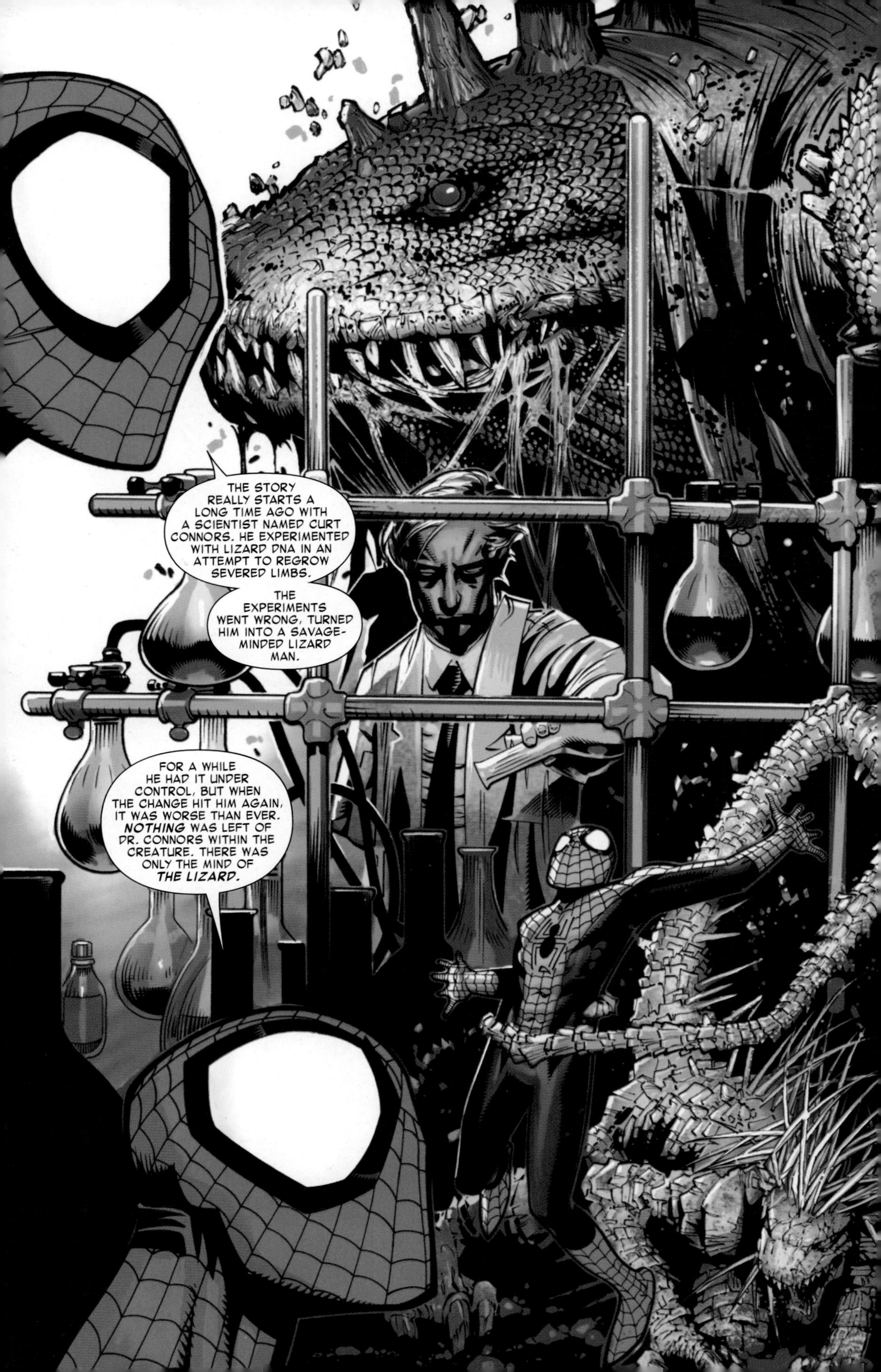
THE STORY REALLY STARTS A LONG TIME AGO WITH A SCIENTIST NAMED CURT CONNORS. HE EXPERIMENTED WITH LIZARD DNA IN AN ATTEMPT TO REGROW SEVERED LIMBS.
THE EXPERIMENTS WENT WRONG, TURNED HIM INTO A SAVAGE-MINDED LIZARD MAN.
FOR A WHILE HE HAD IT UNDER CONTROL, BUT WHEN THE CHANGE HIT HIM AGAIN, IT WAS WORSE THAN EVER. *NOTHING* WAS LEFT OF DR. CONNORS WITHIN THE CREATURE. THERE WAS ONLY THE MIND OF *THE LIZARD.*

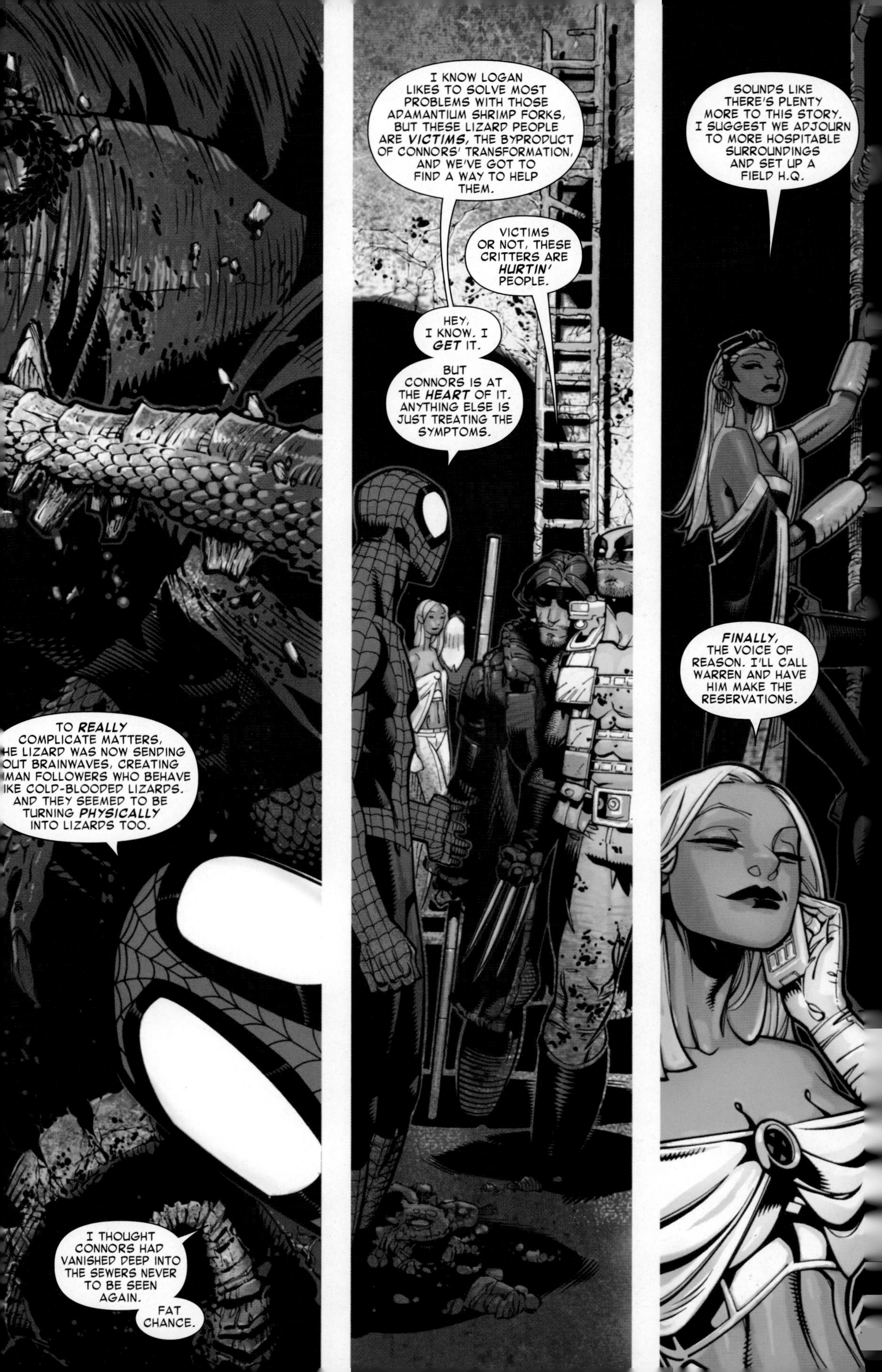
TO REALLY COMPLICATE MATTERS, HE LIZARD WAS NOW SENDING OUT BRAINWAVES, CREATING MAN FOLLOWERS WHO BEHAVE IKE COLD-BLOODED LIZARDS. AND THEY SEEMED TO BE TURNING PHYSICALLY INTO LIZARDS TOO.
I THOUGHT CONNORS HAD VANISHED DEEP INTO THE SEWERS NEVER TO BE SEEN AGAIN.
FAT CHANCE.
I KNOW LOGAN LIKES TO SOLVE MOST PROBLEMS WITH THOSE ADAMANTIUM SHRIMP FORKS, BUT THESE LIZARD PEOPLE ARE VICTIMS, THE BYPRODUCT OF CONNORS' TRANSFORMATION, AND WE'VE GOT TO FIND A WAY TO HELP THEM.
VICTIMS OR NOT, THESE CRITTERS ARE HURTIN' PEOPLE.
HEY, I KNOW. I GET IT.
BUT CONNORS IS AT THE HEART OF IT. ANYTHING ELSE IS JUST TREATING THE SYMPTOMS.
SOUNDS LIKE THERE'S PLENTY MORE TO THIS STORY. I SUGGEST WE ADJOURN TO MORE HOSPITABLE SURROUNDINGS AND SET UP A FIELD H.Q.
FINALLY, THE VOICE OF REASON. I'LL CALL WARREN AND HAVE HIM MAKE THE RESERVATIONS.

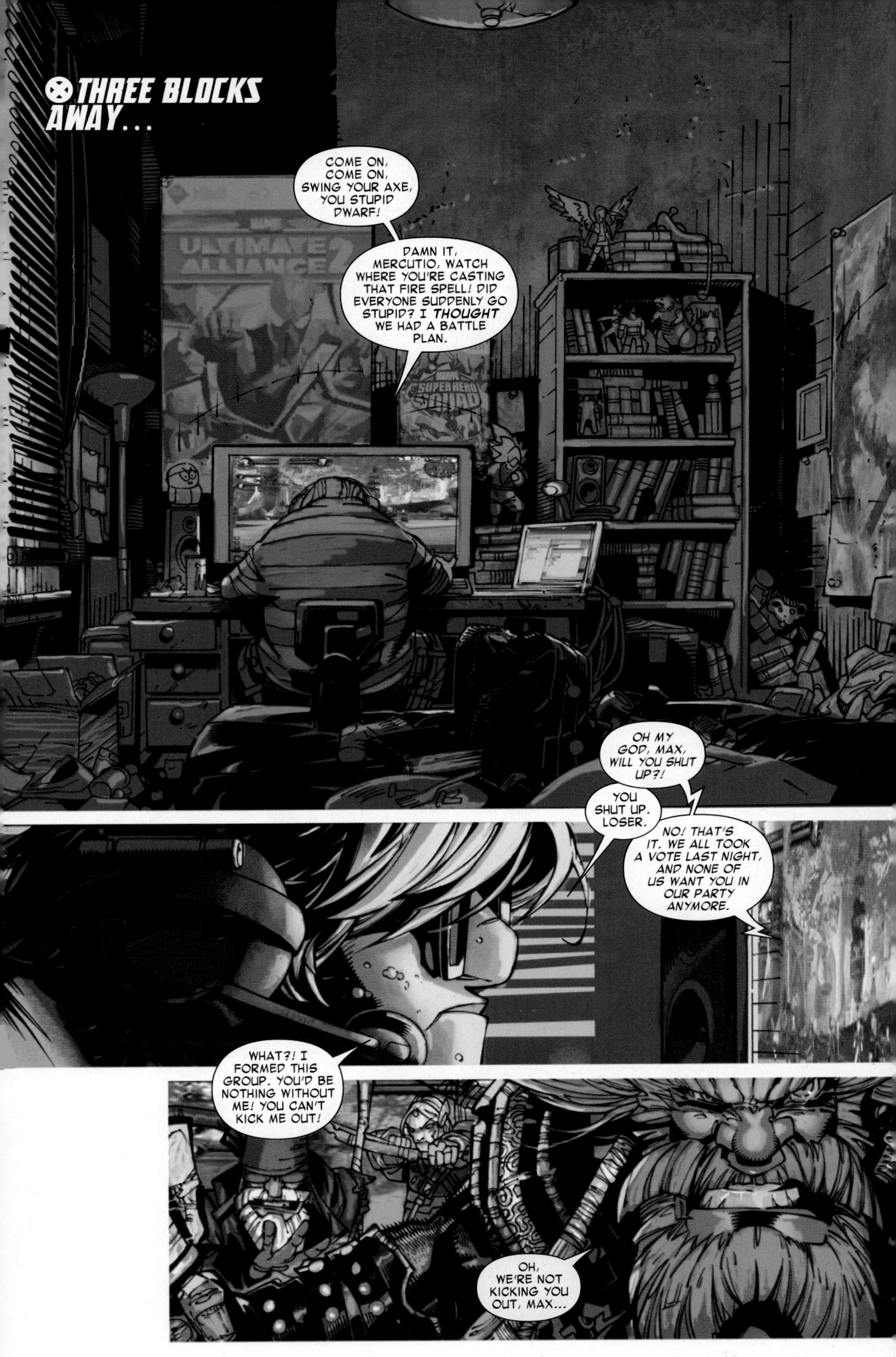
THREE BLOCKS AWAY...
COME ON, COME ON, SWING YOUR AXE, YOU STUPID DWARF!
DAMN IT, MERCUTIO, WATCH WHERE YOU'RE CASTING THAT FIRE SPELL! DID EVERYONE SUDDENLY GO STUPID? I THOUGHT WE HAD A BATTLE PLAN.
ULTIMATE ALLIANCE 2
SUPER HERO SQUAD
OH MY GOD, MAX, WILL YOU SHUT UP?!
YOU SHUT UP. LOSER.
NO! THAT'S IT. WE ALL TOOK A VOTE LAST NIGHT, AND NONE OF US WANT YOU IN OUR PARTY ANYMORE.
WHAT?! I FORMED THIS GROUP. YOU'D BE NOTHING WITHOUT ME! YOU CAN'T KICK ME OUT!
OH, WE'RE NOT KICKING YOU OUT, MAX...

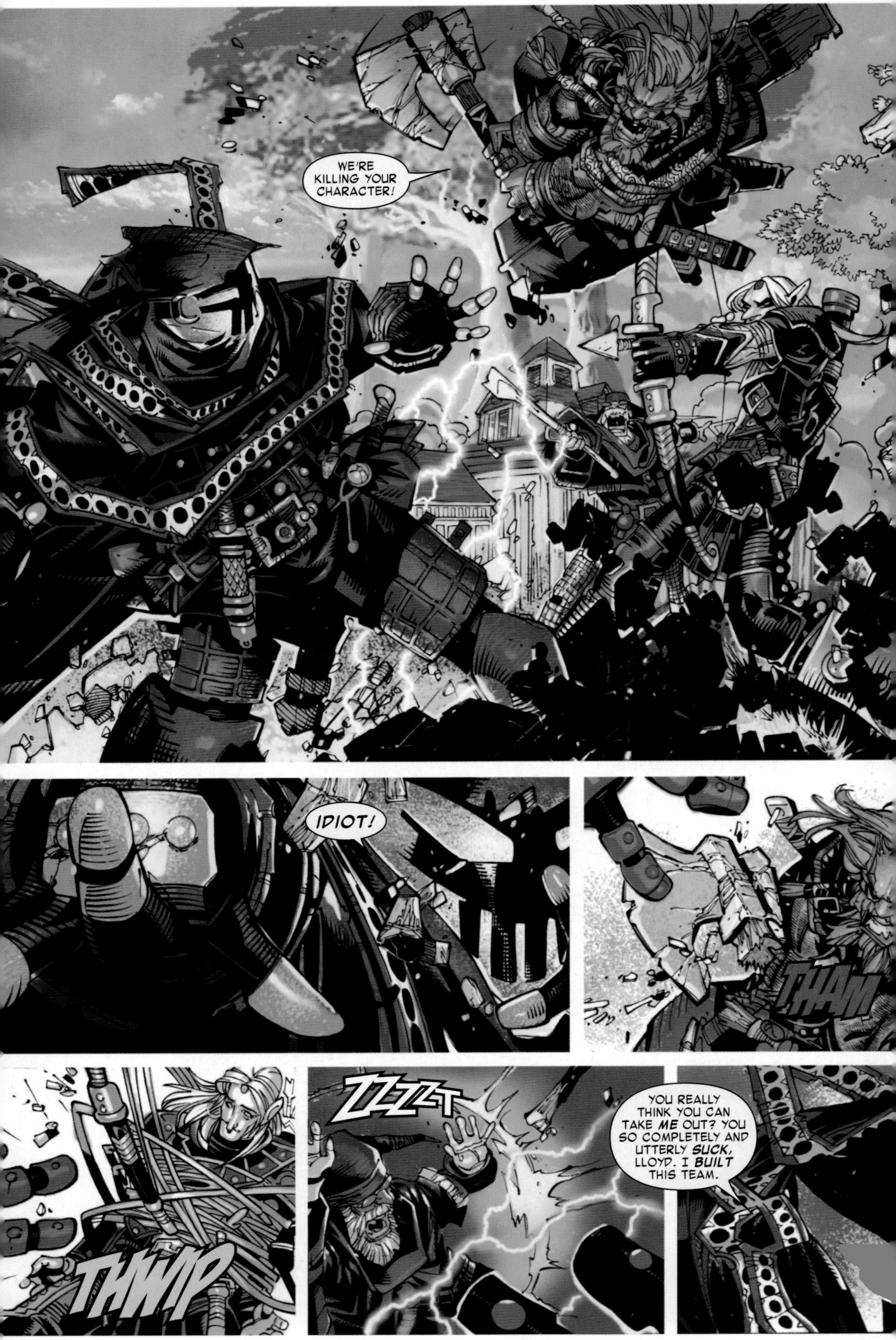
WE'RE KILLING YOUR CHARACTER!
IDIOT!
THAM
THWIP
ZZZZT
YOU REALLY THINK YOU CAN TAKE ME OUT? YOU SO COMPLETELY AND UTTERLY SUCK, LLOYD. I BUILT THIS TEAM.

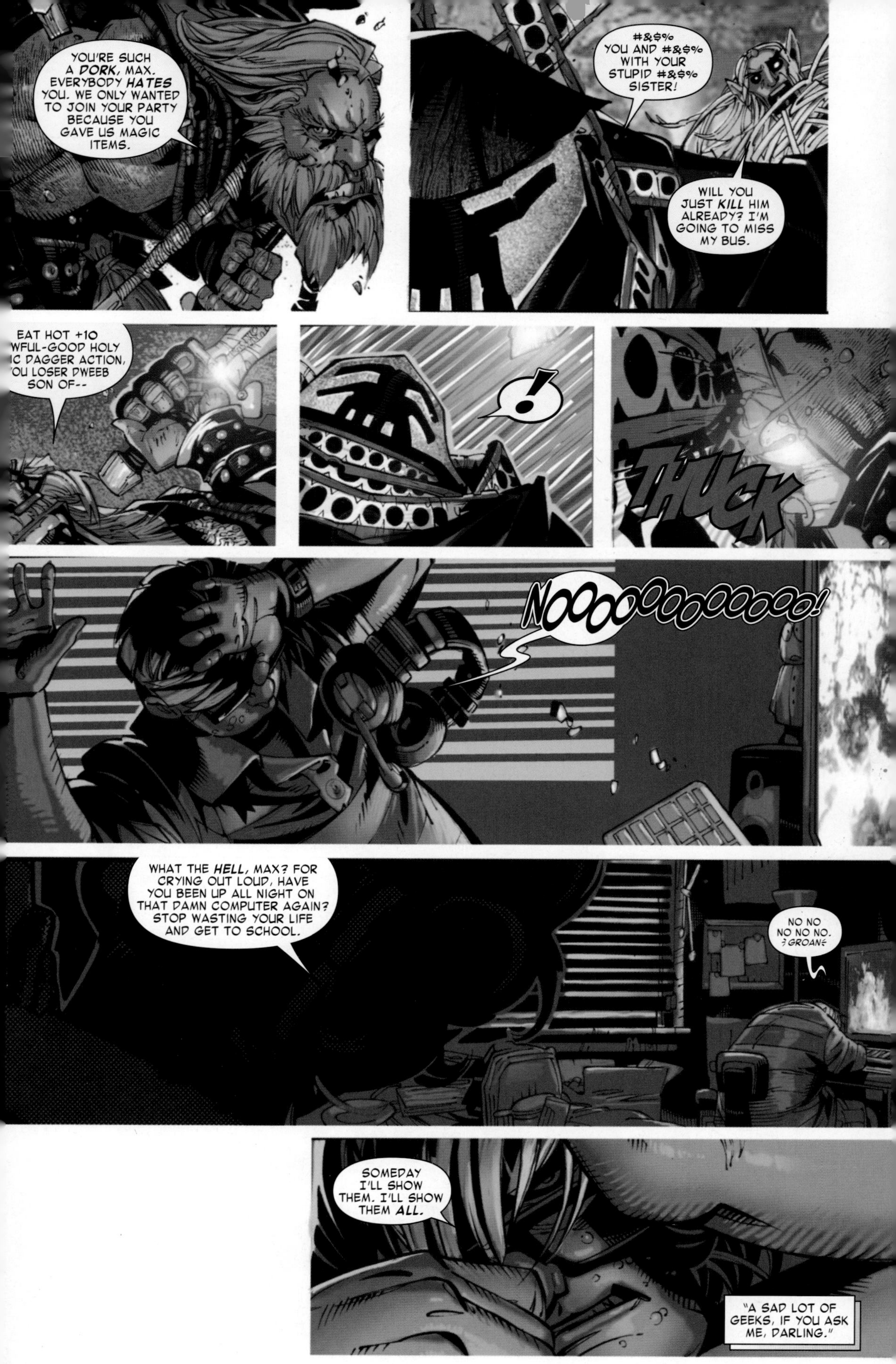
YOU'RE SUCH A DORK, MAX. EVERYBODY HATES YOU. WE ONLY WANTED TO JOIN YOUR PARTY BECAUSE YOU GAVE US MAGIC ITEMS.
#&$% YOU AND #&$% WITH YOUR STUPID #&$% SISTER!
WILL YOU JUST KILL HIM ALREADY? I'M GOING TO MISS MY BUS.
EAT HOT +10 WFUL-GOOD HOLY IC DAGGER ACTION, OU LOSER DWEEB SON OF--
!
THUCK
NOOOOOOOOOOOOO!
WHAT THE HELL, MAX? FOR CRYING OUT LOUD, HAVE YOU BEEN UP ALL NIGHT ON THAT DAMN COMPUTER AGAIN? STOP WASTING YOUR LIFE AND GET TO SCHOOL.
NO NO NO NO NO. GROAN
SOMEDAY I'LL SHOW THEM. I'LL SHOW THEM ALL.
"A SAD LOT OF GEEKS, IF YOU ASK ME, DARLING."

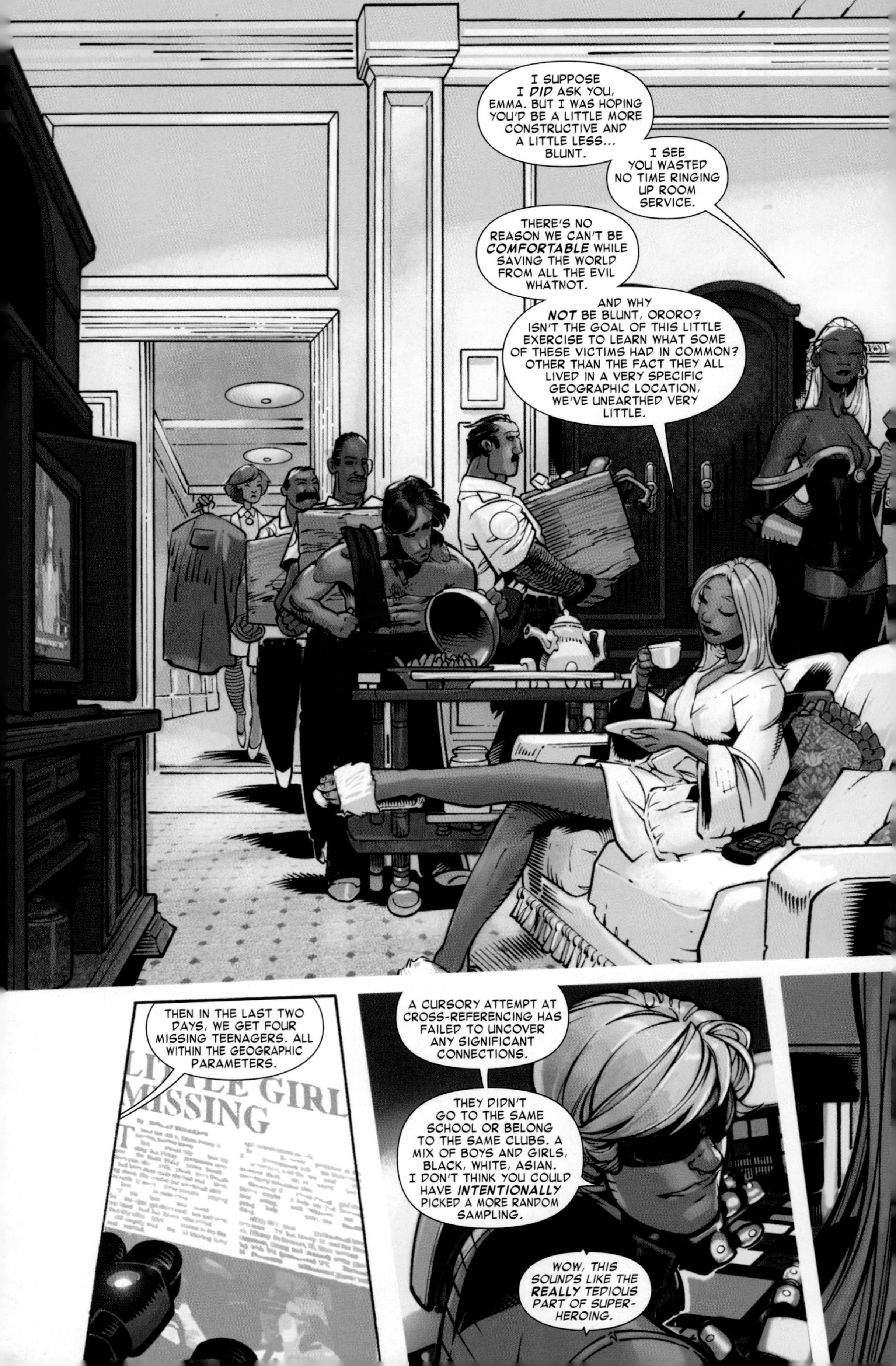
I SUPPOSE I DID ASK YOU, EMMA. BUT I WAS HOPING YOU'D BE A LITTLE MORE CONSTRUCTIVE AND A LITTLE LESS... BLUNT.
I SEE YOU WASTED NO TIME RINGING UP ROOM SERVICE.
THERE'S NO REASON WE CAN'T BE COMFORTABLE WHILE SAVING THE WORLD FROM ALL THE EVIL WHATNOT.
AND WHY NOT BE BLUNT, ORORO? ISN'T THE GOAL OF THIS LITTLE EXERCISE TO LEARN WHAT SOME OF THESE VICTIMS HAD IN COMMON? OTHER THAN THE FACT THEY ALL LIVED IN A VERY SPECIFIC GEOGRAPHIC LOCATION, WE'VE UNEARTHED VERY LITTLE.
THEN IN THE LAST TWO DAYS, WE GET FOUR MISSING TEENAGERS. ALL WITHIN THE GEOGRAPHIC PARAMETERS.
LITTLE GIRL MISSING
A CURSORY ATTEMPT AT CROSS-REFERENCING HAS FAILED TO UNCOVER ANY SIGNIFICANT CONNECTIONS.
THEY DIDN'T GO TO THE SAME SCHOOL OR BELONG TO THE SAME CLUBS. A MIX OF BOYS AND GIRLS, BLACK, WHITE, ASIAN. I DON'T THINK YOU COULD HAVE INTENTIONALLY PICKED A MORE RANDOM SAMPLING.
WOW, THIS SOUNDS LIKE THE REALLY TEDIOUS PART OF SUPER-HEROING.

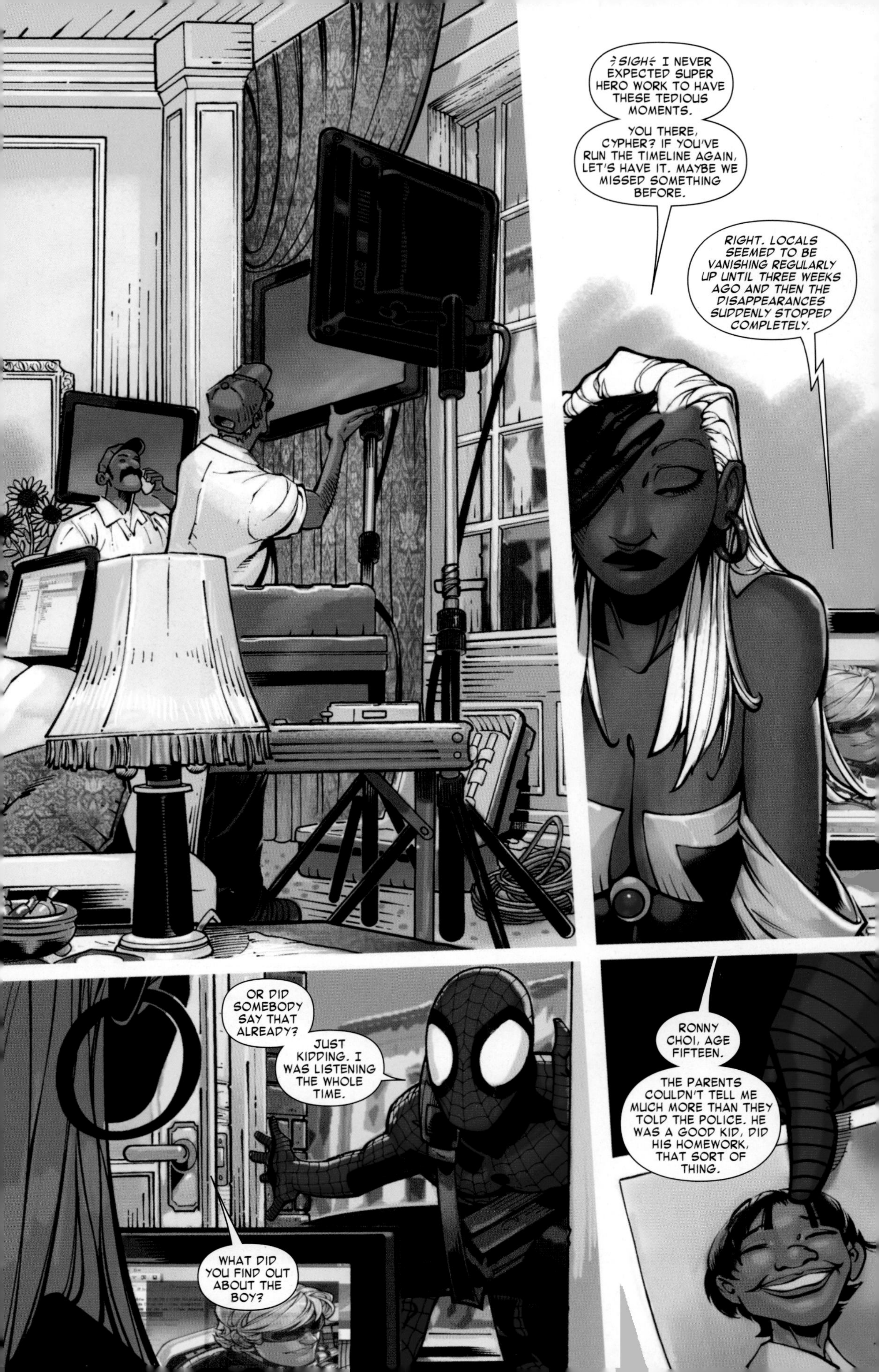

⸗SIGH⸗ I NEVER EXPECTED SUPER HERO WORK TO HAVE THESE TEDIOUS MOMENTS.
YOU THERE, CYPHER? IF YOU'VE RUN THE TIMELINE AGAIN, LET'S HAVE IT. MAYBE WE MISSED SOMETHING BEFORE.
RIGHT. LOCALS SEEMED TO BE VANISHING REGULARLY UP UNTIL THREE WEEKS AGO AND THEN THE DISAPPEARANCES SUDDENLY STOPPED COMPLETELY.
OR DID SOMEBODY SAY THAT ALREADY?
JUST KIDDING. I WAS LISTENING THE WHOLE TIME.
WHAT DID YOU FIND OUT ABOUT THE BOY?
RONNY CHOI, AGE FIFTEEN.
THE PARENTS COULDN'T TELL ME MUCH MORE THAN THEY TOLD THE POLICE. HE WAS A GOOD KID, DID HIS HOMEWORK, THAT SORT OF THING.

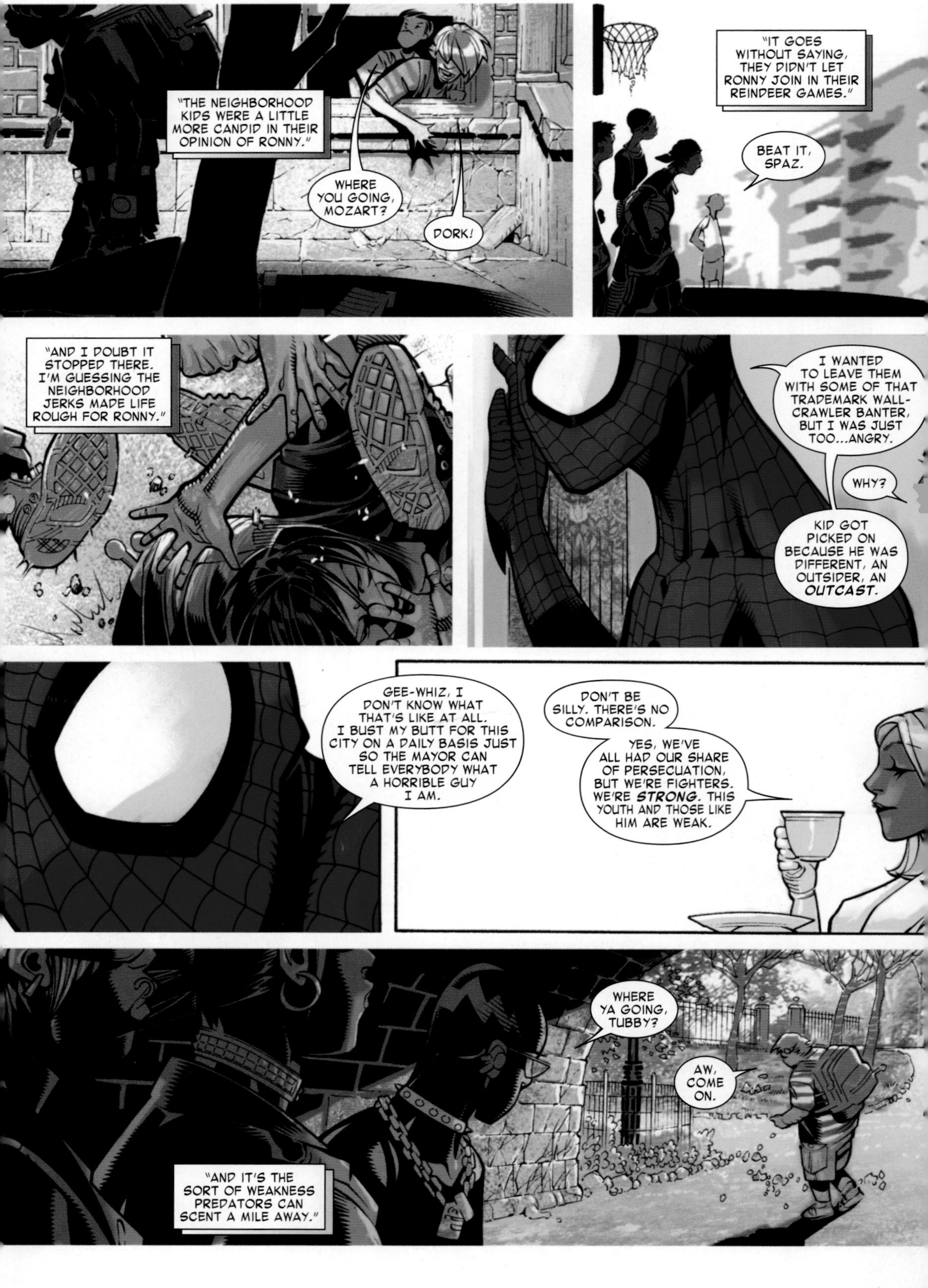
"THE NEIGHBORHOOD KIDS WERE A LITTLE MORE CANDID IN THEIR OPINION OF RONNY."
WHERE YOU GOING, MOZART?
DORK!
"IT GOES WITHOUT SAYING, THEY DIDN'T LET RONNY JOIN IN THEIR REINDEER GAMES."
BEAT IT, SPAZ.
"AND I DOUBT IT STOPPED THERE. I'M GUESSING THE NEIGHBORHOOD JERKS MADE LIFE ROUGH FOR RONNY."
I WANTED TO LEAVE THEM WITH SOME OF THAT TRADEMARK WALL-CRAWLER BANTER, BUT I WAS JUST TOO...ANGRY.
WHY?
KID GOT PICKED ON BECAUSE HE WAS DIFFERENT, AN OUTSIDER, AN OUTCAST.
GEE-WHIZ, I DON'T KNOW WHAT THAT'S LIKE AT ALL. I BUST MY BUTT FOR THIS CITY ON A DAILY BASIS JUST SO THE MAYOR CAN TELL EVERYBODY WHAT A HORRIBLE GUY I AM.
DON'T BE SILLY. THERE'S NO COMPARISON.
YES, WE'VE ALL HAD OUR SHARE OF PERSECUATION, BUT WE'RE FIGHTERS. WE'RE STRONG. THIS YOUTH AND THOSE LIKE HIM ARE WEAK.
WHERE YA GOING, TUBBY?
AW, COME ON.
"AND IT'S THE SORT OF WEAKNESS PREDATORS CAN SCENT A MILE AWAY."

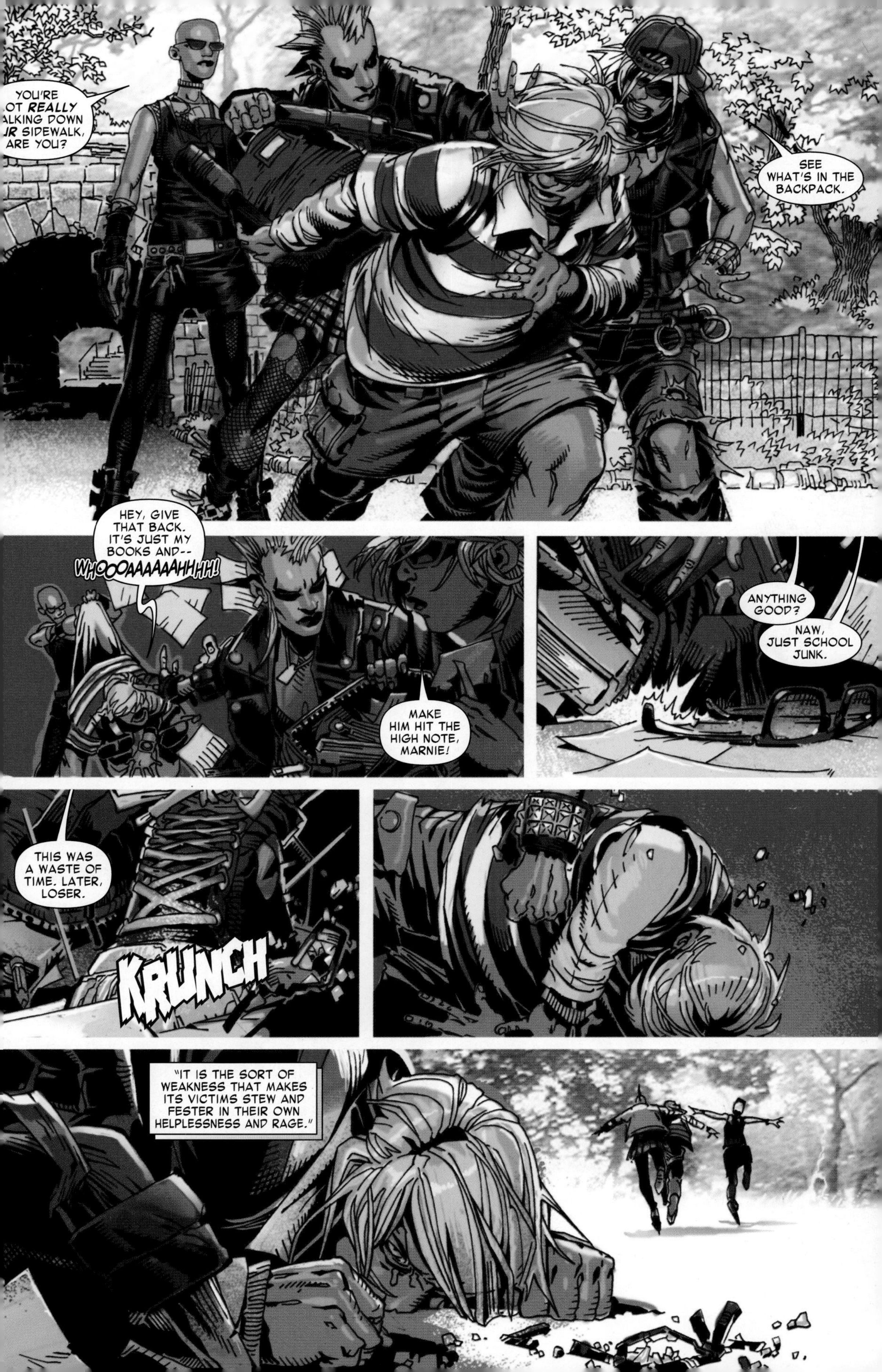
YOU'RE OT *REALLY* ALKING DOWN *UR* SIDEWALK, ARE YOU?
SEE WHAT'S IN THE BACKPACK.
HEY, GIVE THAT BACK. IT'S JUST MY BOOKS AND--
WHOOOAAAAAAHHHH!
MAKE HIM HIT THE HIGH NOTE, MARNIE!
ANYTHING GOOD?
NAW, JUST SCHOOL JUNK.
THIS WAS A WASTE OF TIME. LATER, LOSER.
KRUNCH
"IT IS THE SORT OF WEAKNESS THAT MAKES ITS VICTIMS STEW AND FESTER IN THEIR OWN HELPLESSNESS AND RAGE."

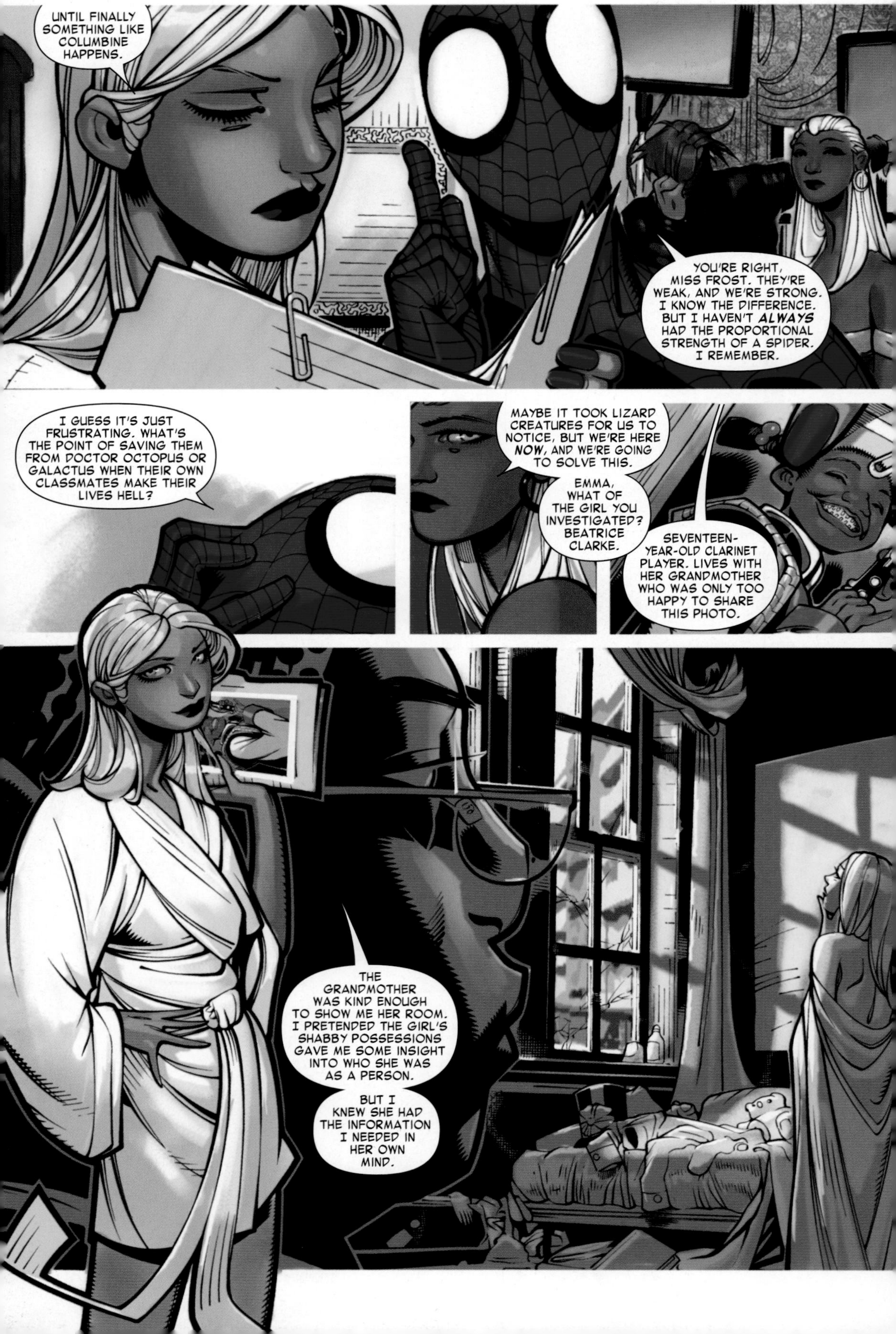

UNTIL FINALLY SOMETHING LIKE COLUMBINE HAPPENS.
YOU'RE RIGHT, MISS FROST. THEY'RE WEAK, AND WE'RE STRONG. I KNOW THE DIFFERENCE. BUT I HAVEN'T *ALWAYS* HAD THE PROPORTIONAL STRENGTH OF A SPIDER. I REMEMBER.
I GUESS IT'S JUST FRUSTRATING. WHAT'S THE POINT OF SAVING THEM FROM DOCTOR OCTOPUS OR GALACTUS WHEN THEIR OWN CLASSMATES MAKE THEIR LIVES HELL?
MAYBE IT TOOK LIZARD CREATURES FOR US TO NOTICE, BUT WE'RE HERE *NOW*, AND WE'RE GOING TO SOLVE THIS.
EMMA, WHAT OF THE GIRL YOU INVESTIGATED? BEATRICE CLARKE.
SEVENTEEN-YEAR-OLD CLARINET PLAYER. LIVES WITH HER GRANDMOTHER WHO WAS ONLY TOO HAPPY TO SHARE THIS PHOTO.
THE GRANDMOTHER WAS KIND ENOUGH TO SHOW ME HER ROOM. I PRETENDED THE GIRL'S SHABBY POSSESSIONS GAVE ME SOME INSIGHT INTO WHO SHE WAS AS A PERSON.
BUT I KNEW SHE HAD THE INFORMATION I NEEDED IN HER OWN MIND.

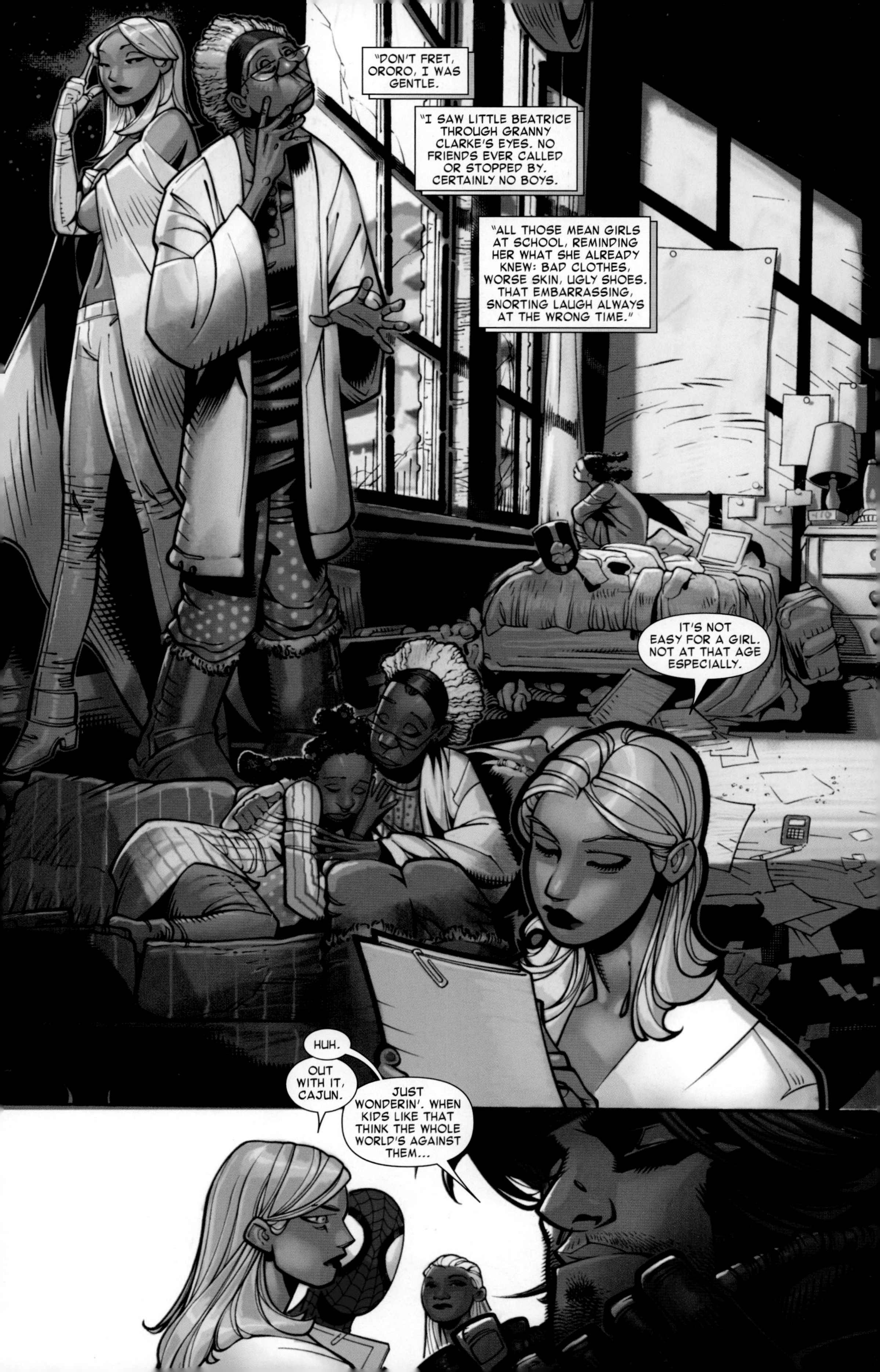
"DON'T FRET, ORORO, I WAS GENTLE.
"I SAW LITTLE BEATRICE THROUGH GRANNY CLARKE'S EYES. NO FRIENDS EVER CALLED OR STOPPED BY. CERTAINLY NO BOYS.
"ALL THOSE MEAN GIRLS AT SCHOOL, REMINDING HER WHAT SHE ALREADY KNEW: BAD CLOTHES, WORSE SKIN, UGLY SHOES. THAT EMBARRASSING, SNORTING LAUGH ALWAYS AT THE WRONG TIME."
IT'S NOT EASY FOR A GIRL. NOT AT THAT AGE ESPECIALLY.
HUH.
OUT WITH IT, CAJUN.
JUST WONDERIN'. WHEN KIDS LIKE THAT THINK THE WHOLE WORLD'S AGAINST THEM...

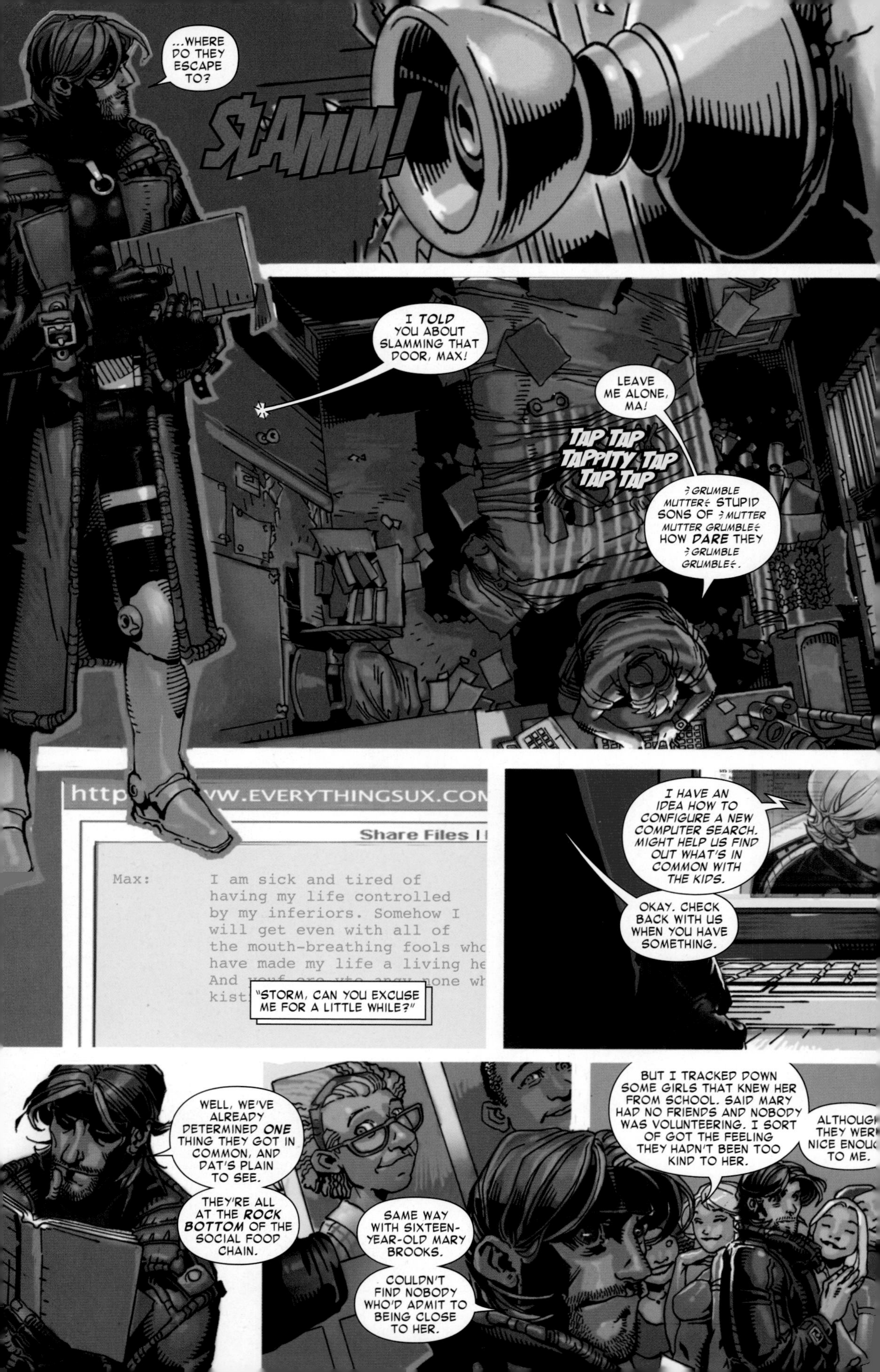
...WHERE DO THEY ESCAPE TO?
SLAMM!
I TOLD YOU ABOUT SLAMMING THAT DOOR, MAX!
LEAVE ME ALONE, MA!
TAP TAP TAPPITY TAP TAP TAP
GRUMBLE MUTTER STUPID SONS OF MUTTER MUTTER GRUMBLE HOW DARE THEY GRUMBLE GRUMBLE.
http:// WWW.EVERYTHINGSUX.COM
Share Files
Max: I am sick and tired of having my life controlled by my inferiors. Somehow I will get even with all of the mouth-breathing fools who have made my life a living he
"STORM, CAN YOU EXCUSE ME FOR A LITTLE WHILE?"
I HAVE AN IDEA HOW TO CONFIGURE A NEW COMPUTER SEARCH. MIGHT HELP US FIND OUT WHAT'S IN COMMON WITH THE KIDS.
OKAY. CHECK BACK WITH US WHEN YOU HAVE SOMETHING.
WELL, WE'VE ALREADY DETERMINED ONE THING THEY GOT IN COMMON, AND DAT'S PLAIN TO SEE.
THEY'RE ALL AT THE ROCK BOTTOM OF THE SOCIAL FOOD CHAIN.
SAME WAY WITH SIXTEEN-YEAR-OLD MARY BROOKS.
COULDN'T FIND NOBODY WHO'D ADMIT TO BEING CLOSE TO HER.
BUT I TRACKED DOWN SOME GIRLS THAT KNEW HER FROM SCHOOL. SAID MARY HAD NO FRIENDS AND NOBODY WAS VOLUNTEERING. I SORT OF GOT THE FEELING THEY HADN'T BEEN TOO KIND TO HER.

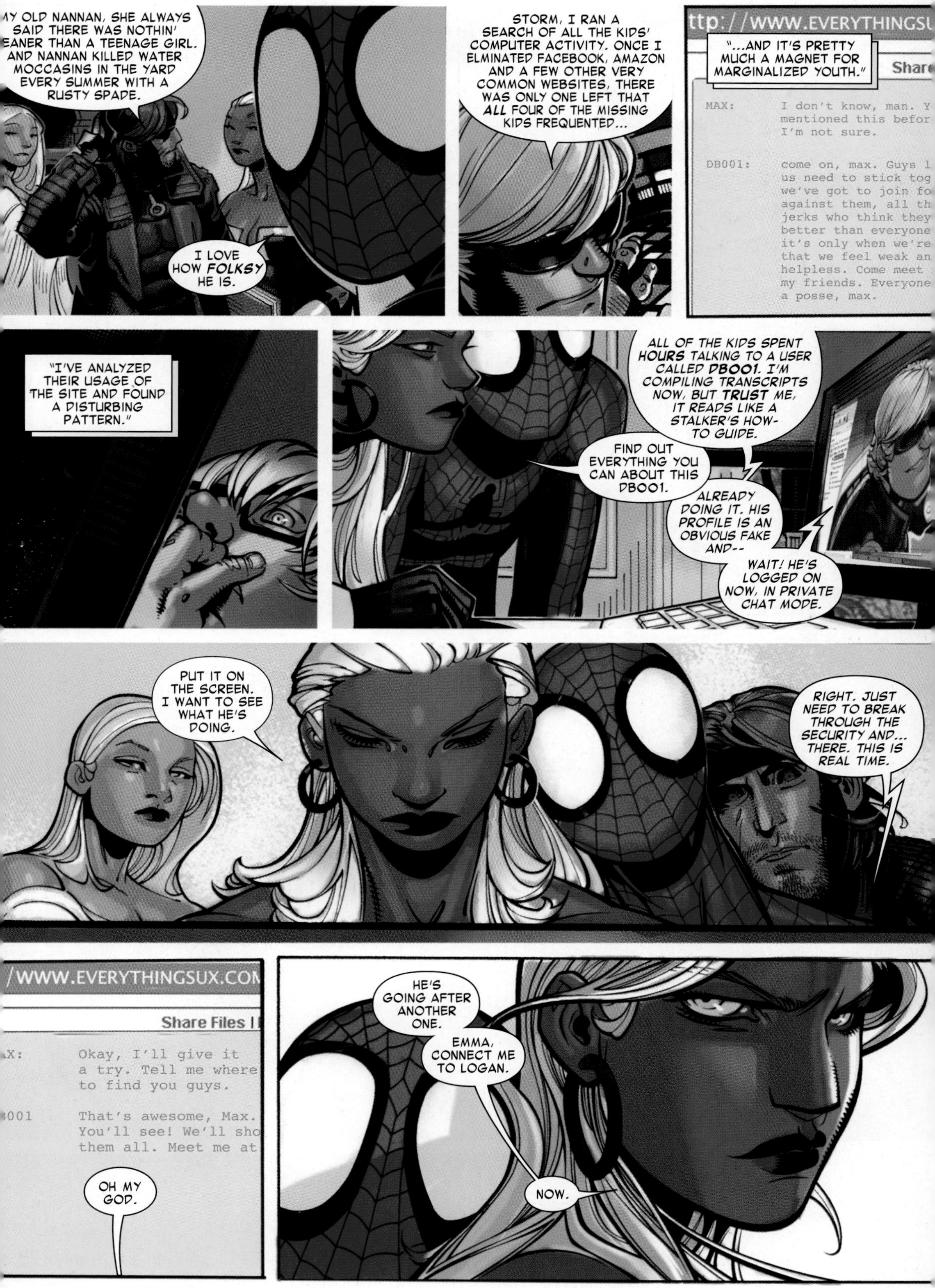
MY OLD NANNAN, SHE ALWAYS SAID THERE WAS NOTHIN' MEANER THAN A TEENAGE GIRL. AND NANNAN KILLED WATER MOCCASINS IN THE YARD EVERY SUMMER WITH A RUSTY SPADE.
I LOVE HOW FOLKSY HE IS.
STORM, I RAN A SEARCH OF ALL THE KIDS' COMPUTER ACTIVITY. ONCE I ELMINATED FACEBOOK, AMAZON AND A FEW OTHER VERY COMMON WEBSITES, THERE WAS ONLY ONE LEFT THAT ALL FOUR OF THE MISSING KIDS FREQUENTED...
ttp://WWW.EVERYTHINGSU
"...AND IT'S PRETTY MUCH A MAGNET FOR MARGINALIZED YOUTH."
Share
MAX: I don't know, man. Y mentioned this befor I'm not sure.
DB001: come on, max. Guys l us need to stick tog we've got to join fo against them, all th jerks who think they better than everyone it's only when we're that we feel weak an helpless. Come meet my friends. Everyone a posse, max.
"I'VE ANALYZED THEIR USAGE OF THE SITE AND FOUND A DISTURBING PATTERN."
ALL OF THE KIDS SPENT HOURS TALKING TO A USER CALLED DB001. I'M COMPILING TRANSCRIPTS NOW, BUT TRUST ME, IT READS LIKE A STALKER'S HOW-TO GUIDE.
FIND OUT EVERYTHING YOU CAN ABOUT THIS DB001.
ALREADY DOING IT. HIS PROFILE IS AN OBVIOUS FAKE AND--
WAIT! HE'S LOGGED ON NOW, IN PRIVATE CHAT MODE.
PUT IT ON THE SCREEN. I WANT TO SEE WHAT HE'S DOING.
RIGHT. JUST NEED TO BREAK THROUGH THE SECURITY AND... THERE. THIS IS REAL TIME.
/WWW.EVERYTHINGSUX.COM
Share Files
AX: Okay, I'll give it a try. Tell me where to find you guys.
001 That's awesome, Max. You'll see! We'll sho them all. Meet me at
OH MY GOD.
HE'S GOING AFTER ANOTHER ONE.
EMMA, CONNECT ME TO LOGAN.
NOW.

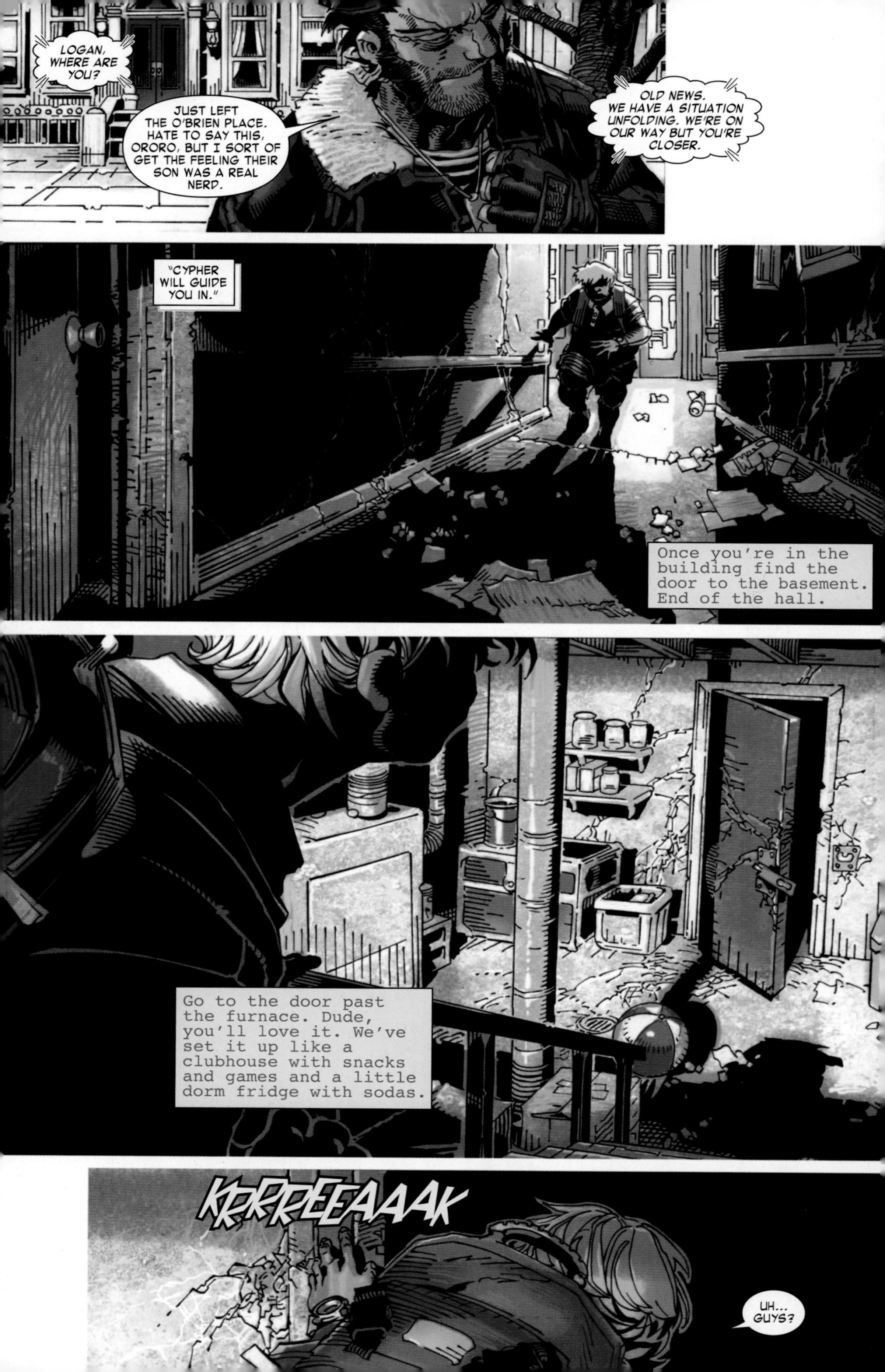
LOGAN, WHERE ARE YOU?
JUST LEFT THE O'BRIEN PLACE. HATE TO SAY THIS, ORORO, BUT I SORT OF GET THE FEELING THEIR SON WAS A REAL NERD.
OLD NEWS. WE HAVE A SITUATION UNFOLDING. WE'RE ON OUR WAY BUT YOU'RE CLOSER.
"CYPHER WILL GUIDE YOU IN."
Once you're in the building find the door to the basement. End of the hall.
Go to the door past the furnace. Dude, you'll love it. We've set it up like a clubhouse with snacks and games and a little dorm fridge with sodas.
KRRRREEAAAK
UH... GUYS?

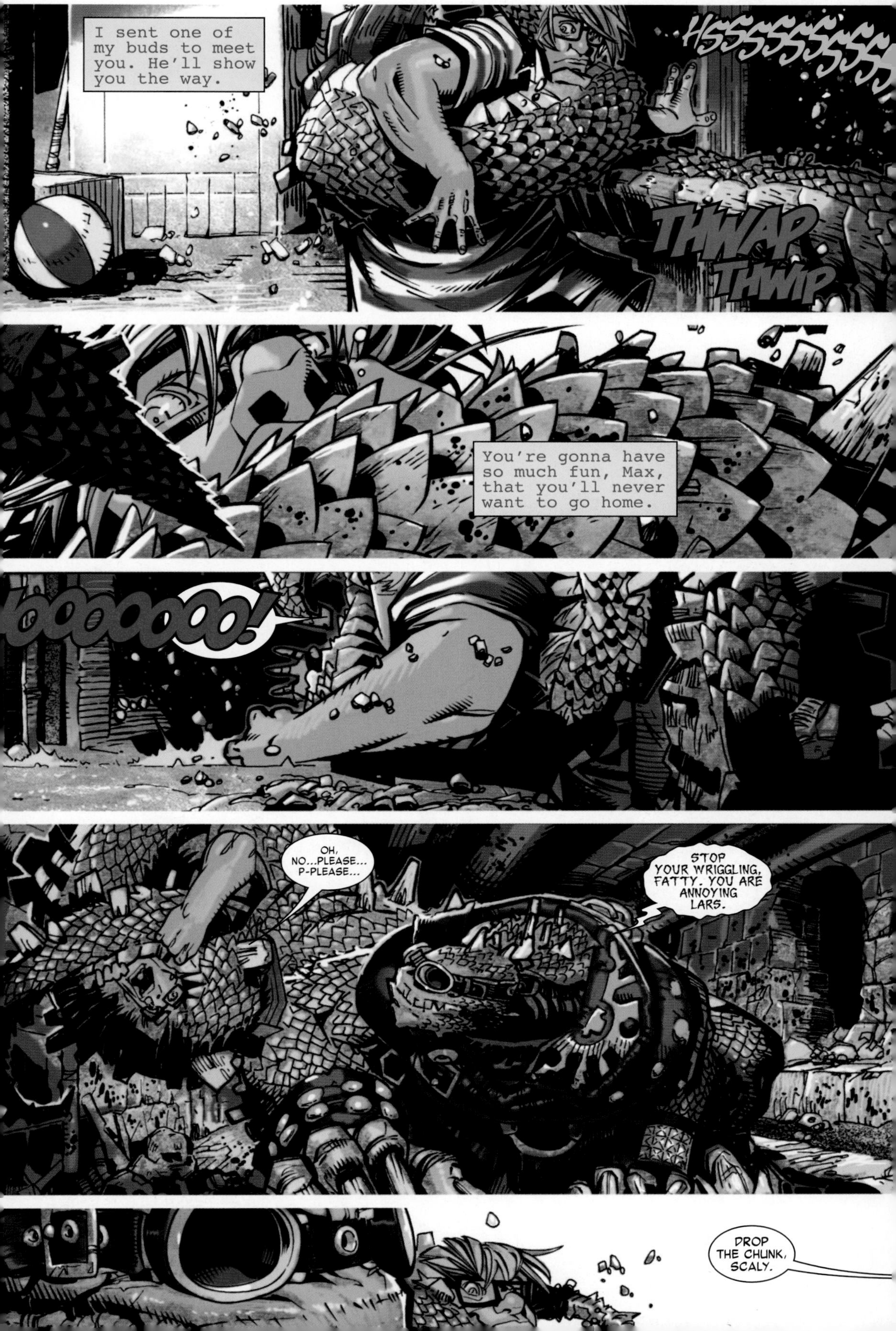
I sent one of my buds to meet you. He'll show you the way.
HSSSSSSSSS
THWAP
THWIP
You're gonna have so much fun, Max, that you'll never want to go home.
OOOOOOO!
OH, NO...PLEASE... P-PLEASE...
STOP YOUR WRIGGLING, FATTY. YOU ARE ANNOYING LARS.
DROP THE CHUNK, SCALY.

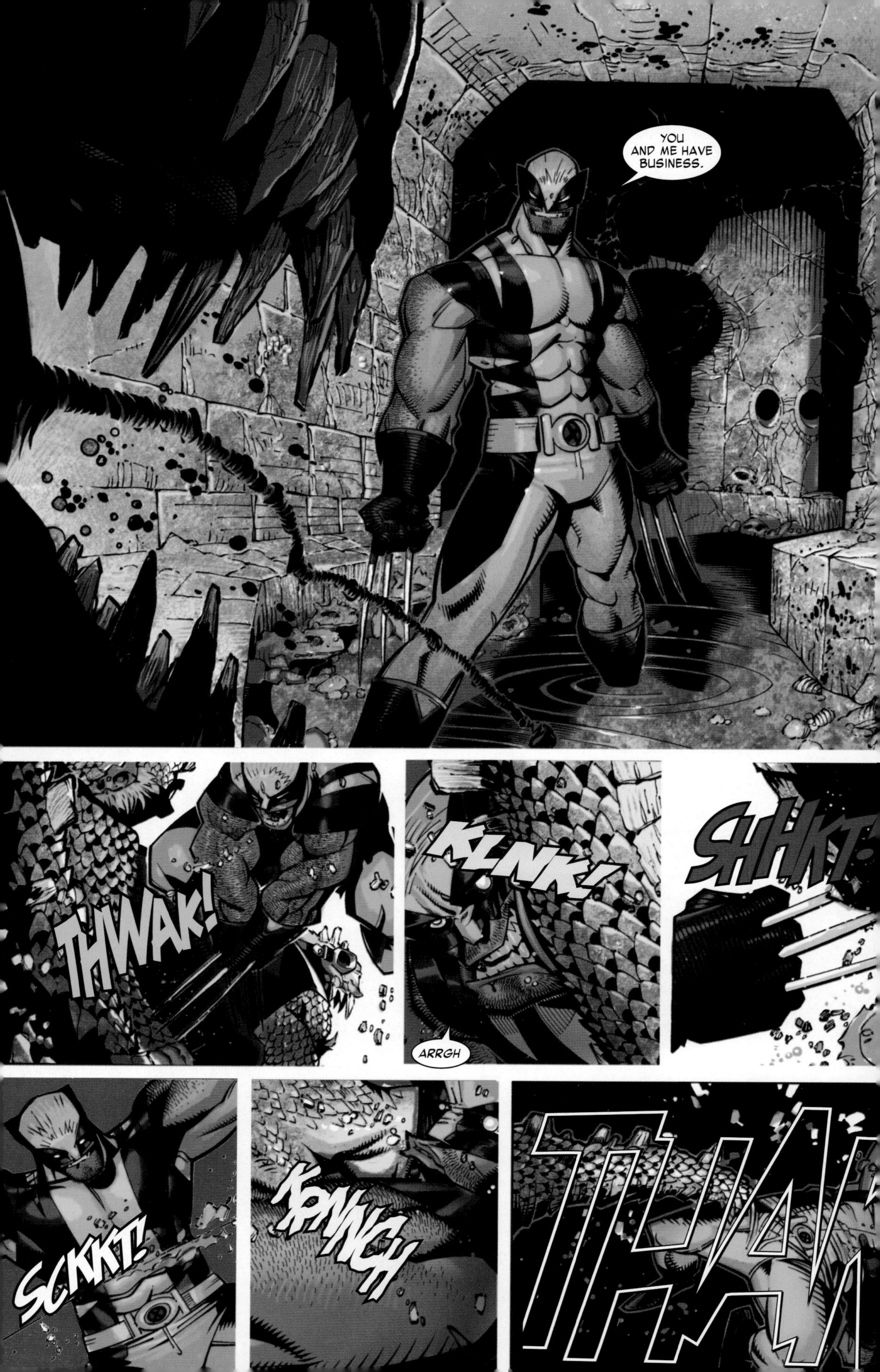
YOU AND ME HAVE BUSINESS.
THWAK!
KLNK!
ARRGH
SHHKT
SCKKT!
KRNNCH

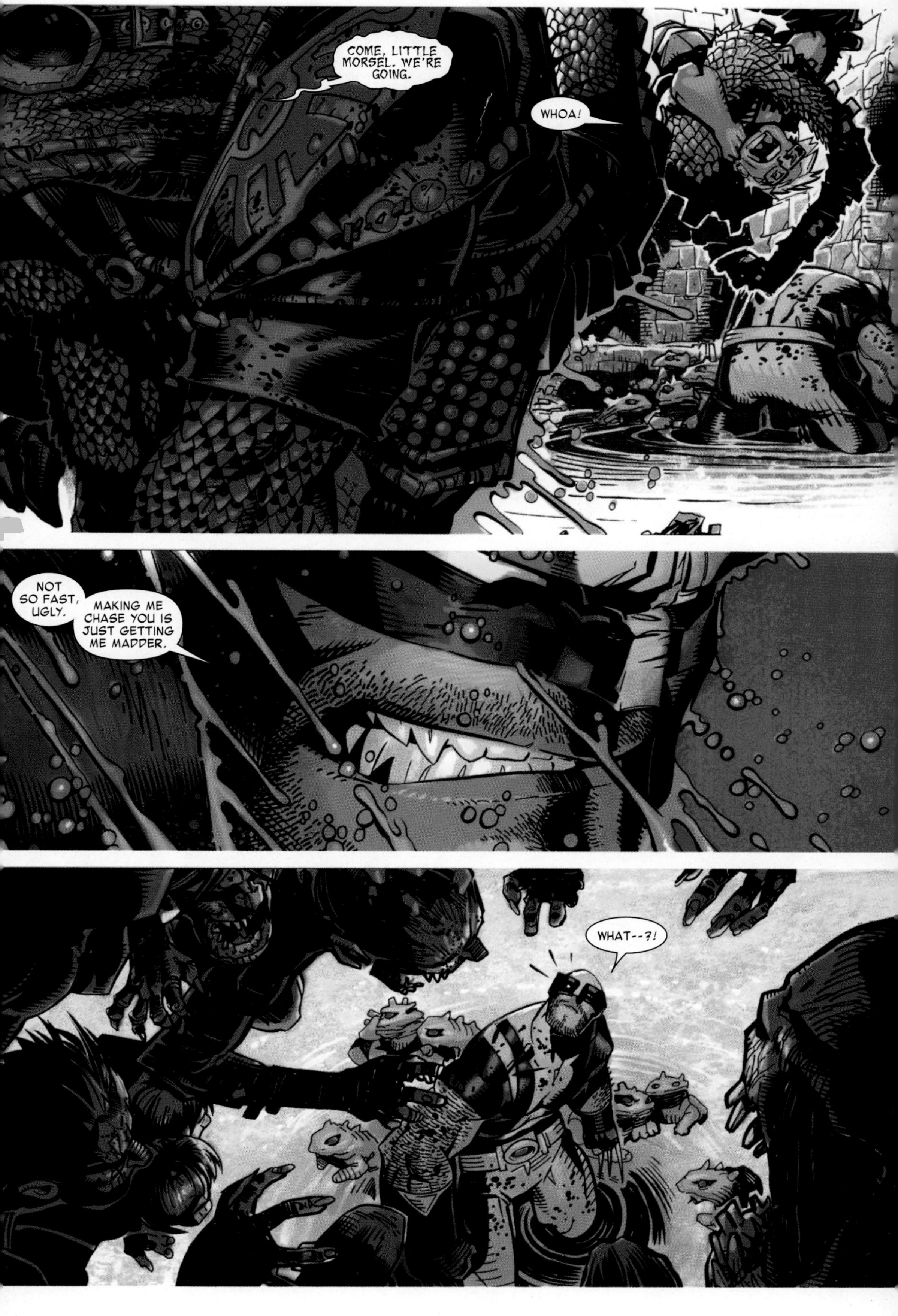
COME, LITTLE MORSEL. WE'RE GOING.
WHOA!
NOT SO FAST, UGLY.
MAKING ME CHASE YOU IS JUST GETTING ME MADDER.
WHAT--?!

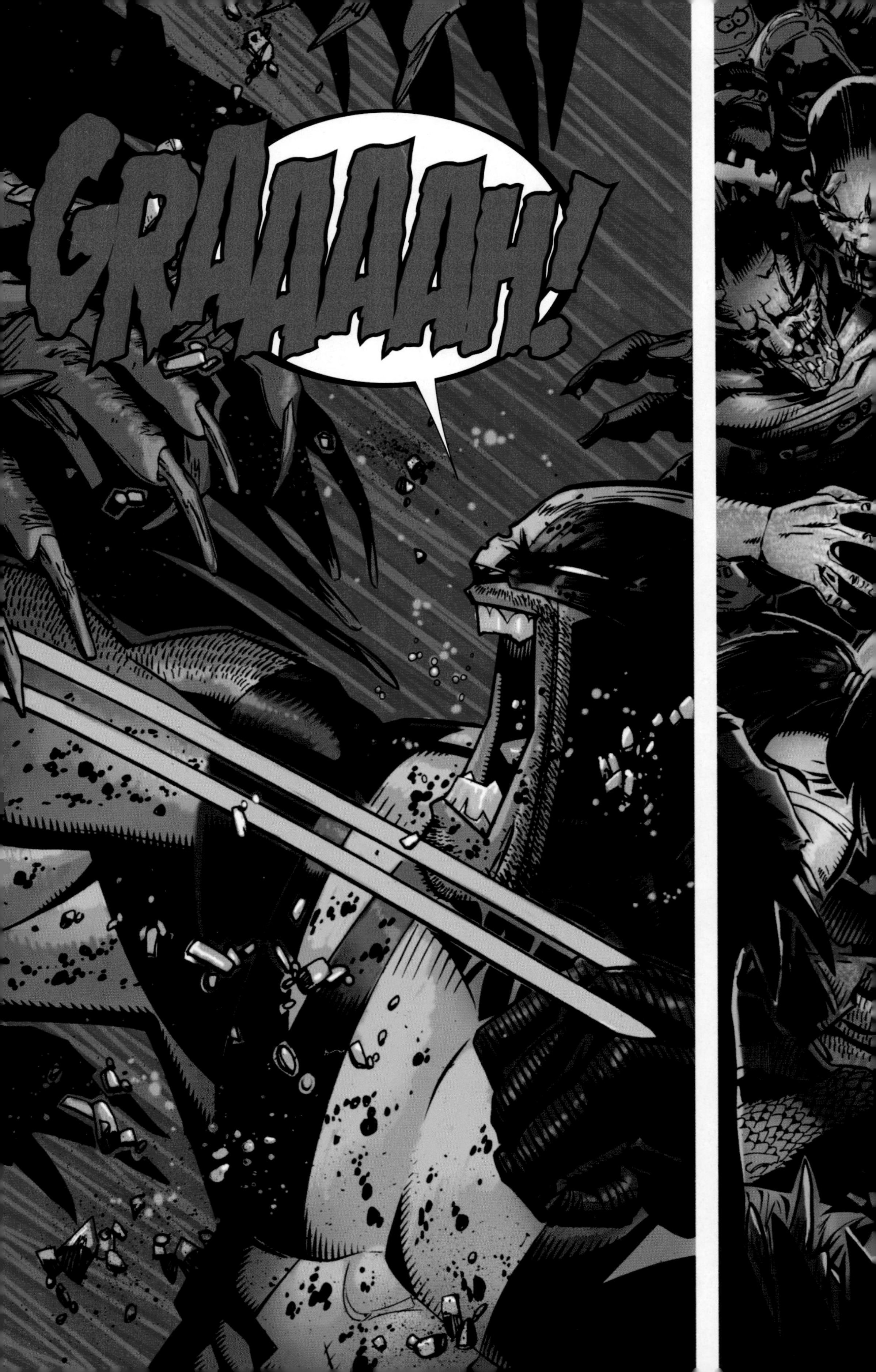
GRAAAAH!

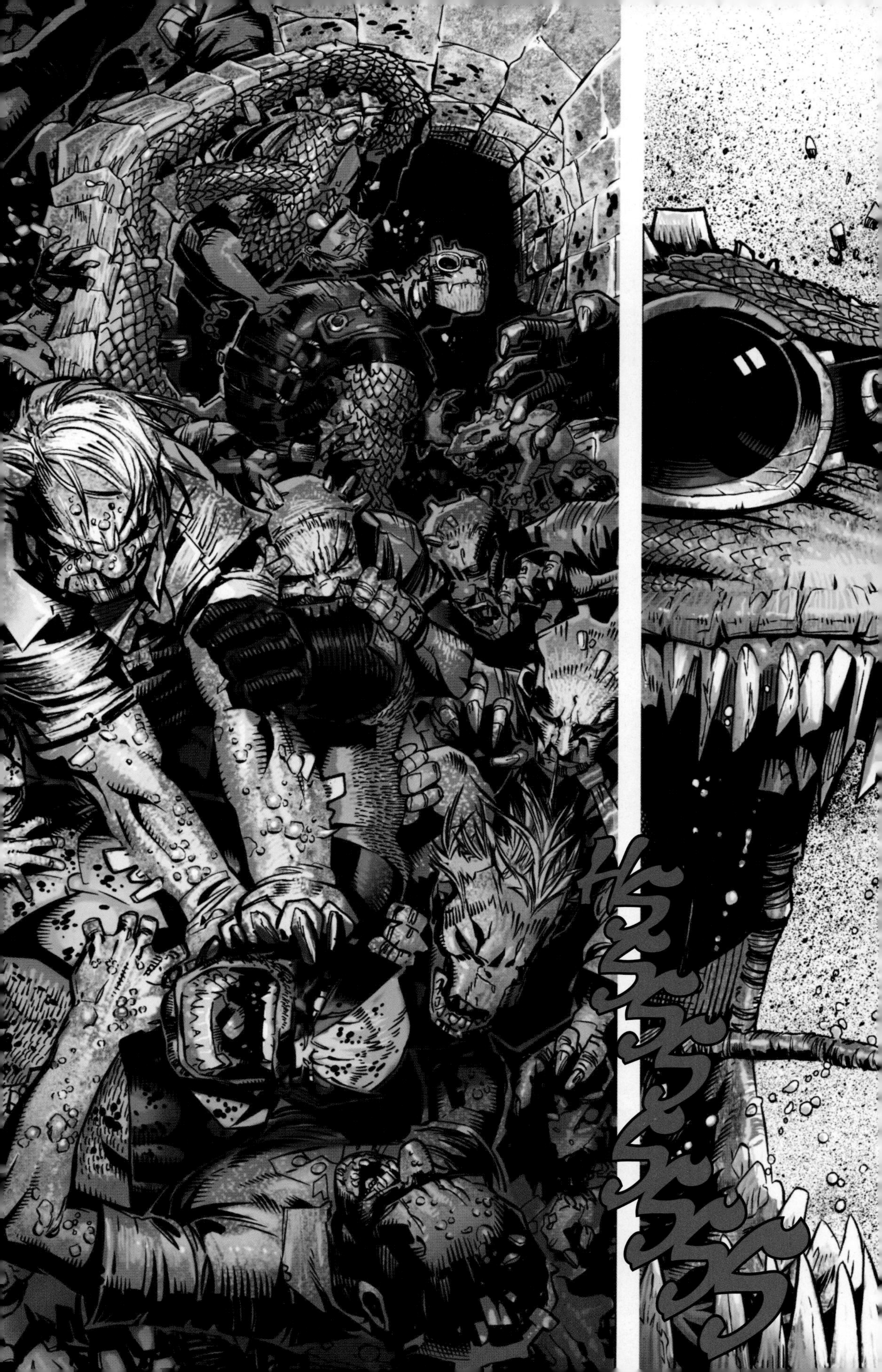
HSSSSSSS

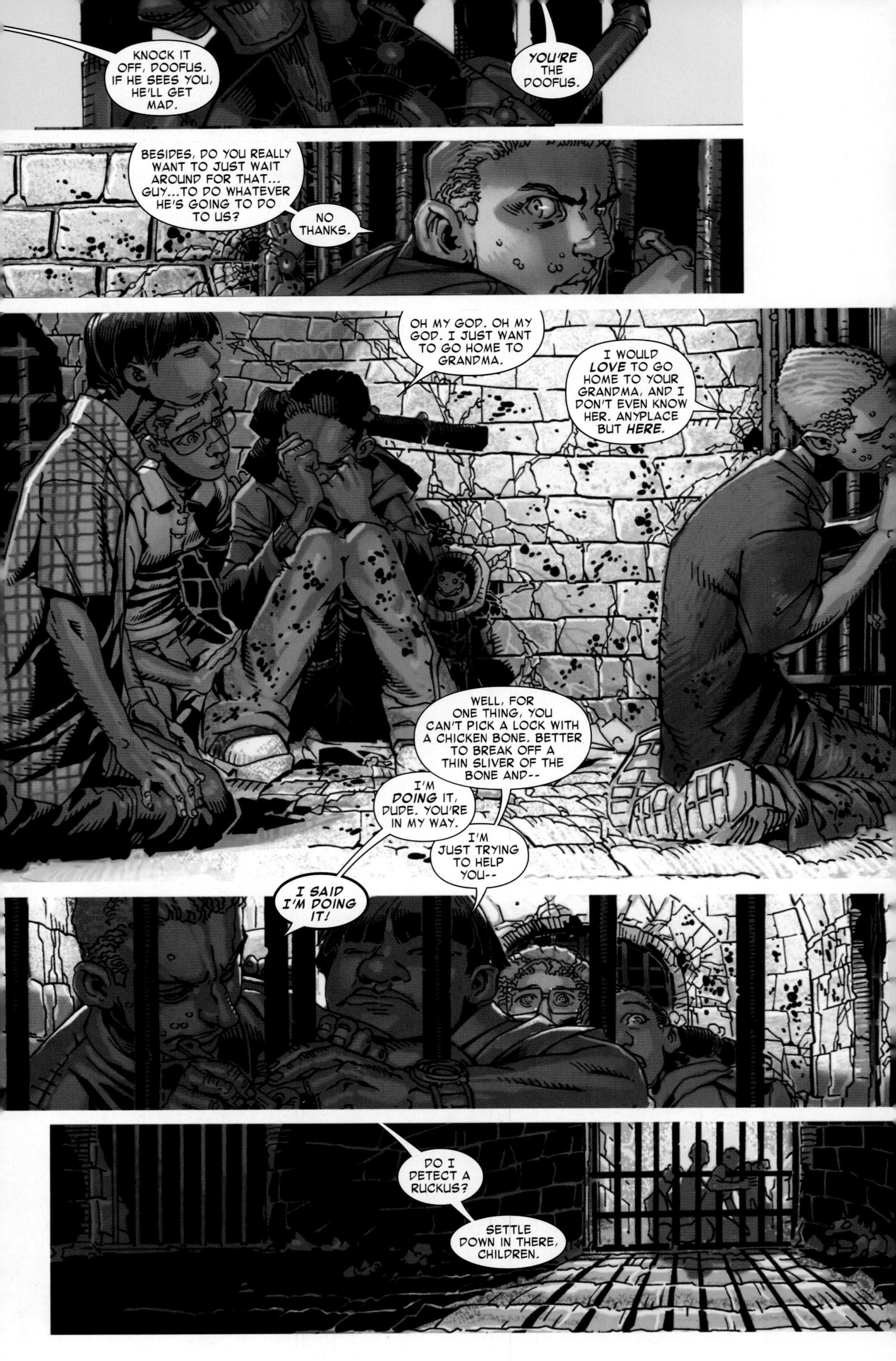
KNOCK IT OFF, DOOFUS. IF HE SEES YOU, HE'LL GET MAD.
YOU'RE THE DOOFUS.
BESIDES, DO YOU REALLY WANT TO JUST WAIT AROUND FOR THAT... GUY...TO DO WHATEVER HE'S GOING TO DO TO US?
NO THANKS.
OH MY GOD. OH MY GOD. I JUST WANT TO GO HOME TO GRANDMA.
I WOULD *LOVE* TO GO HOME TO YOUR GRANDMA, AND I DON'T EVEN KNOW HER. ANYPLACE BUT *HERE.*
WELL, FOR ONE THING, YOU CAN'T PICK A LOCK WITH A CHICKEN BONE. BETTER TO BREAK OFF A THIN SLIVER OF THE BONE AND--
I'M *DOING* IT, DUDE. YOU'RE IN MY WAY.
I'M JUST TRYING TO HELP YOU--
I SAID I'M DOING IT!
DO I DETECT A RUCKUS?
SETTLE DOWN IN THERE, CHILDREN.

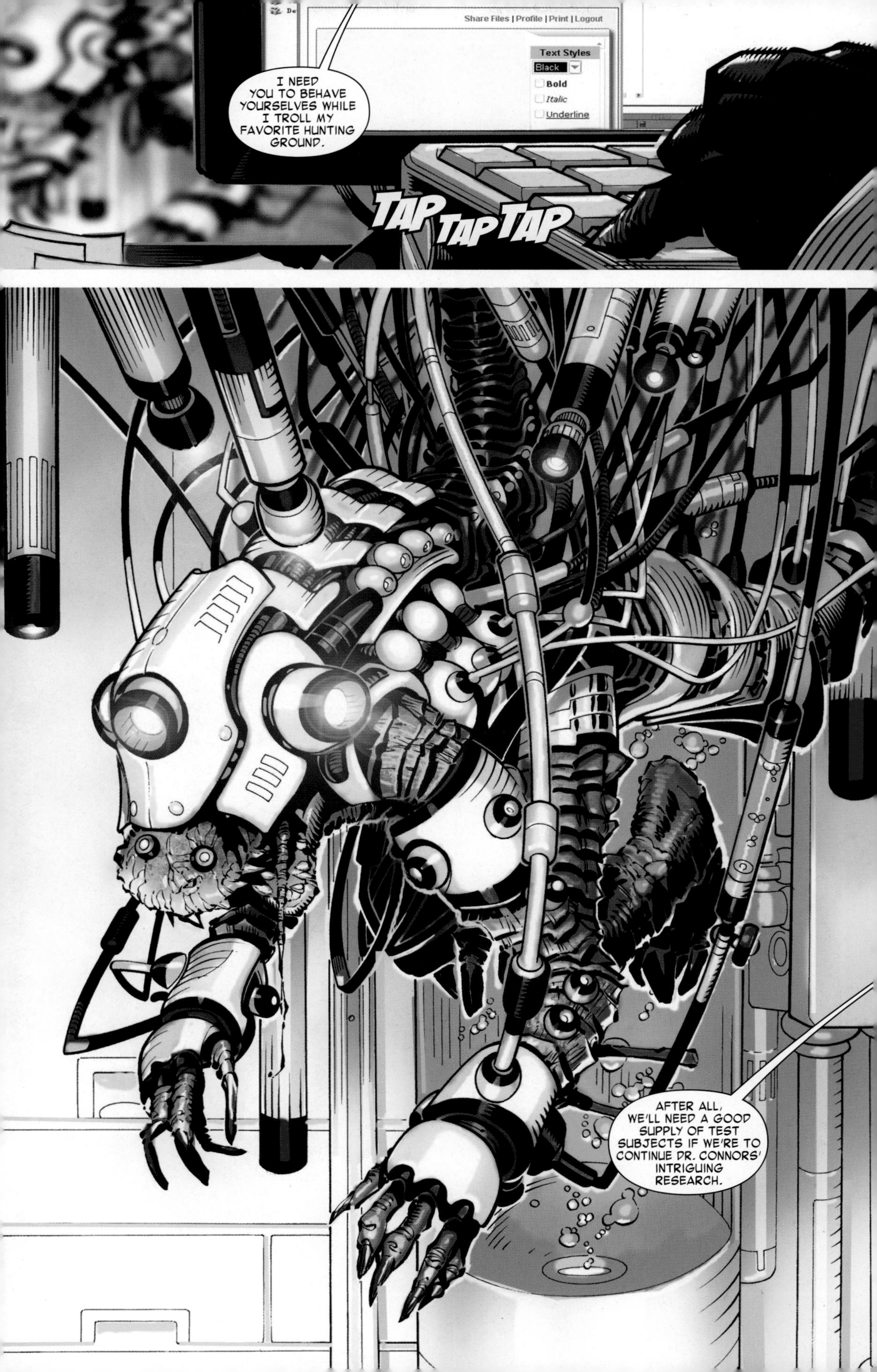
Share Files | Profile | Print | Logout
Text Styles
Black
Bold
Italic
Underline
I NEED YOU TO BEHAVE YOURSELVES WHILE I TROLL MY FAVORITE HUNTING GROUND.
TAP TAP TAP
AFTER ALL, WE'LL NEED A GOOD SUPPLY OF TEST SUBJECTS IF WE'RE TO CONTINUE DR. CONNORS' INTRIGUING RESEARCH.

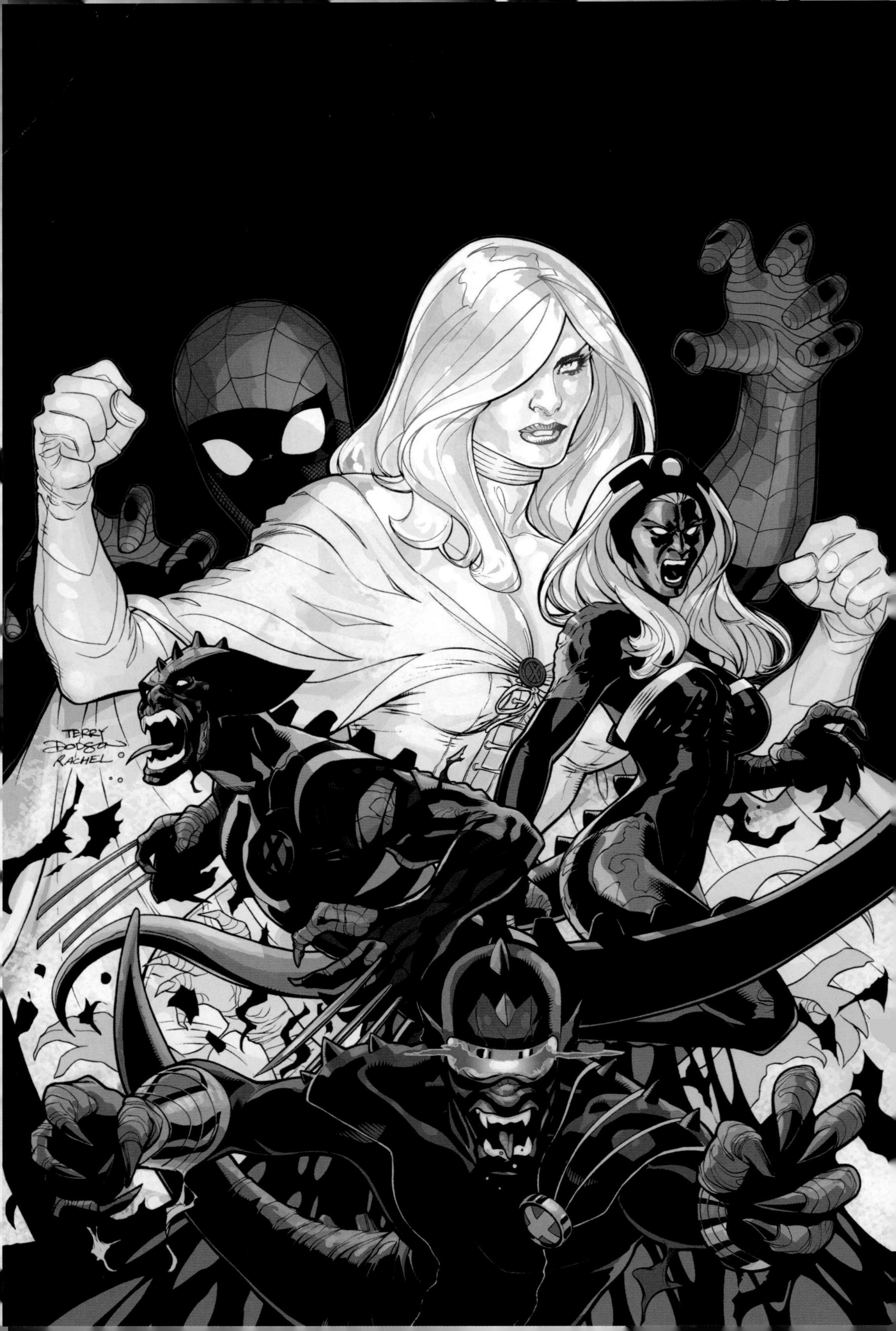
TERRY
DODSON
RACHEL

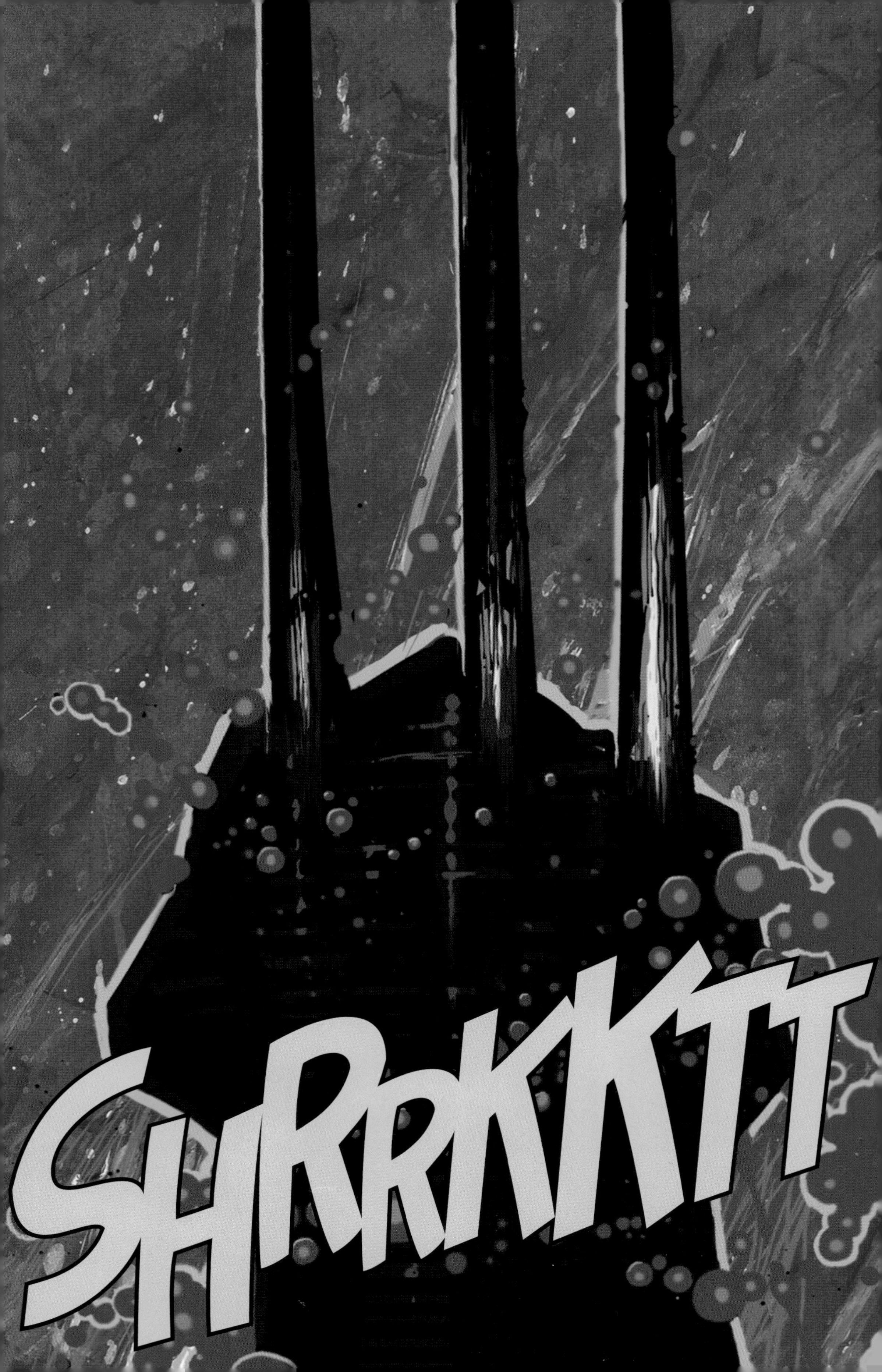
SHRRKKTT

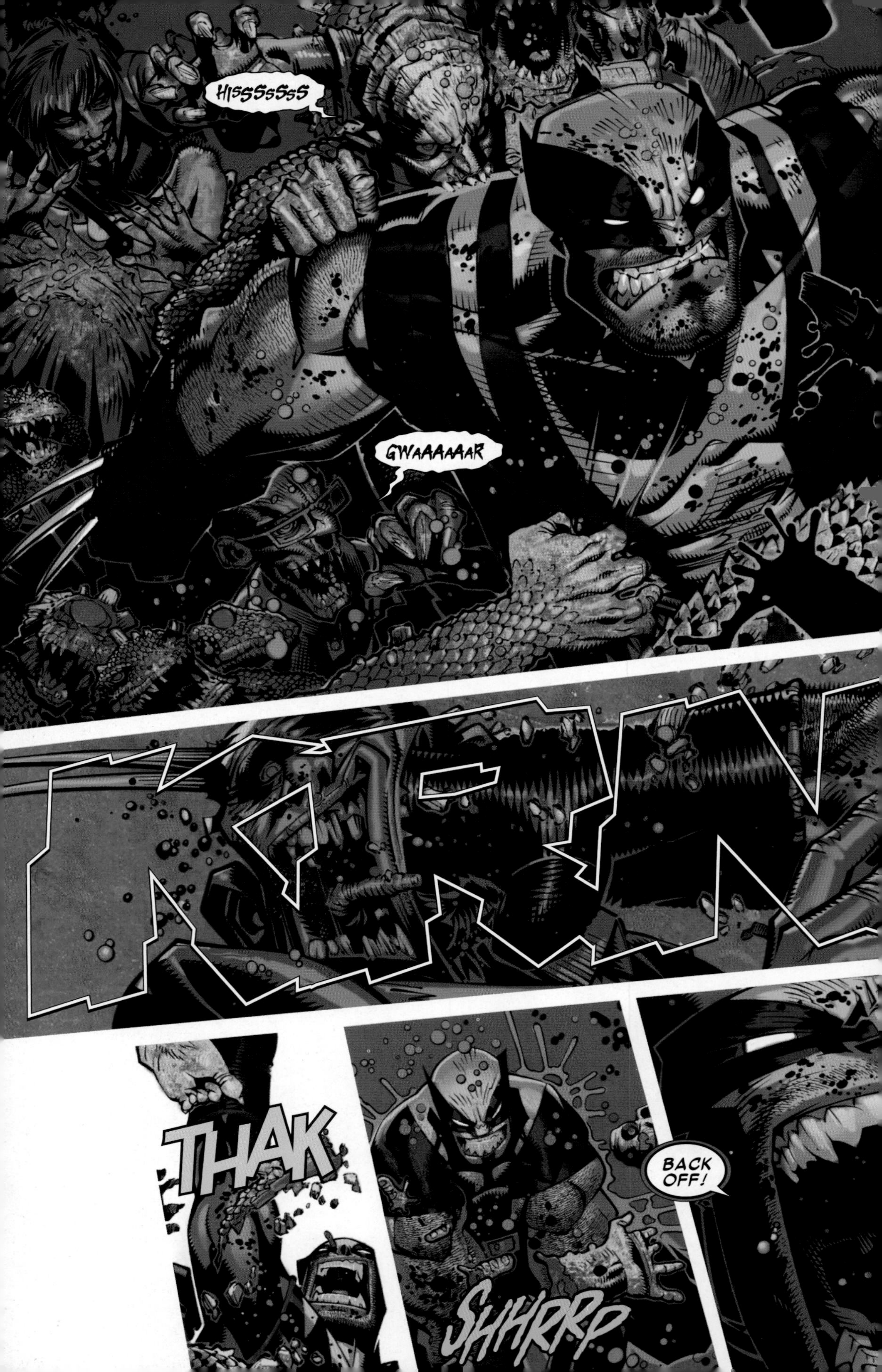
HISSSSSSS
GWAAAAAAR
THAK
SHHRP
BACK OFF!

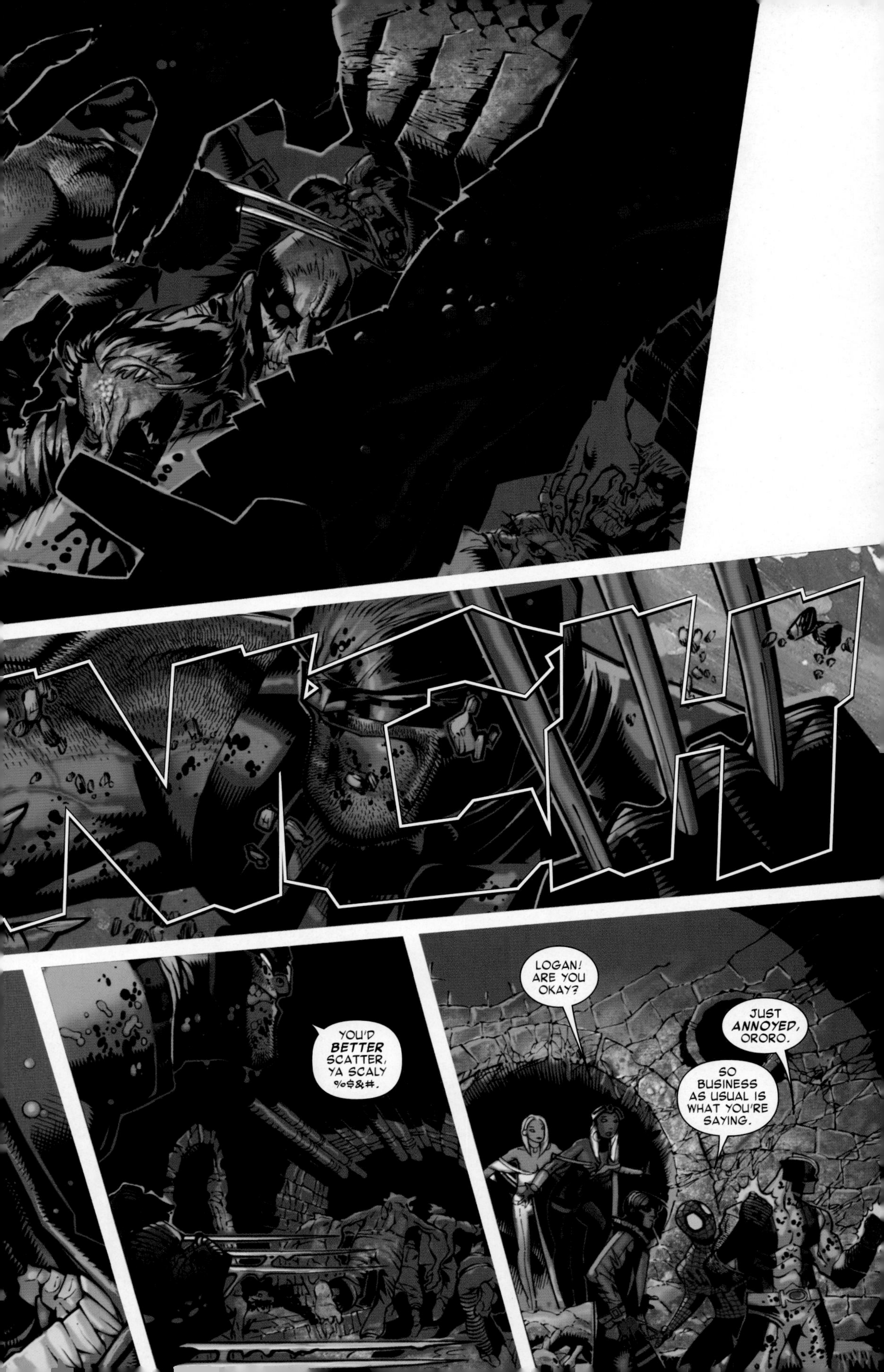

YOU'D BETTER SCATTER, YA SCALY %$&#.
LOGAN! ARE YOU OKAY?
JUST ANNOYED, ORORO.
SO BUSINESS AS USUAL IS WHAT YOU'RE SAYING.

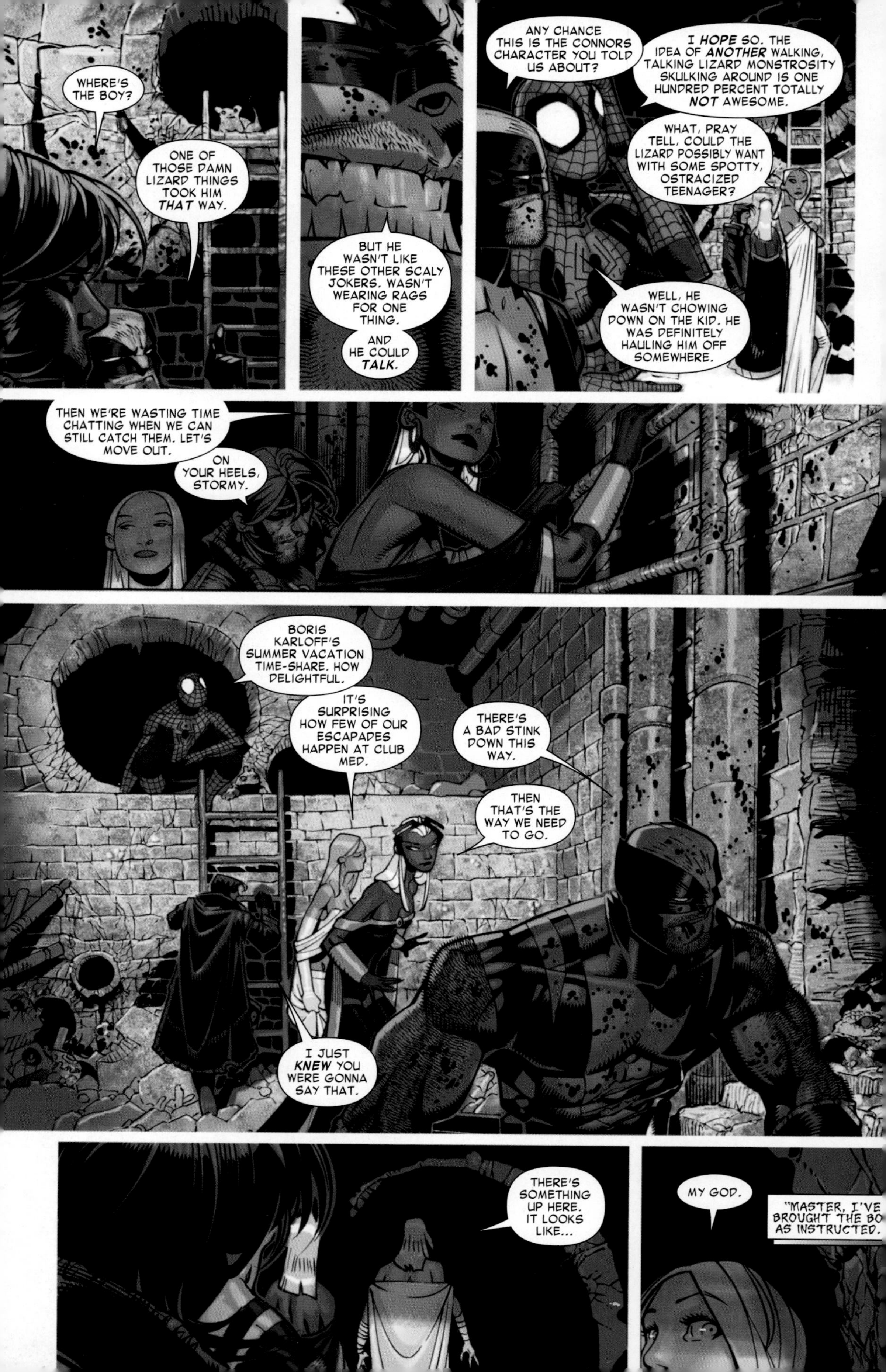

WHERE'S THE BOY?
ONE OF THOSE DAMN LIZARD THINGS TOOK HIM *THAT* WAY.
BUT HE WASN'T LIKE THESE OTHER SCALY JOKERS. WASN'T WEARING RAGS FOR ONE THING.
AND HE COULD *TALK*.
ANY CHANCE THIS IS THE CONNORS CHARACTER YOU TOLD US ABOUT?
I *HOPE* SO. THE IDEA OF *ANOTHER* WALKING, TALKING LIZARD MONSTROSITY SKULKING AROUND IS ONE HUNDRED PERCENT TOTALLY *NOT* AWESOME.
WHAT, PRAY TELL, COULD THE LIZARD POSSIBLY WANT WITH SOME SPOTTY, OSTRACIZED TEENAGER?
WELL, HE WASN'T CHOWING DOWN ON THE KID. HE WAS DEFINITELY HAULING HIM OFF SOMEWHERE.
THEN WE'RE WASTING TIME CHATTING WHEN WE CAN STILL CATCH THEM. LET'S MOVE OUT.
ON YOUR HEELS, STORMY.
BORIS KARLOFF'S SUMMER VACATION TIME-SHARE. HOW DELIGHTFUL.
IT'S SURPRISING HOW FEW OF OUR ESCAPADES HAPPEN AT CLUB MED.
THERE'S A BAD STINK DOWN THIS WAY.
THEN THAT'S THE WAY WE NEED TO GO.
I JUST *KNEW* YOU WERE GONNA SAY THAT.
THERE'S SOMETHING UP HERE. IT LOOKS LIKE...
MY GOD.
"MASTER, I'VE BROUGHT THE BO AS INSTRUCTED.

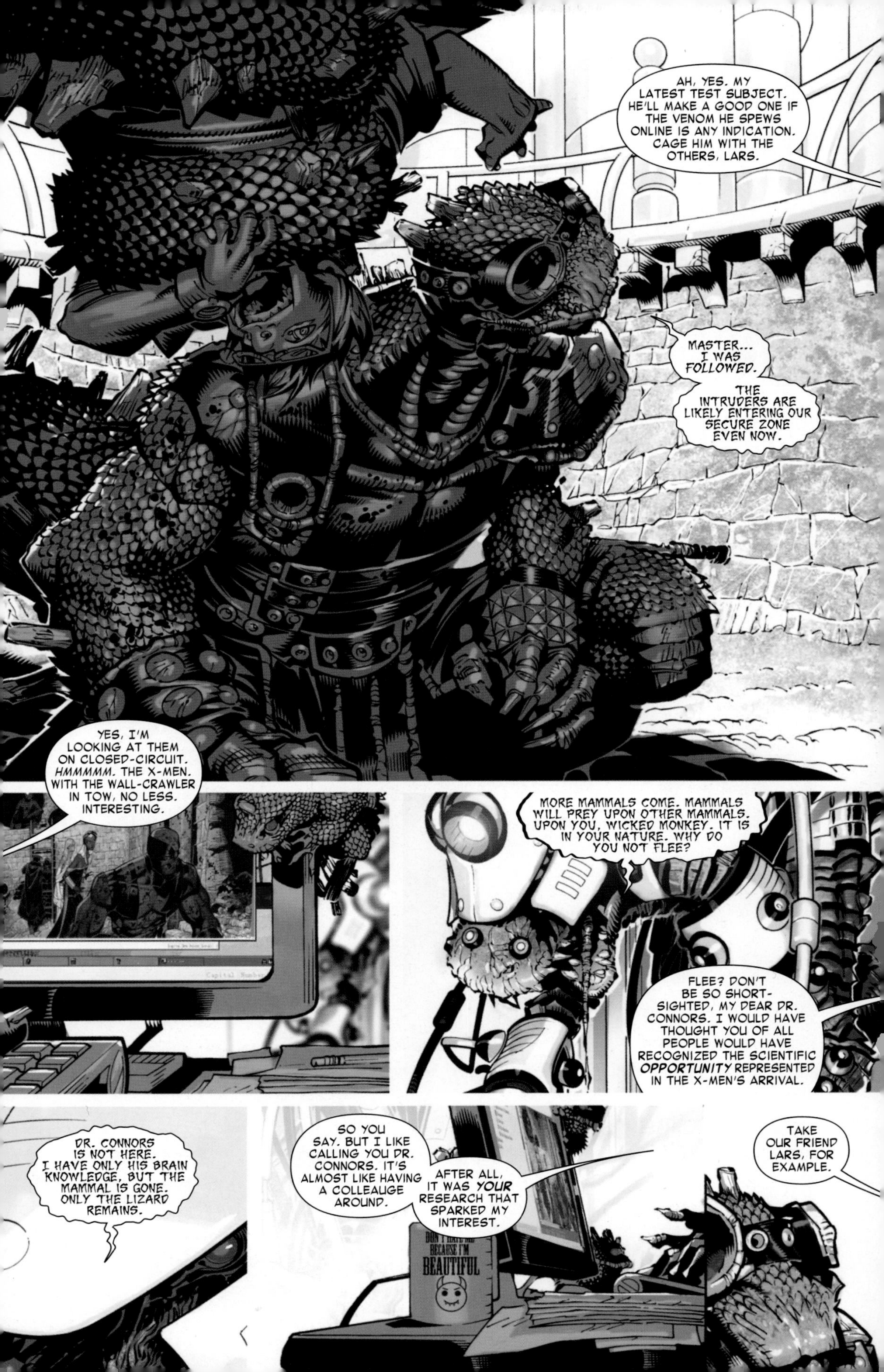
AH, YES. MY LATEST TEST SUBJECT. HE'LL MAKE A GOOD ONE IF THE VENOM HE SPEWS ONLINE IS ANY INDICATION. CAGE HIM WITH THE OTHERS, LARS.
MASTER... I WAS *FOLLOWED*.
THE INTRUDERS ARE LIKELY ENTERING OUR SECURE ZONE EVEN NOW.
YES, I'M LOOKING AT THEM ON CLOSED-CIRCUIT. *HMMMMM.* THE X-MEN. WITH THE WALL-CRAWLER IN TOW, NO LESS. INTERESTING.
MORE MAMMALS COME. MAMMALS WILL PREY UPON OTHER MAMMALS. UPON YOU, WICKED MONKEY. IT IS IN YOUR NATURE. WHY DO YOU NOT FLEE?
FLEE? DON'T BE SO SHORT-SIGHTED, MY DEAR DR. CONNORS. I WOULD HAVE THOUGHT YOU OF ALL PEOPLE WOULD HAVE RECOGNIZED THE SCIENTIFIC *OPPORTUNITY* REPRESENTED IN THE X-MEN'S ARRIVAL.
DR. CONNORS IS NOT HERE. I HAVE ONLY HIS BRAIN KNOWLEDGE, BUT THE MAMMAL IS GONE. ONLY THE LIZARD REMAINS.
SO YOU SAY. BUT I LIKE CALLING YOU DR. CONNORS. IT'S ALMOST LIKE HAVING A COLLEAUGE AROUND.
AFTER ALL, IT WAS *YOUR* RESEARCH THAT SPARKED MY INTEREST.
DON'T HATE ME BECAUSE I'M BEAUTIFUL
TAKE OUR FRIEND LARS, FOR EXAMPLE.

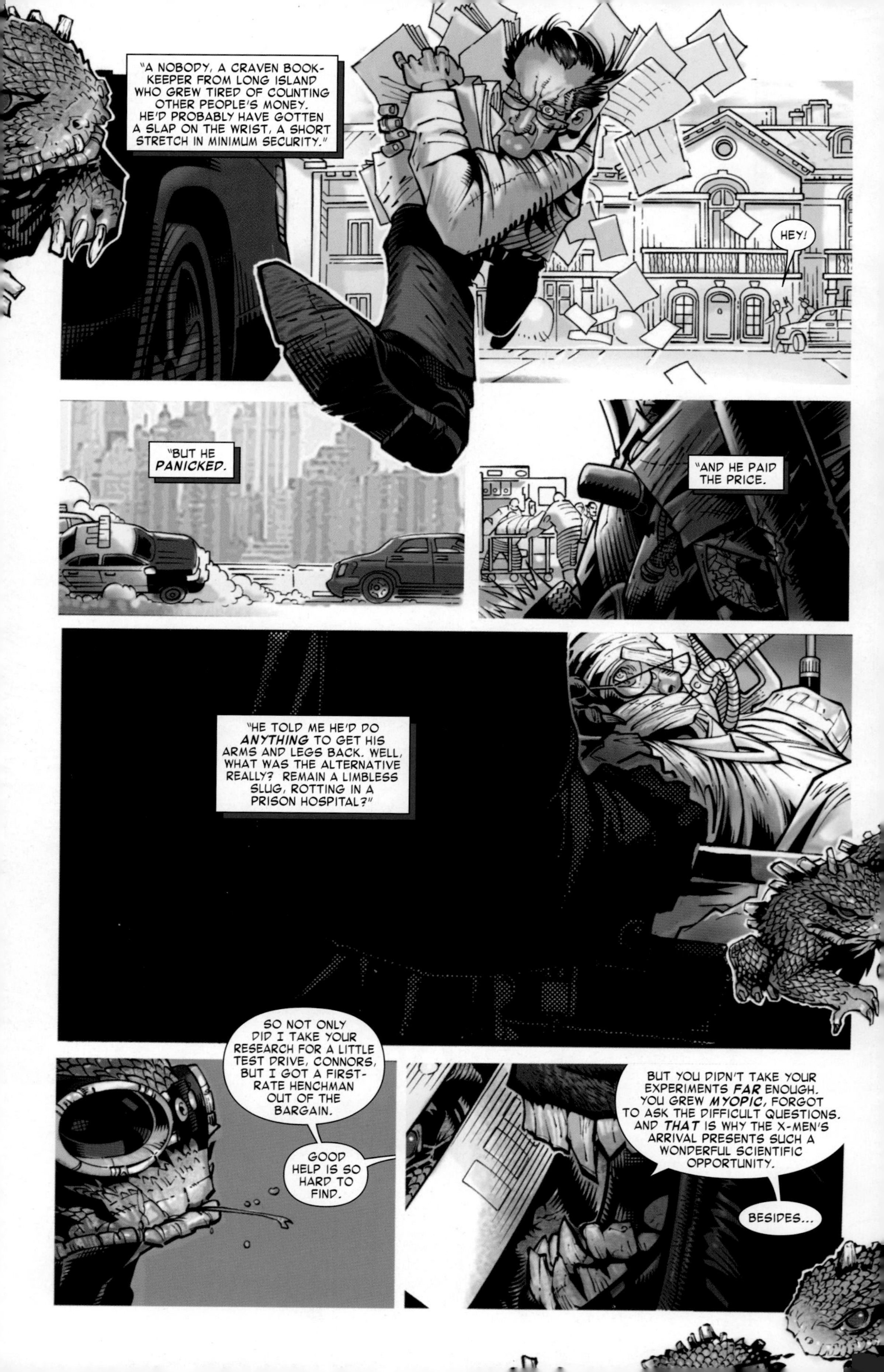
"A NOBODY, A CRAVEN BOOK-KEEPER FROM LONG ISLAND WHO GREW TIRED OF COUNTING OTHER PEOPLE'S MONEY. HE'D PROBABLY HAVE GOTTEN A SLAP ON THE WRIST, A SHORT STRETCH IN MINIMUM SECURITY."
HEY!
"BUT HE PANICKED.
"AND HE PAID THE PRICE.
"HE TOLD ME HE'D DO ANYTHING TO GET HIS ARMS AND LEGS BACK. WELL, WHAT WAS THE ALTERNATIVE REALLY? REMAIN A LIMBLESS SLUG, ROTTING IN A PRISON HOSPITAL?"
SO NOT ONLY DID I TAKE YOUR RESEARCH FOR A LITTLE TEST DRIVE, CONNORS, BUT I GOT A FIRST-RATE HENCHMAN OUT OF THE BARGAIN.
GOOD HELP IS SO HARD TO FIND.
BUT YOU DIDN'T TAKE YOUR EXPERIMENTS FAR ENOUGH. YOU GREW MYOPIC, FORGOT TO ASK THE DIFFICULT QUESTIONS. AND THAT IS WHY THE X-MEN'S ARRIVAL PRESENTS SUCH A WONDERFUL SCIENTIFIC OPPORTUNITY.
BESIDES...

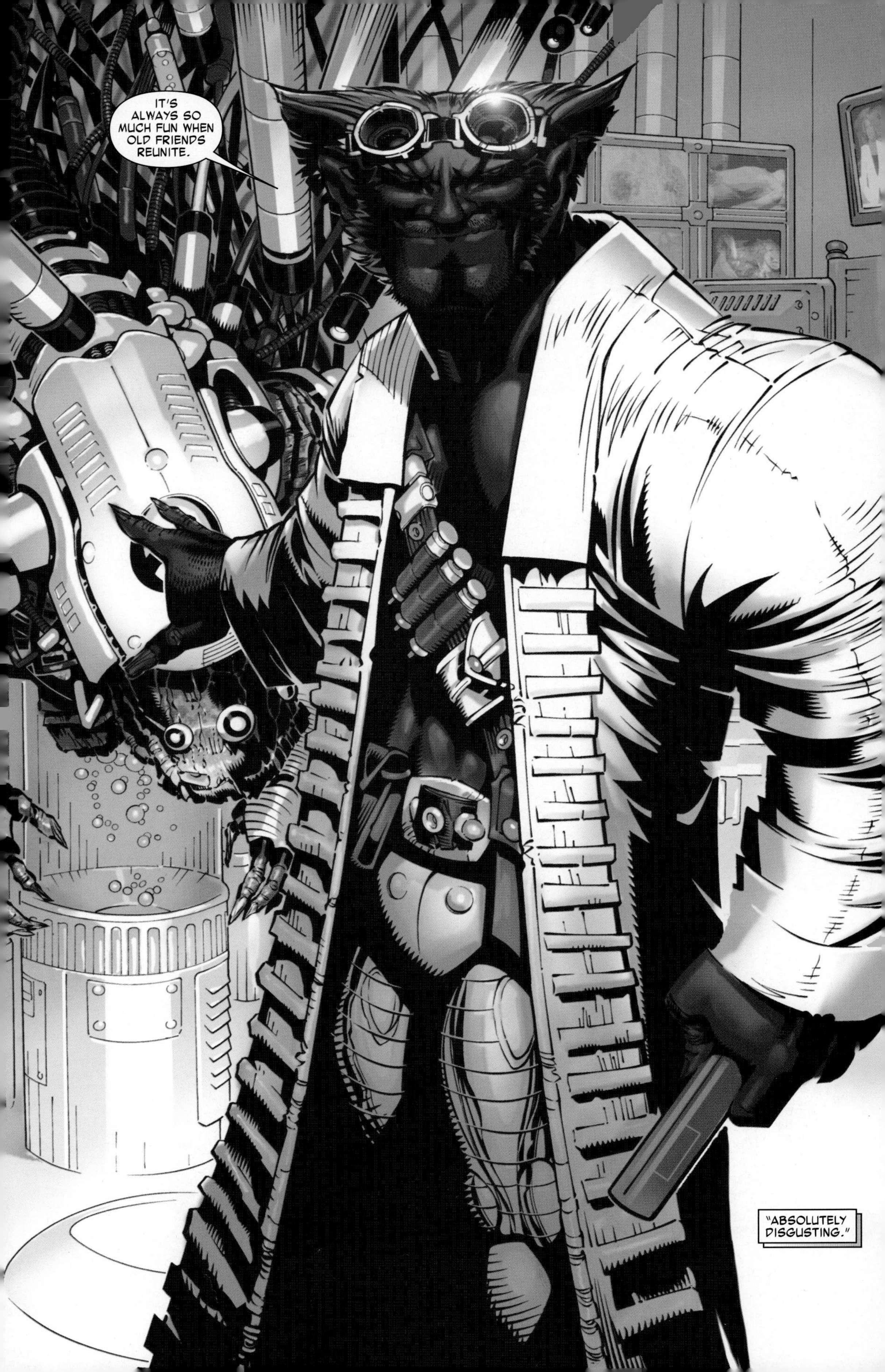
IT'S ALWAYS SO MUCH FUN WHEN OLD FRIENDS REUNITE.
"ABSOLUTELY DISGUSTING."

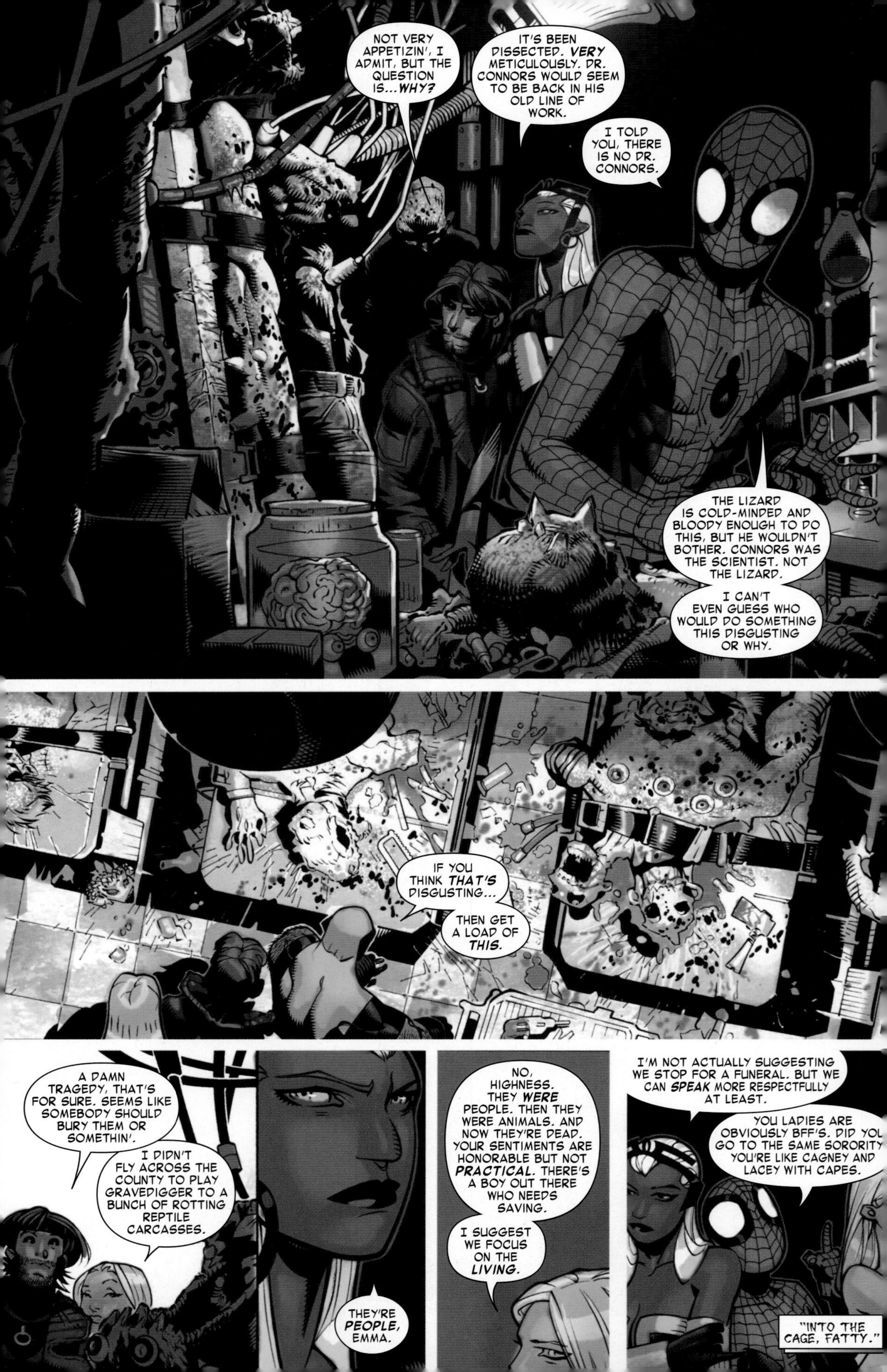
NOT VERY APPETIZIN', I ADMIT, BUT THE QUESTION IS...WHY?
IT'S BEEN DISSECTED. VERY METICULOUSLY. DR. CONNORS WOULD SEEM TO BE BACK IN HIS OLD LINE OF WORK.
I TOLD YOU, THERE IS NO DR. CONNORS.
THE LIZARD IS COLD-MINDED AND BLOODY ENOUGH TO DO THIS, BUT HE WOULDN'T BOTHER. CONNORS WAS THE SCIENTIST. NOT THE LIZARD.
I CAN'T EVEN GUESS WHO WOULD DO SOMETHING THIS DISGUSTING OR WHY.
IF YOU THINK THAT'S DISGUSTING...
THEN GET A LOAD OF THIS.
A DAMN TRAGEDY, THAT'S FOR SURE. SEEMS LIKE SOMEBODY SHOULD BURY THEM OR SOMETHIN'.
I DIDN'T FLY ACROSS THE COUNTY TO PLAY GRAVEDIGGER TO A BUNCH OF ROTTING REPTILE CARCASSES.
THEY'RE PEOPLE, EMMA.
NO, HIGHNESS. THEY WERE PEOPLE. THEN THEY WERE ANIMALS. AND NOW THEY'RE DEAD. YOUR SENTIMENTS ARE HONORABLE BUT NOT PRACTICAL. THERE'S A BOY OUT THERE WHO NEEDS SAVING.
I SUGGEST WE FOCUS ON THE LIVING.
I'M NOT ACTUALLY SUGGESTING WE STOP FOR A FUNERAL. BUT WE CAN SPEAK MORE RESPECTFULLY AT LEAST.
YOU LADIES ARE OBVIOUSLY BFF'S. DID YOU GO TO THE SAME SORORITY? YOU'RE LIKE CAGNEY AND LACEY WITH CAPES.
"INTO THE CAGE, FATTY."

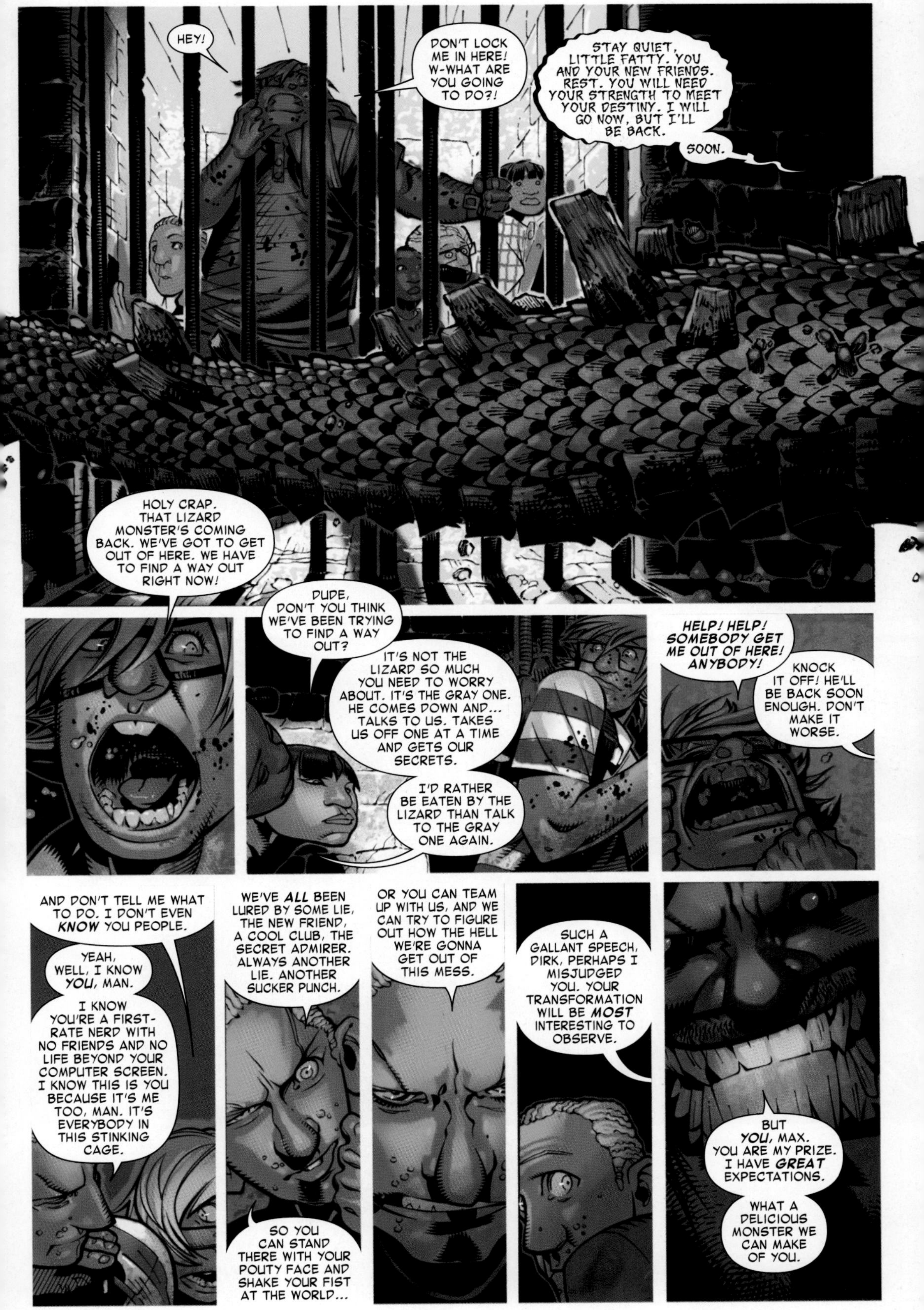
HEY!
DON'T LOCK ME IN HERE! W-WHAT ARE YOU GOING TO DO?!
STAY QUIET, LITTLE FATTY. YOU AND YOUR NEW FRIENDS. REST. YOU WILL NEED YOUR STRENGTH TO MEET YOUR DESTINY. I WILL GO NOW, BUT I'LL BE BACK.
SOON.
HOLY CRAP. THAT LIZARD MONSTER'S COMING BACK. WE'VE GOT TO GET OUT OF HERE. WE HAVE TO FIND A WAY OUT RIGHT NOW!
DUDE, DON'T YOU THINK WE'VE BEEN TRYING TO FIND A WAY OUT?
IT'S NOT THE LIZARD SO MUCH YOU NEED TO WORRY ABOUT. IT'S THE GRAY ONE. HE COMES DOWN AND... TALKS TO US. TAKES US OFF ONE AT A TIME AND GETS OUR SECRETS.
I'D RATHER BE EATEN BY THE LIZARD THAN TALK TO THE GRAY ONE AGAIN.
HELP! HELP! SOMEBODY GET ME OUT OF HERE! ANYBODY!
KNOCK IT OFF! HE'LL BE BACK SOON ENOUGH. DON'T MAKE IT WORSE.
AND DON'T TELL ME WHAT TO DO. I DON'T EVEN KNOW YOU PEOPLE.
YEAH, WELL, I KNOW YOU, MAN.
I KNOW YOU'RE A FIRST-RATE NERD WITH NO FRIENDS AND NO LIFE BEYOND YOUR COMPUTER SCREEN. I KNOW THIS IS YOU BECAUSE IT'S ME TOO, MAN. IT'S EVERYBODY IN THIS STINKING CAGE.
WE'VE ALL BEEN LURED BY SOME LIE, THE NEW FRIEND, A COOL CLUB, THE SECRET ADMIRER. ALWAYS ANOTHER LIE. ANOTHER SUCKER PUNCH.
SO YOU CAN STAND THERE WITH YOUR POUTY FACE AND SHAKE YOUR FIST AT THE WORLD...
OR YOU CAN TEAM UP WITH US, AND WE CAN TRY TO FIGURE OUT HOW THE HELL WE'RE GONNA GET OUT OF THIS MESS.
SUCH A GALLANT SPEECH, DIRK, PERHAPS I MISJUDGED YOU. YOUR TRANSFORMATION WILL BE MOST INTERESTING TO OBSERVE.
BUT YOU, MAX. YOU ARE MY PRIZE. I HAVE GREAT EXPECTATIONS.
WHAT A DELICIOUS MONSTER WE CAN MAKE OF YOU.

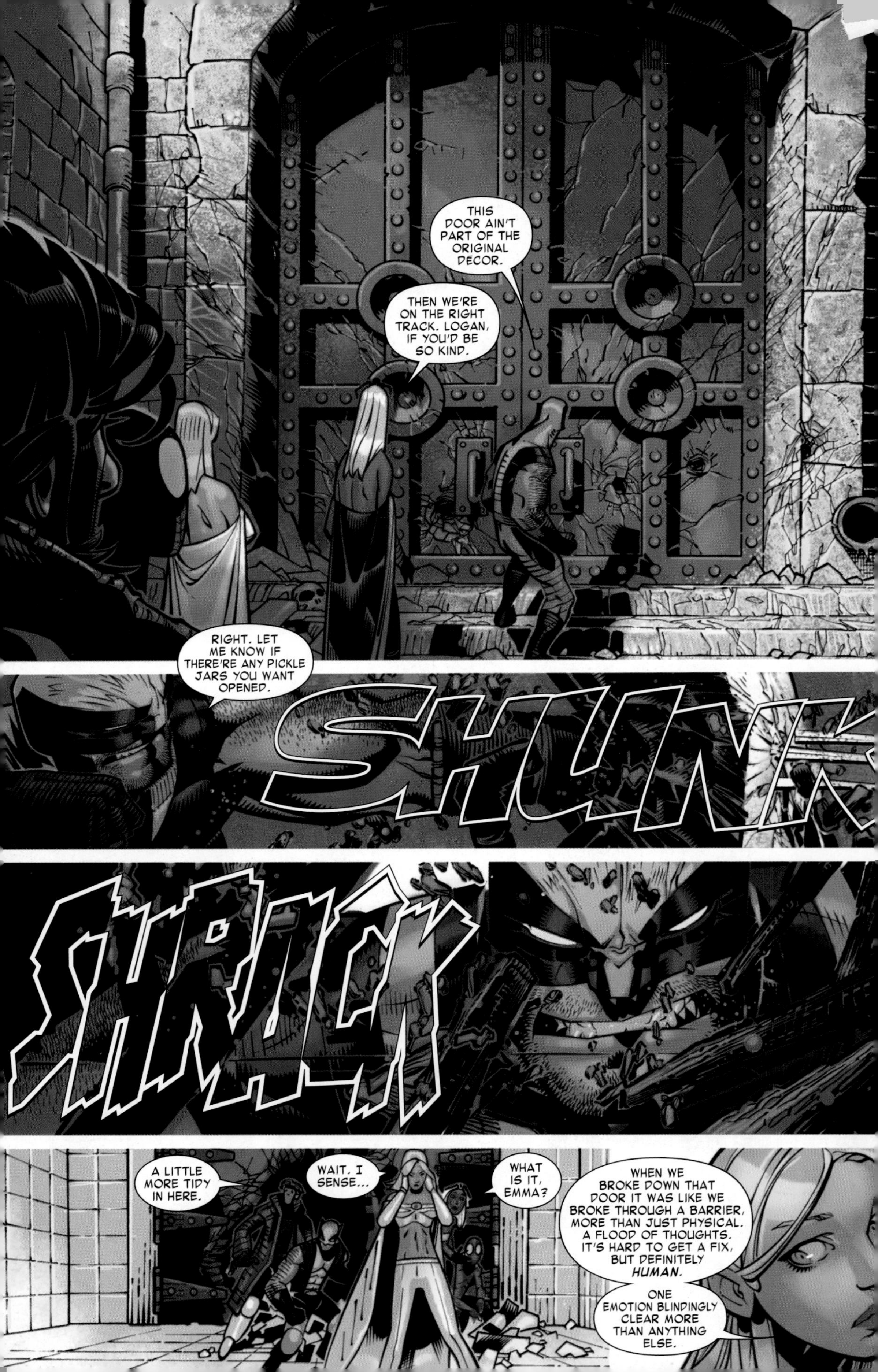
THIS DOOR AIN'T PART OF THE ORIGINAL DECOR.
THEN WE'RE ON THE RIGHT TRACK. LOGAN, IF YOU'D BE SO KIND.
RIGHT. LET ME KNOW IF THERE'RE ANY PICKLE JARS YOU WANT OPENED.
SHUNK
SHRACK
A LITTLE MORE TIDY IN HERE.
WAIT. I SENSE...
WHAT IS IT, EMMA?
WHEN WE BROKE DOWN THAT DOOR IT WAS LIKE WE BROKE THROUGH A BARRIER, MORE THAN JUST PHYSICAL. A FLOOD OF THOUGHTS. IT'S HARD TO GET A FIX, BUT DEFINITELY *HUMAN.*
ONE EMOTION BLINDINGLY CLEAR MORE THAN ANYTHING ELSE.

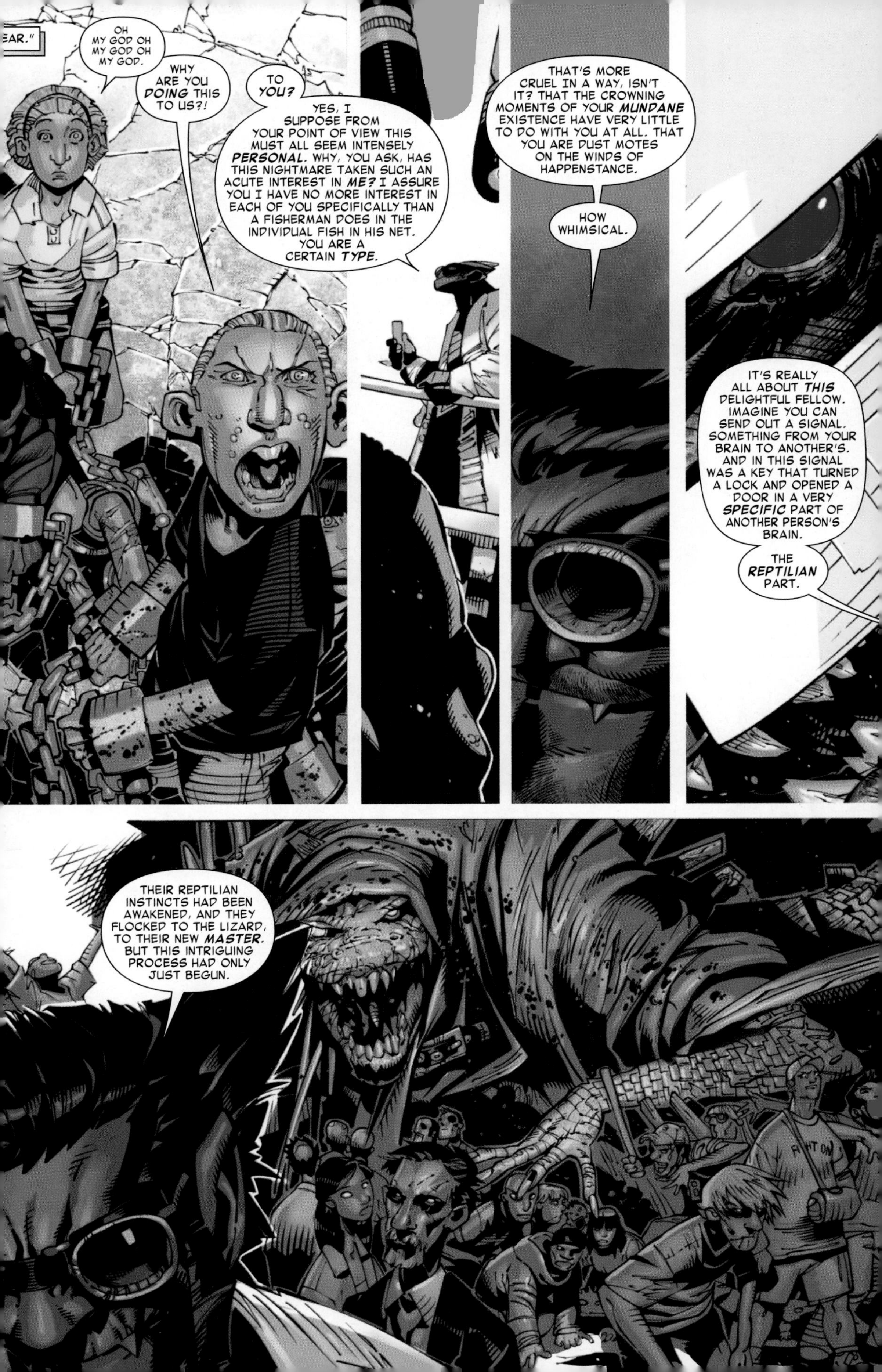

EAR."
OH MY GOD OH MY GOD OH MY GOD.
WHY ARE YOU DOING THIS TO US?!
TO YOU?
YES, I SUPPOSE FROM YOUR POINT OF VIEW THIS MUST ALL SEEM INTENSELY PERSONAL. WHY, YOU ASK, HAS THIS NIGHTMARE TAKEN SUCH AN ACUTE INTEREST IN ME? I ASSURE YOU I HAVE NO MORE INTEREST IN EACH OF YOU SPECIFICALLY THAN A FISHERMAN DOES IN THE INDIVIDUAL FISH IN HIS NET. YOU ARE A CERTAIN TYPE.
THAT'S MORE CRUEL IN A WAY, ISN'T IT? THAT THE CROWNING MOMENTS OF YOUR MUNDANE EXISTENCE HAVE VERY LITTLE TO DO WITH YOU AT ALL. THAT YOU ARE DUST MOTES ON THE WINDS OF HAPPENSTANCE.
HOW WHIMSICAL.
IT'S REALLY ALL ABOUT THIS DELIGHTFUL FELLOW. IMAGINE YOU CAN SEND OUT A SIGNAL. SOMETHING FROM YOUR BRAIN TO ANOTHER'S. AND IN THIS SIGNAL WAS A KEY THAT TURNED A LOCK AND OPENED A DOOR IN A VERY SPECIFIC PART OF ANOTHER PERSON'S BRAIN.
THE REPTILIAN PART.
THEIR REPTILIAN INSTINCTS HAD BEEN AWAKENED, AND THEY FLOCKED TO THE LIZARD, TO THEIR NEW MASTER. BUT THIS INTRIGUING PROCESS HAD ONLY JUST BEGUN.

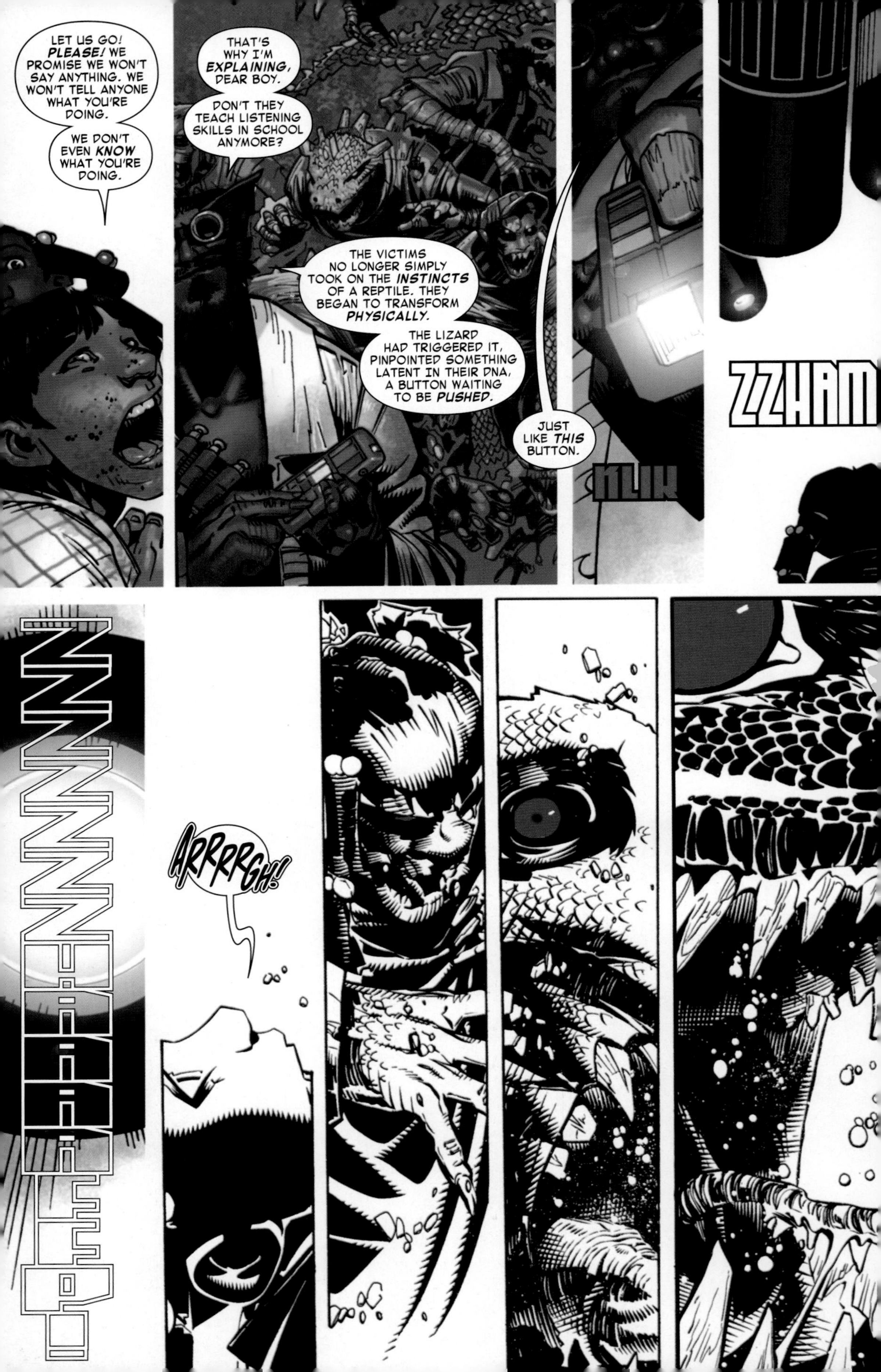
LET US GO! PLEASE! WE PROMISE WE WON'T SAY ANYTHING. WE WON'T TELL ANYONE WHAT YOU'RE DOING.
WE DON'T EVEN KNOW WHAT YOU'RE DOING.
THAT'S WHY I'M EXPLAINING, DEAR BOY.
DON'T THEY TEACH LISTENING SKILLS IN SCHOOL ANYMORE?
THE VICTIMS NO LONGER SIMPLY TOOK ON THE INSTINCTS OF A REPTILE. THEY BEGAN TO TRANSFORM PHYSICALLY.
THE LIZARD HAD TRIGGERED IT, PINPOINTED SOMETHING LATENT IN THEIR DNA, A BUTTON WAITING TO BE PUSHED.
JUST LIKE THIS BUTTON.
KLIK
ZZHAM
ARRRRGH!

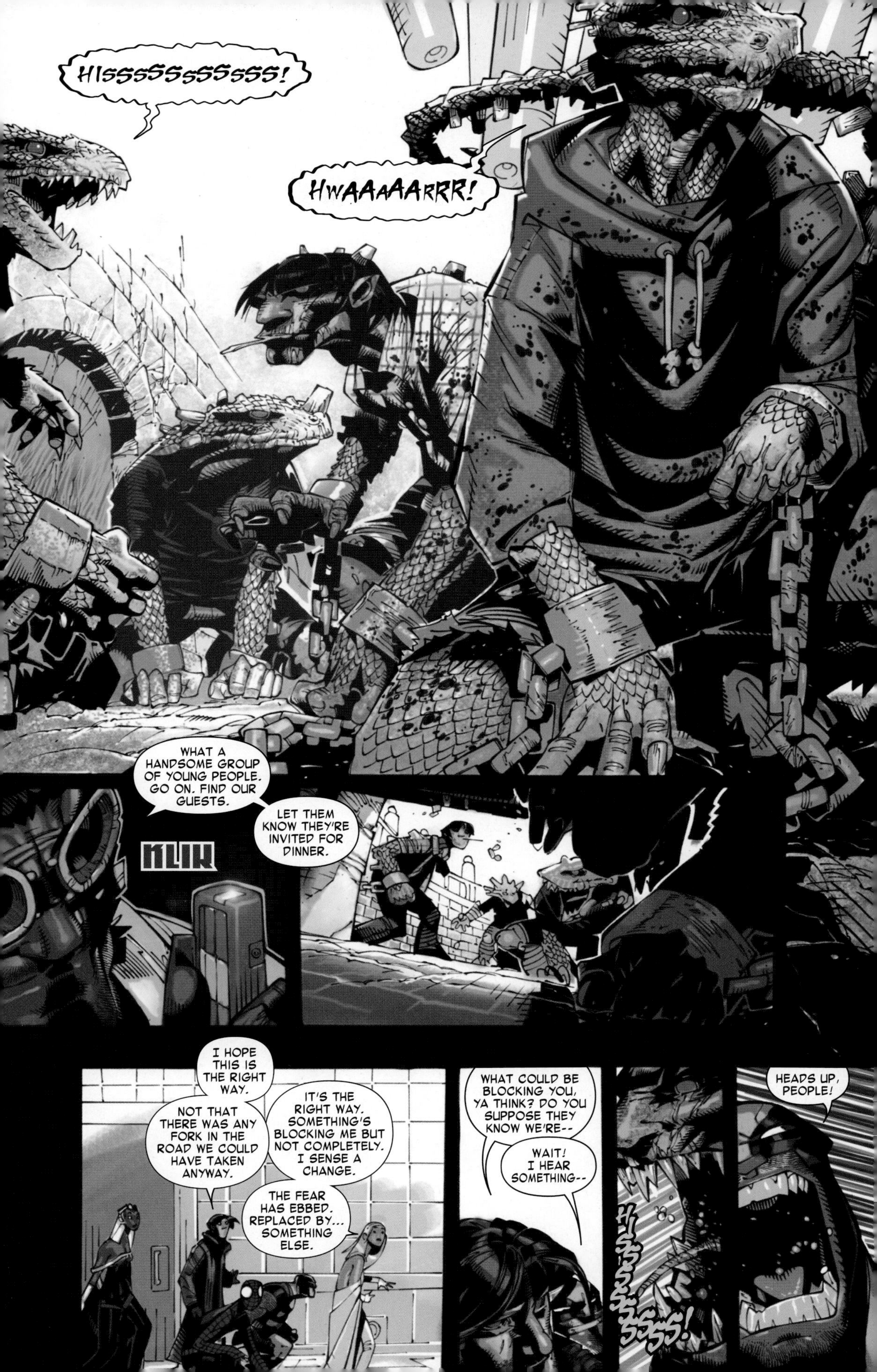
HISSSSSSSSSSS!
HWAAAAARRR!
WHAT A HANDSOME GROUP OF YOUNG PEOPLE. GO ON. FIND OUR GUESTS.
LET THEM KNOW THEY'RE INVITED FOR DINNER.
KLIK
I HOPE THIS IS THE RIGHT WAY.
NOT THAT THERE WAS ANY FORK IN THE ROAD WE COULD HAVE TAKEN ANYWAY.
IT'S THE RIGHT WAY. SOMETHING'S BLOCKING ME BUT NOT COMPLETELY. I SENSE A CHANGE.
THE FEAR HAS EBBED. REPLACED BY... SOMETHING ELSE.
WHAT COULD BE BLOCKING YOU, YA THINK? DO YOU SUPPOSE THEY KNOW WE'RE--
WAIT! I HEAR SOMETHING--
HISSSSSSSS!
HEADS UP, PEOPLE!

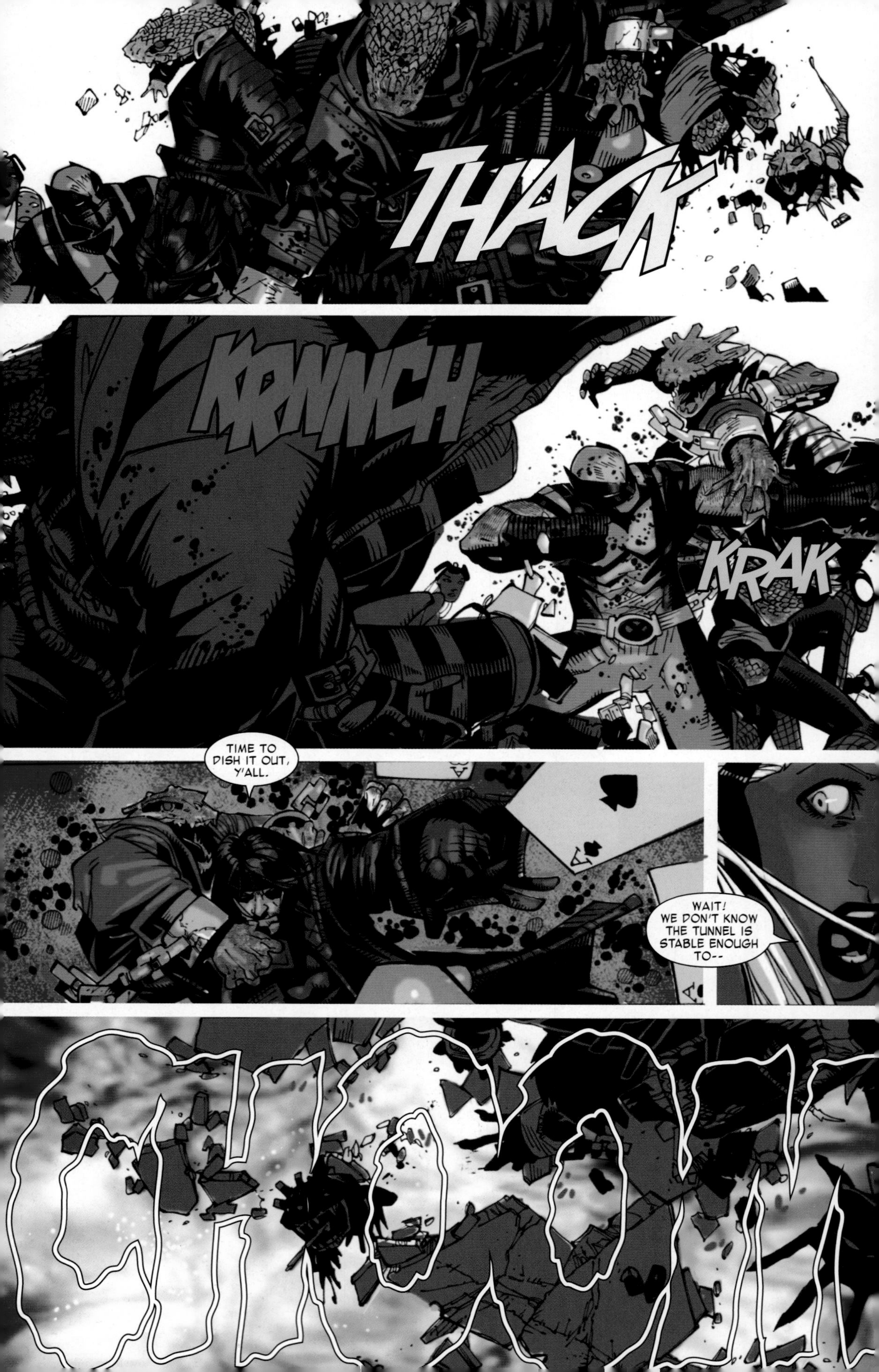
THACK
KRNNCH
KRAK
TIME TO DISH IT OUT, Y'ALL.
WAIT! WE DON'T KNOW THE TUNNEL IS STABLE ENOUGH TO--

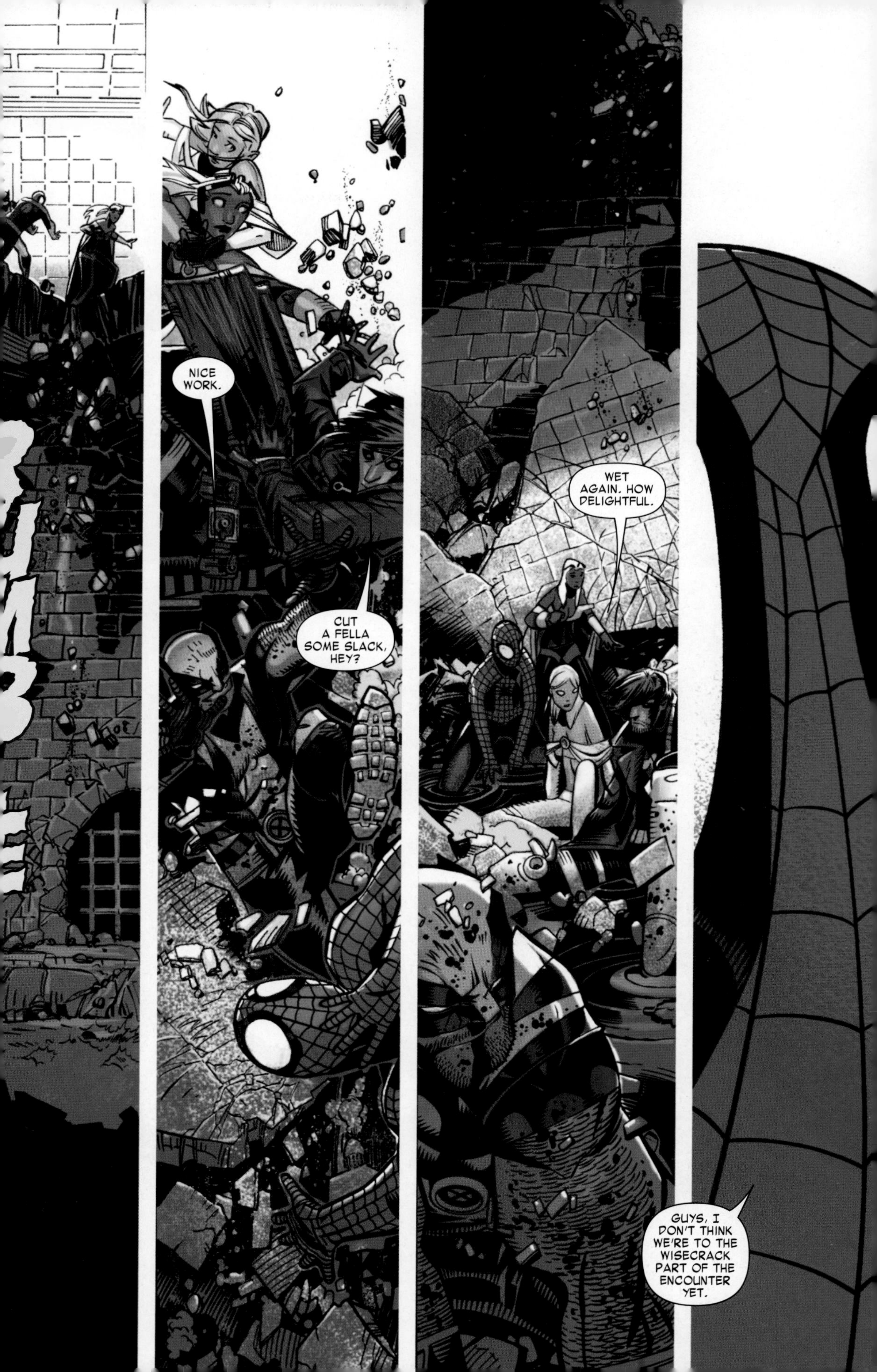
NICE WORK.
CUT A FELLA SOME SLACK, HEY?
WET AGAIN. HOW DELIGHTFUL.
GUYS, I DON'T THINK WE'RE TO THE WISECRACK PART OF THE ENCOUNTER YET.

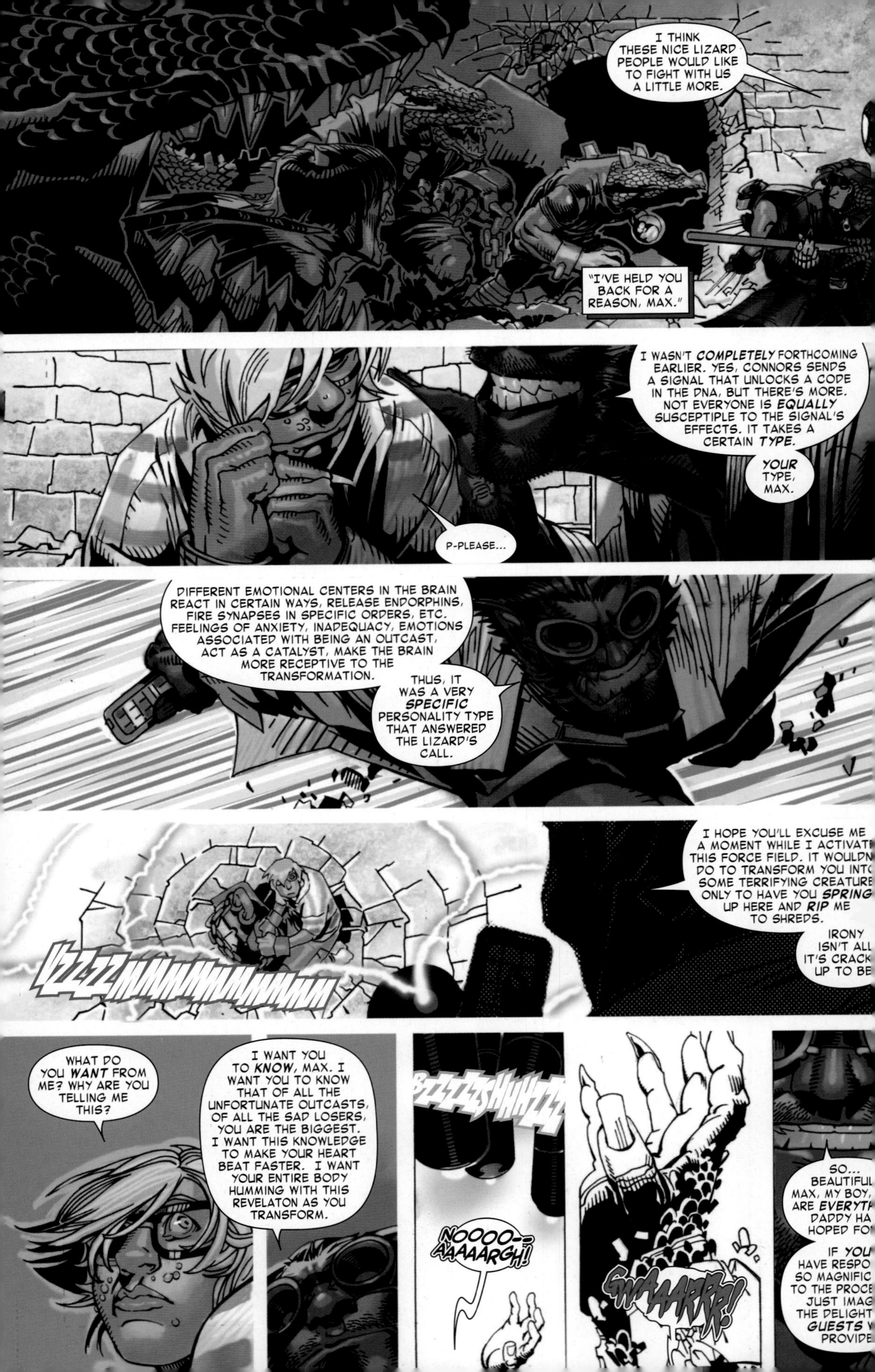

I THINK THESE NICE LIZARD PEOPLE WOULD LIKE TO FIGHT WITH US A LITTLE MORE.
"I'VE HELD YOU BACK FOR A REASON, MAX."
I WASN'T COMPLETELY FORTHCOMING EARLIER. YES, CONNORS SENDS A SIGNAL THAT UNLOCKS A CODE IN THE DNA, BUT THERE'S MORE. NOT EVERYONE IS EQUALLY SUSCEPTIPLE TO THE SIGNAL'S EFFECTS. IT TAKES A CERTAIN TYPE.
YOUR TYPE, MAX.
P-PLEASE...
DIFFERENT EMOTIONAL CENTERS IN THE BRAIN REACT IN CERTAIN WAYS, RELEASE ENDORPHINS, FIRE SYNAPSES IN SPECIFIC ORDERS, ETC. FEELINGS OF ANXIETY, INADEQUACY, EMOTIONS ASSOCIATED WITH BEING AN OUTCAST, ACT AS A CATALYST, MAKE THE BRAIN MORE RECEPTIVE TO THE TRANSFORMATION.
THUS, IT WAS A VERY SPECIFIC PERSONALITY TYPE THAT ANSWERED THE LIZARD'S CALL.
I HOPE YOU'LL EXCUSE ME A MOMENT WHILE I ACTIVATE THIS FORCE FIELD. IT WOULDN' DO TO TRANSFORM YOU INTO SOME TERRIFYING CREATURE ONLY TO HAVE YOU SPRING UP HERE AND RIP ME TO SHREDS.
IRONY ISN'T ALL IT'S CRACK UP TO BE
VZZZZMMMMMMMMMMMMM
WHAT DO YOU WANT FROM ME? WHY ARE YOU TELLING ME THIS?
I WANT YOU TO KNOW, MAX. I WANT YOU TO KNOW THAT OF ALL THE UNFORTUNATE OUTCASTS, OF ALL THE SAD LOSERS, YOU ARE THE BIGGEST. I WANT THIS KNOWLEDGE TO MAKE YOUR HEART BEAT FASTER. I WANT YOUR ENTIRE BODY HUMMING WITH THIS REVELATON AS YOU TRANSFORM.
BZZZZSHHHZZZ
NOOOO--AAAAARGH!
GWAAAARRR!
SO... BEAUTIFUL. MAX, MY BOY, ARE EVERYT DADDY HA HOPED FO
IF YOU HAVE RESPO SO MAGNIFIC TO THE PROCE JUST IMAG THE DELIGHT GUESTS PROVIDE

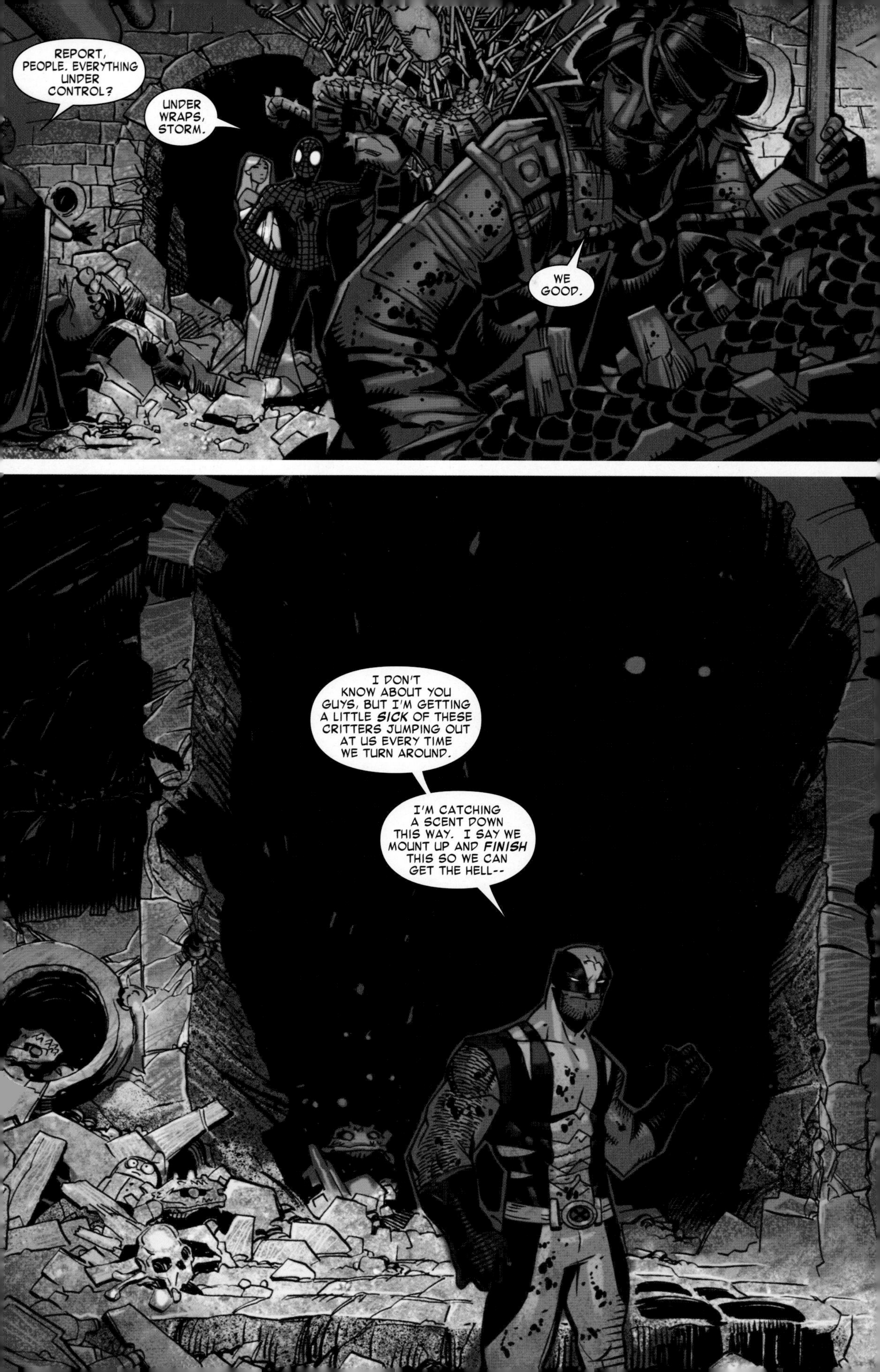
REPORT, PEOPLE. EVERYTHING UNDER CONTROL?
UNDER WRAPS, STORM.
WE GOOD.
I DON'T KNOW ABOUT YOU GUYS, BUT I'M GETTING A LITTLE *SICK* OF THESE CRITTERS JUMPING OUT AT US EVERY TIME WE TURN AROUND.
I'M CATCHING A SCENT DOWN THIS WAY. I SAY WE MOUNT UP AND *FINISH* THIS SO WE CAN GET THE HELL--

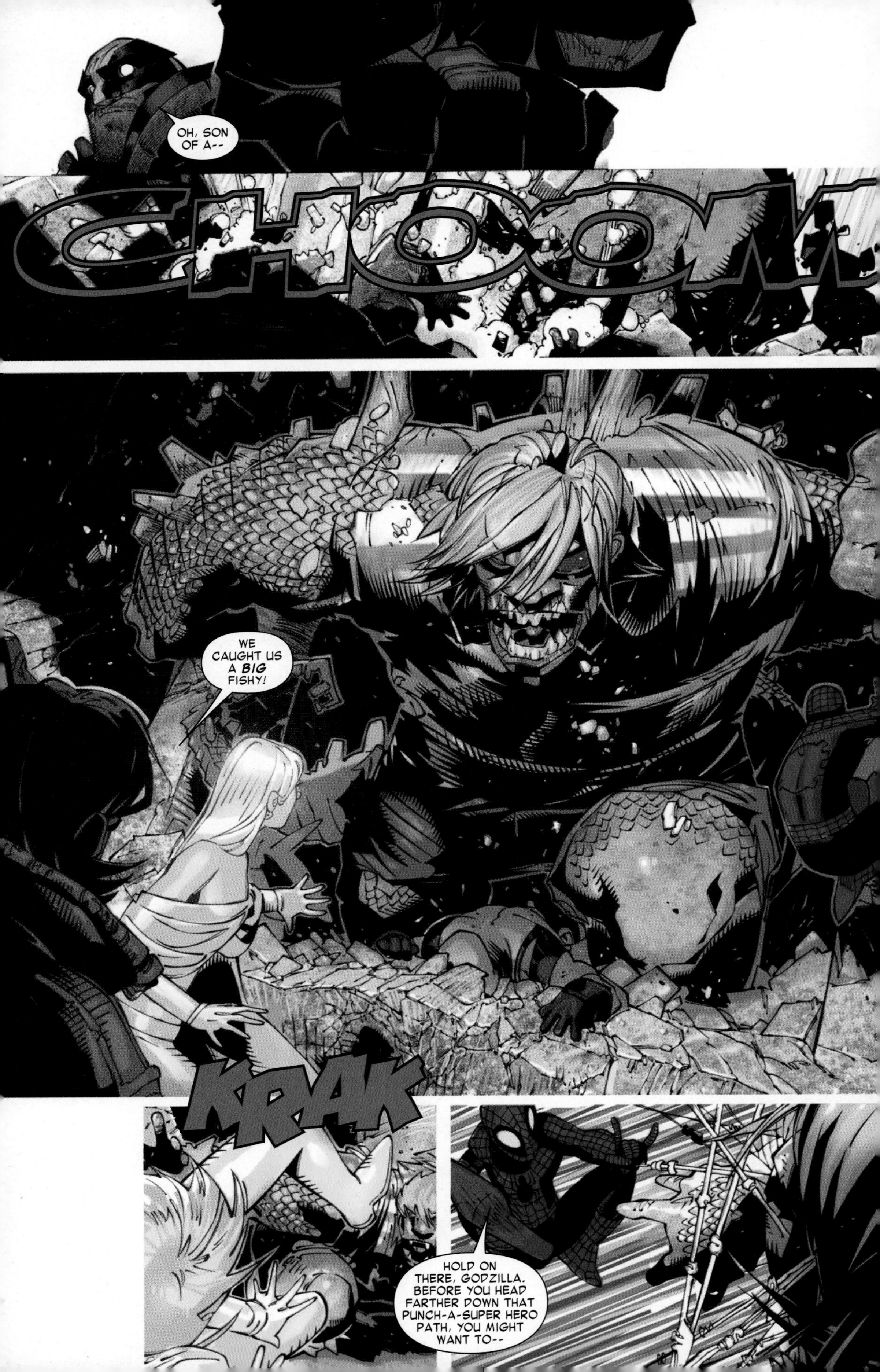
OH, SON OF A--
CHOOM
WE CAUGHT US A BIG FISHY!
KRAK
HOLD ON THERE, GODZILLA. BEFORE YOU HEAD FARTHER DOWN THAT PUNCH-A-SUPER HERO PATH, YOU MIGHT WANT TO--

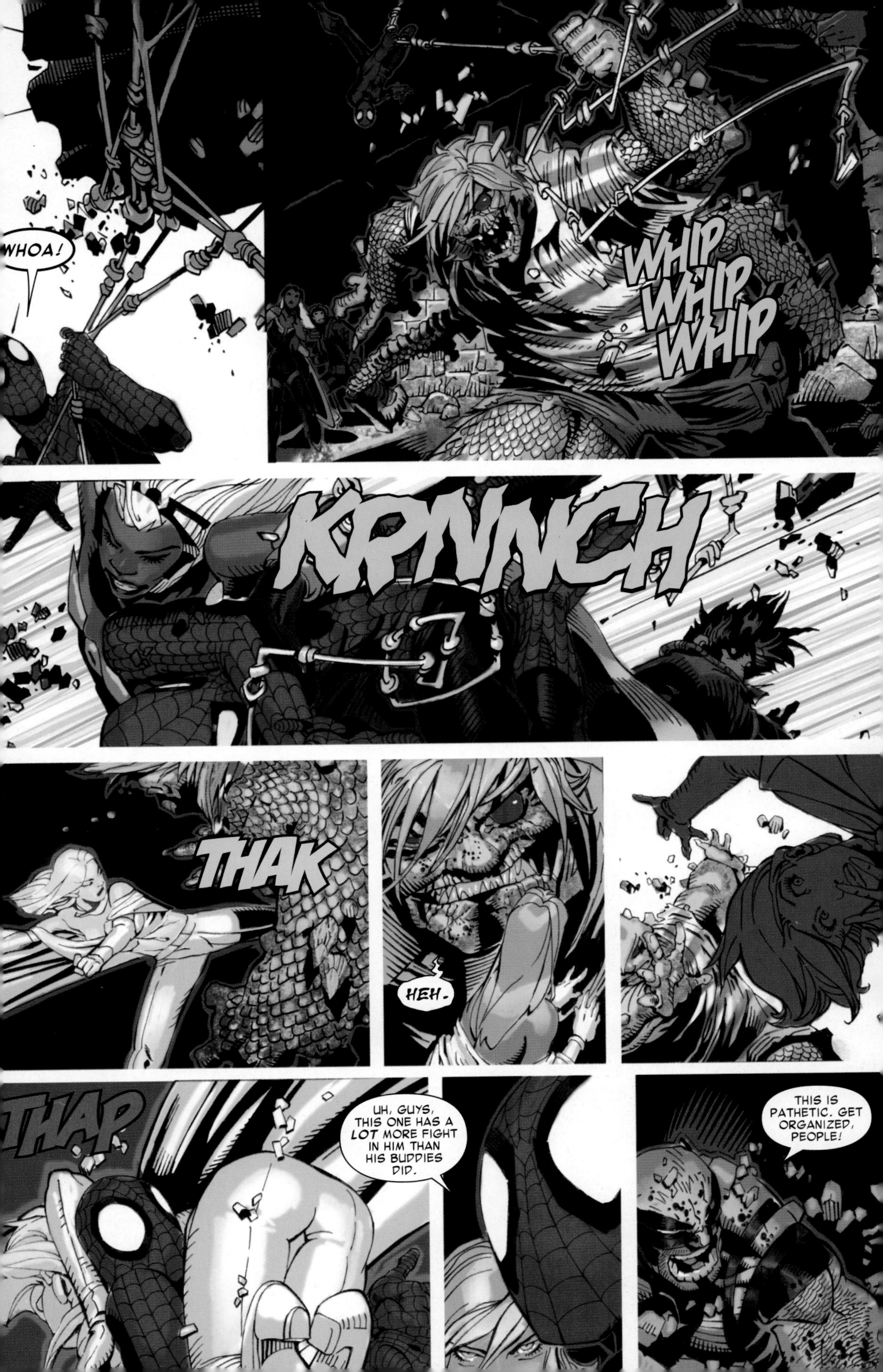

WHOA!
WHIP WHIP WHIP
KRNNCH
THAK
HEH.
THAP
UH, GUYS, THIS ONE HAS A **LOT** MORE FIGHT IN HIM THAN HIS BUDDIES DID.
THIS IS PATHETIC. GET ORGANIZED, PEOPLE!

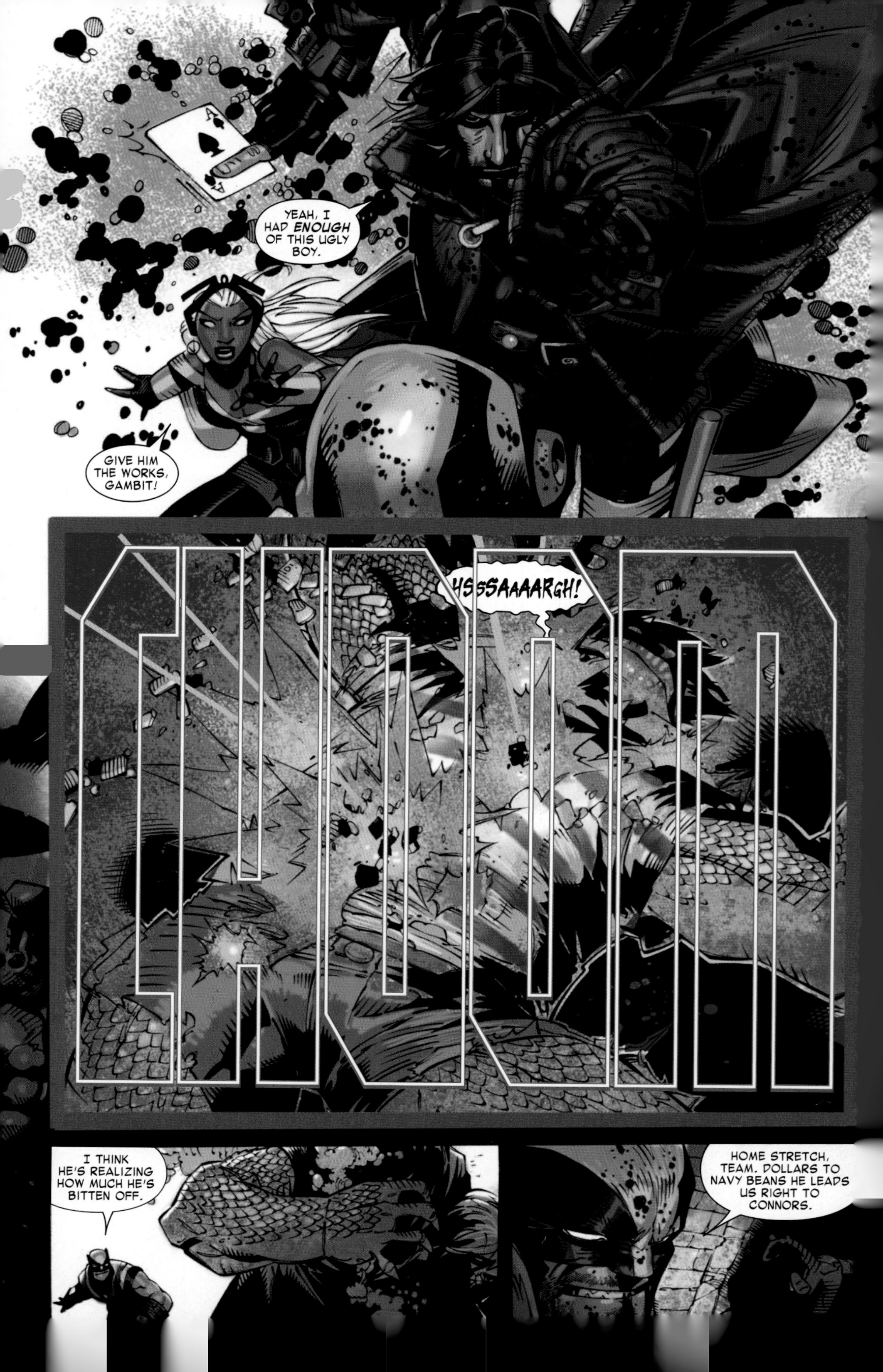
YEAH, I HAD ENOUGH OF THIS UGLY BOY.
GIVE HIM THE WORKS, GAMBIT!
HSSSAAAARGH!
I THINK HE'S REALIZING HOW MUCH HE'S BITTEN OFF.
HOME STRETCH, TEAM. DOLLARS TO NAVY BEANS HE LEADS US RIGHT TO CONNORS.

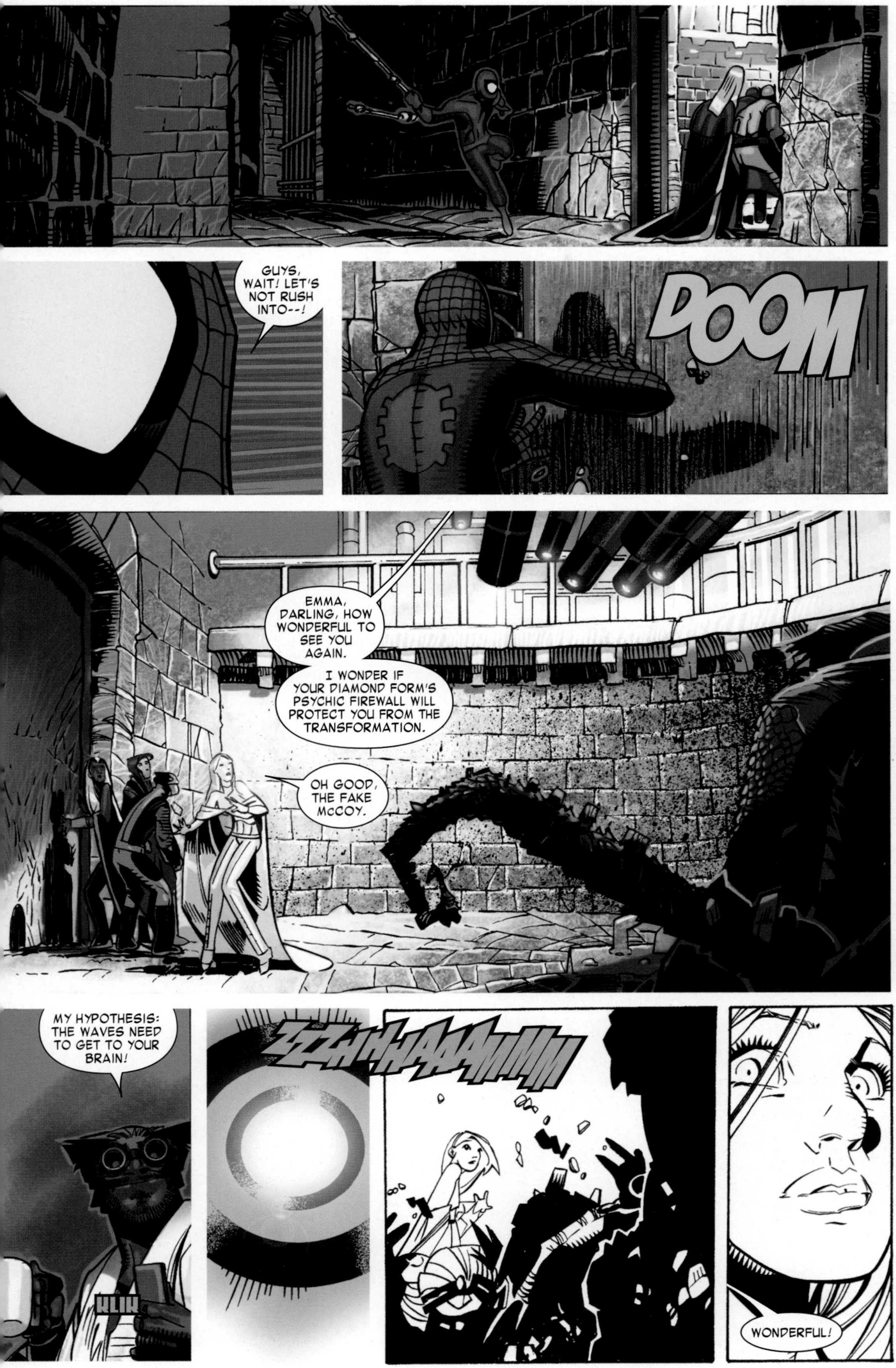
GUYS, WAIT! LET'S NOT RUSH INTO--!
DOOM
EMMA, DARLING, HOW WONDERFUL TO SEE YOU AGAIN.
I WONDER IF YOUR DIAMOND FORM'S PSYCHIC FIREWALL WILL PROTECT YOU FROM THE TRANSFORMATION.
OH GOOD, THE FAKE McCOY.
MY HYPOTHESIS: THE WAVES NEED TO GET TO YOUR BRAIN!
KLIK
ZZZHHHAAAAMMM
WONDERFUL!

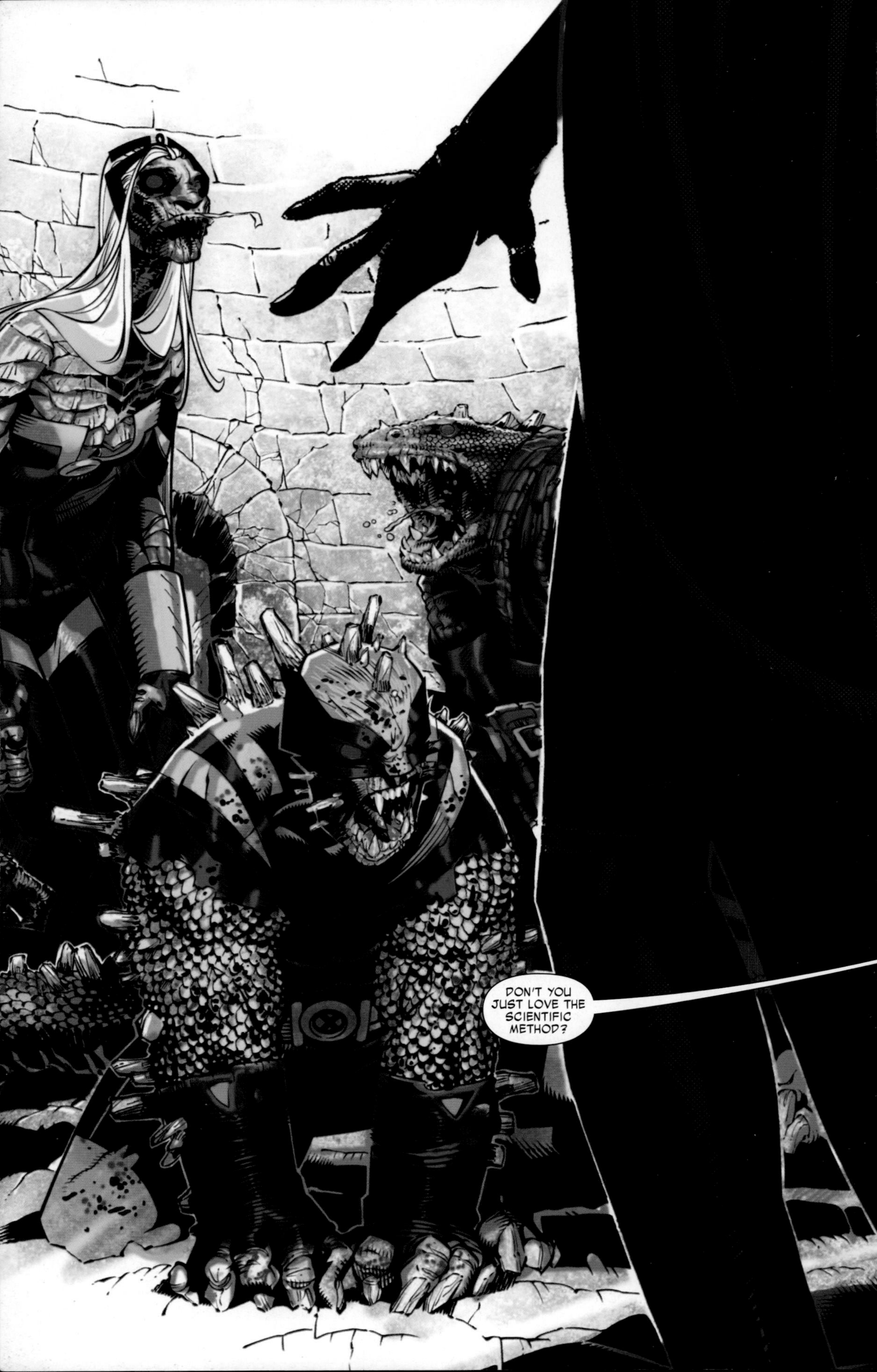
DON'T YOU JUST LOVE THE SCIENTIFIC METHOD?

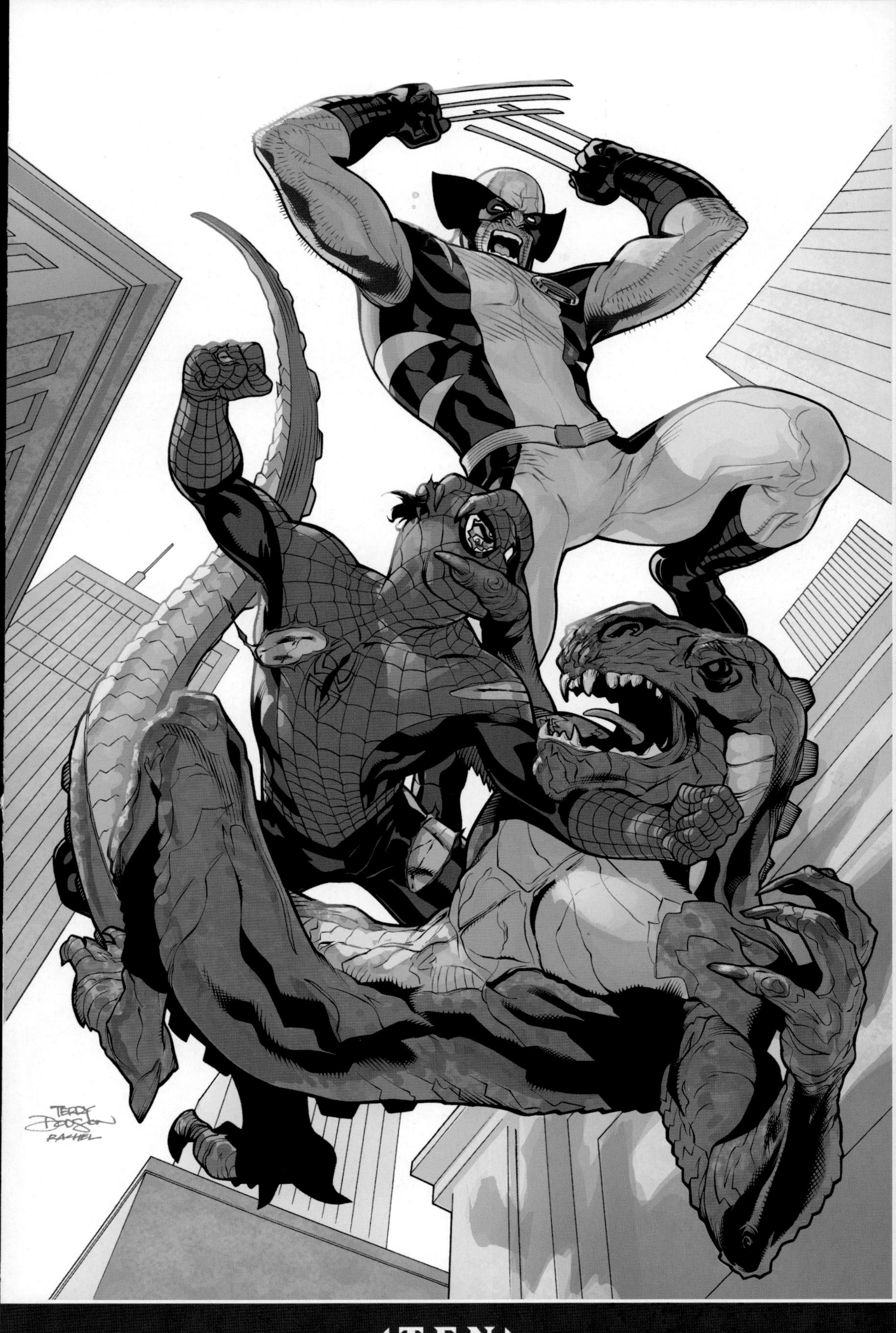
TERRY DODSON
RACHEL

TEN

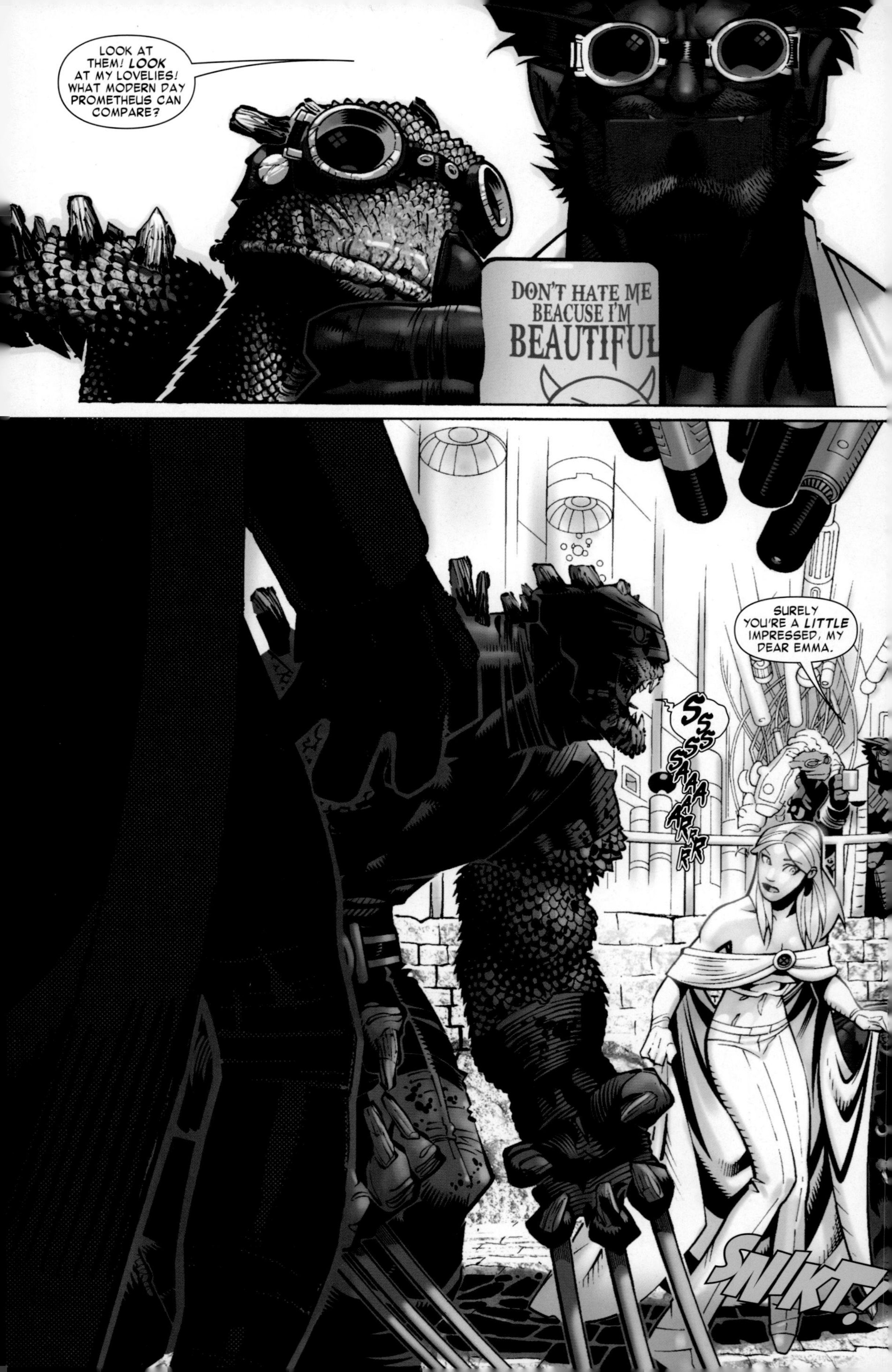
LOOK AT THEM! LOOK AT MY LOVELIES! WHAT MODERN DAY PROMETHEUS CAN COMPARE?
DON'T HATE ME BEACUSE I'M BEAUTIFUL
SURELY YOU'RE A LITTLE IMPRESSED, MY DEAR EMMA.
SSSSAAAARRRR
SNIKT!

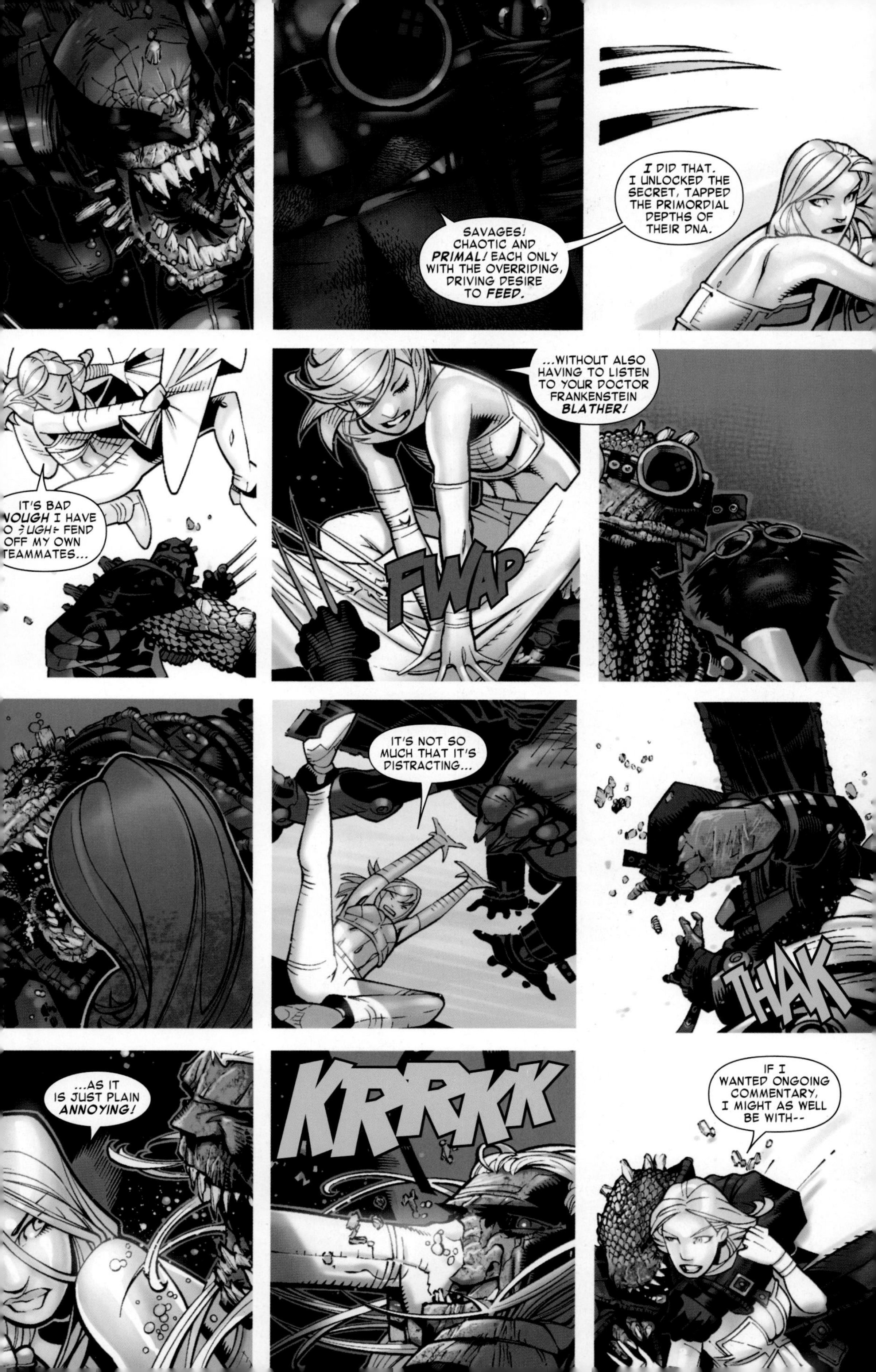
SAVAGES! CHAOTIC AND PRIMAL! EACH ONLY WITH THE OVERRIDING, DRIVING DESIRE TO FEED.
I DID THAT. I UNLOCKED THE SECRET, TAPPED THE PRIMORDIAL DEPTHS OF THEIR DNA.
IT'S BAD NOUGH I HAVE O -UGH- FEND OFF MY OWN TEAMMATES...
...WITHOUT ALSO HAVING TO LISTEN TO YOUR DOCTOR FRANKENSTEIN BLATHER!
FWAP
IT'S NOT SO MUCH THAT IT'S DISTRACTING...
THAK
...AS IT IS JUST PLAIN ANNOYING!
KRRKK
IF I WANTED ONGOING COMMENTARY, I MIGHT AS WELL BE WITH--

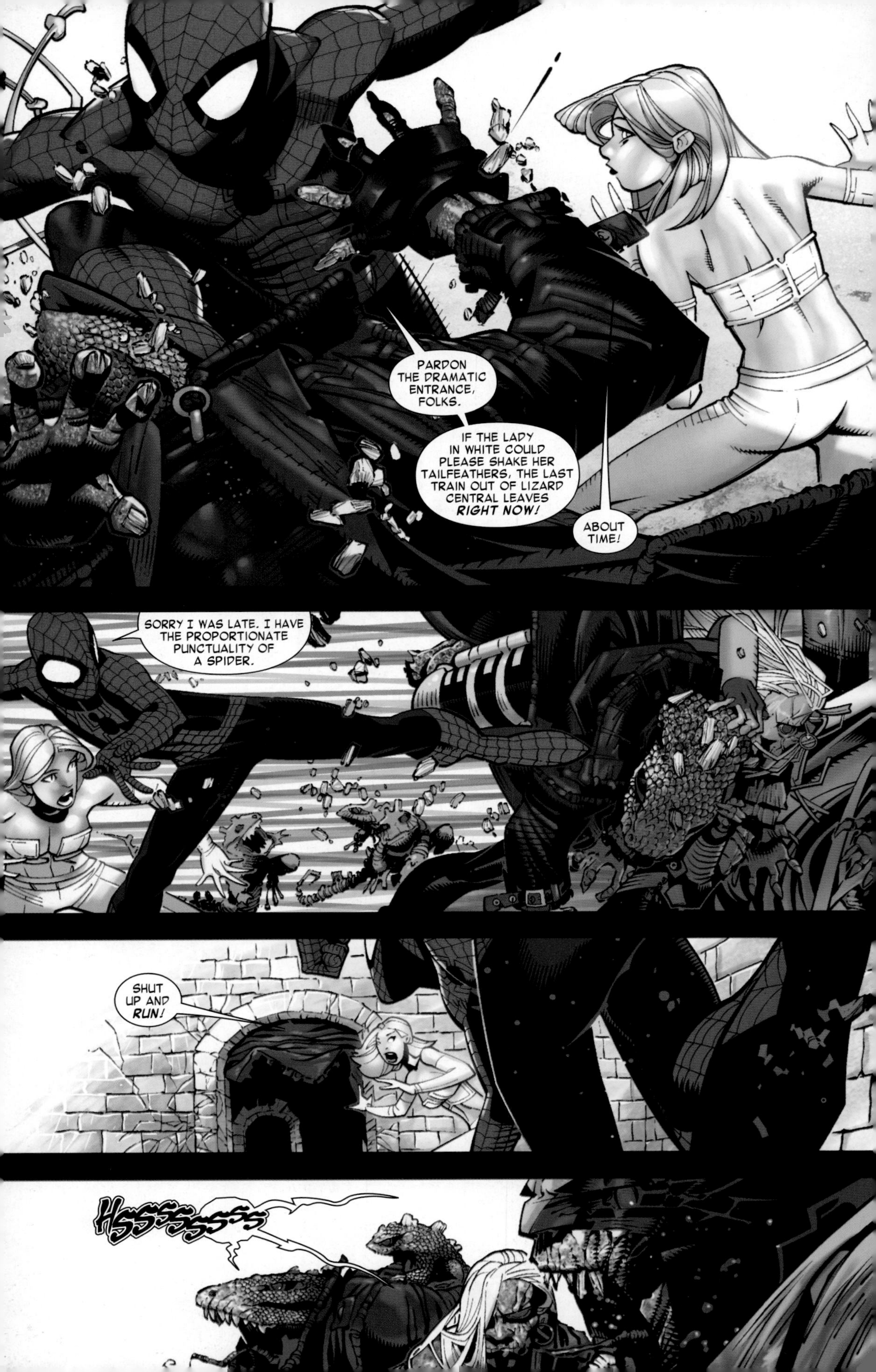
PARDON THE DRAMATIC ENTRANCE, FOLKS.
IF THE LADY IN WHITE COULD PLEASE SHAKE HER TAILFEATHERS, THE LAST TRAIN OUT OF LIZARD CENTRAL LEAVES *RIGHT NOW!*
ABOUT TIME!
SORRY I WAS LATE. I HAVE THE PROPORTIONATE PUNCTUALITY OF A SPIDER.
SHUT UP AND *RUN!*
HSSSSSSSS

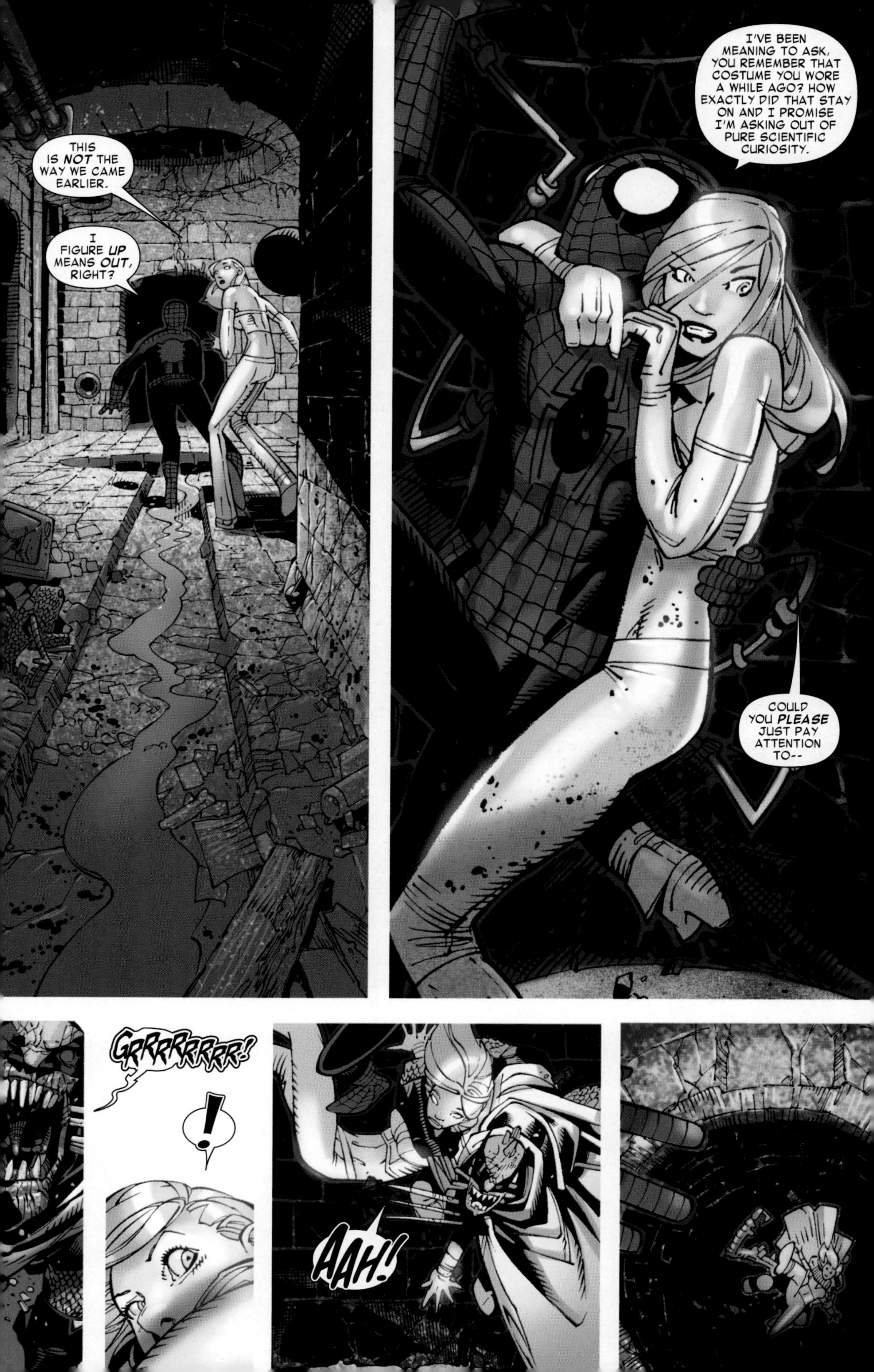
THIS IS NOT THE WAY WE CAME EARLIER.
I FIGURE UP MEANS OUT, RIGHT?
I'VE BEEN MEANING TO ASK, YOU REMEMBER THAT COSTUME YOU WORE A WHILE AGO? HOW EXACTLY DID THAT STAY ON AND I PROMISE I'M ASKING OUT OF PURE SCIENTIFIC CURIOSITY.
COULD YOU PLEASE JUST PAY ATTENTION TO--
GRRRRRRRR!
!
AAH!

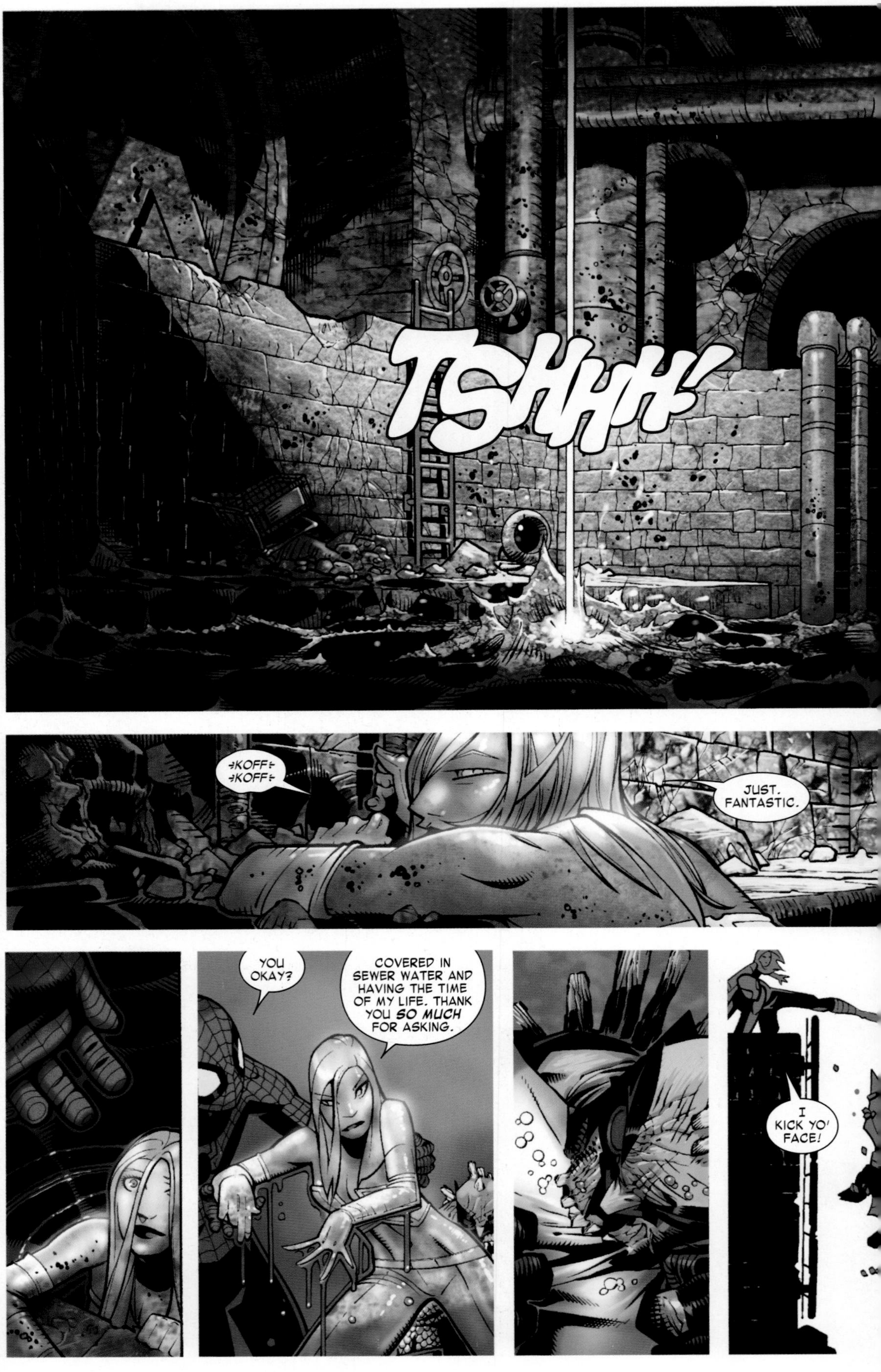
TSHHH!
=KOFF=
=KOFF=
JUST. FANTASTIC.
YOU OKAY?
COVERED IN SEWER WATER AND HAVING THE TIME OF MY LIFE. THANK YOU SO MUCH FOR ASKING.
I KICK YO' FACE!

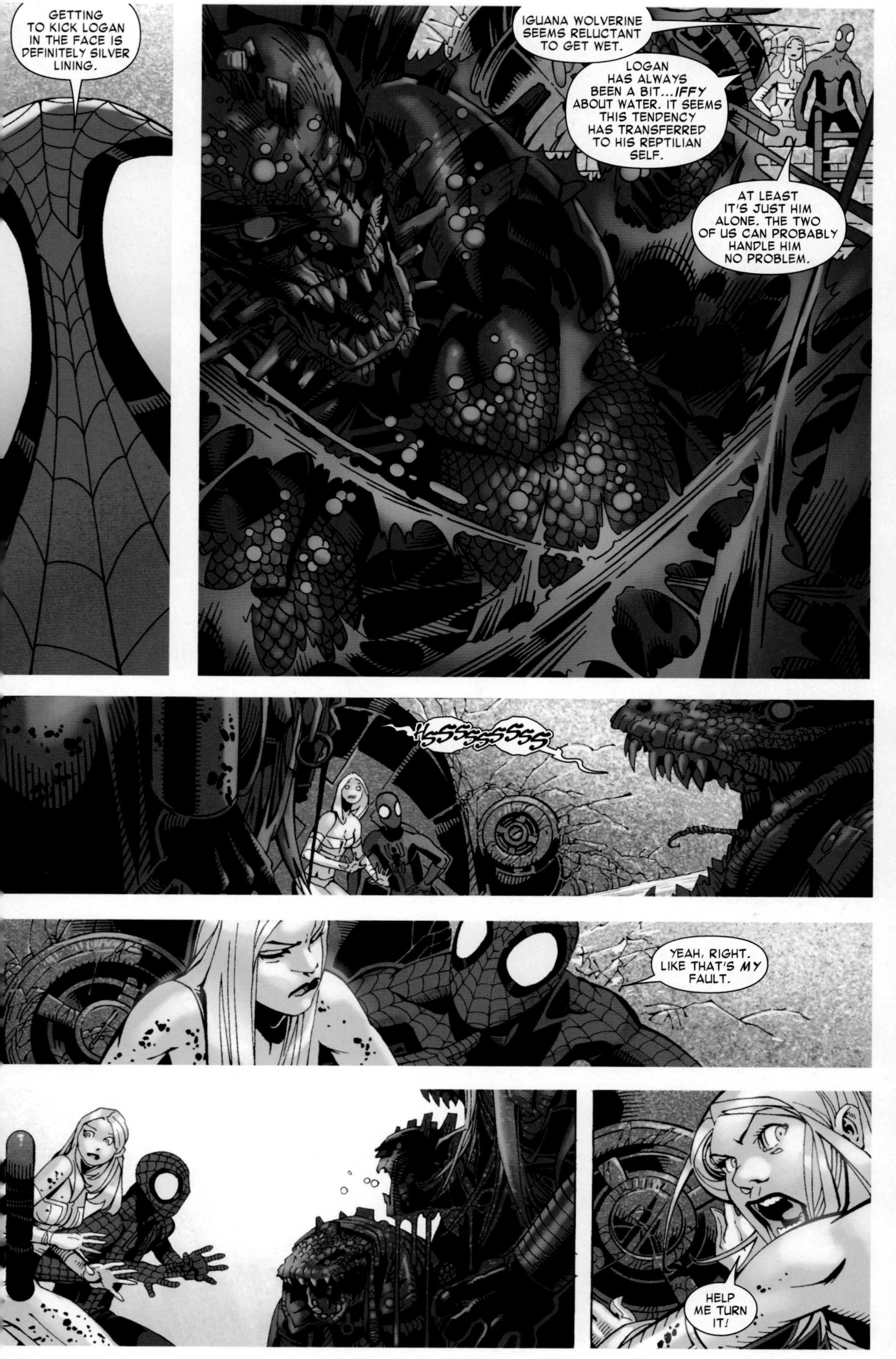
GETTING TO KICK LOGAN IN THE FACE IS DEFINITELY SILVER LINING.
IGUANA WOLVERINE SEEMS RELUCTANT TO GET WET.
LOGAN HAS ALWAYS BEEN A BIT...IFFY ABOUT WATER. IT SEEMS THIS TENDENCY HAS TRANSFERRED TO HIS REPTILIAN SELF.
AT LEAST IT'S JUST HIM ALONE. THE TWO OF US CAN PROBABLY HANDLE HIM NO PROBLEM.
HSSSSSSSSS
YEAH, RIGHT. LIKE THAT'S MY FAULT.
HELP ME TURN IT!

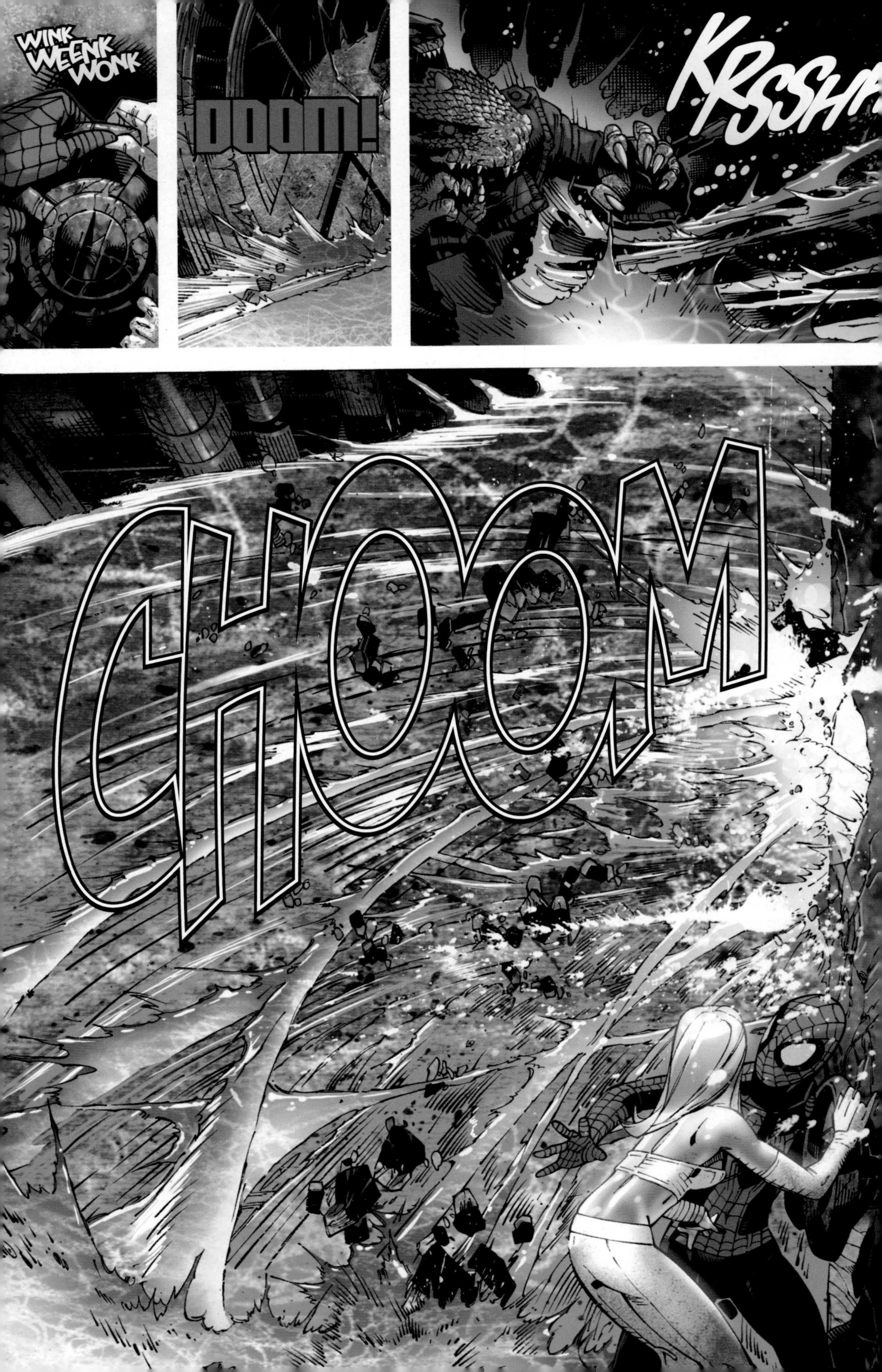
WINK
WEENK
WONK
DOOM!
KRSSH
CHOOM

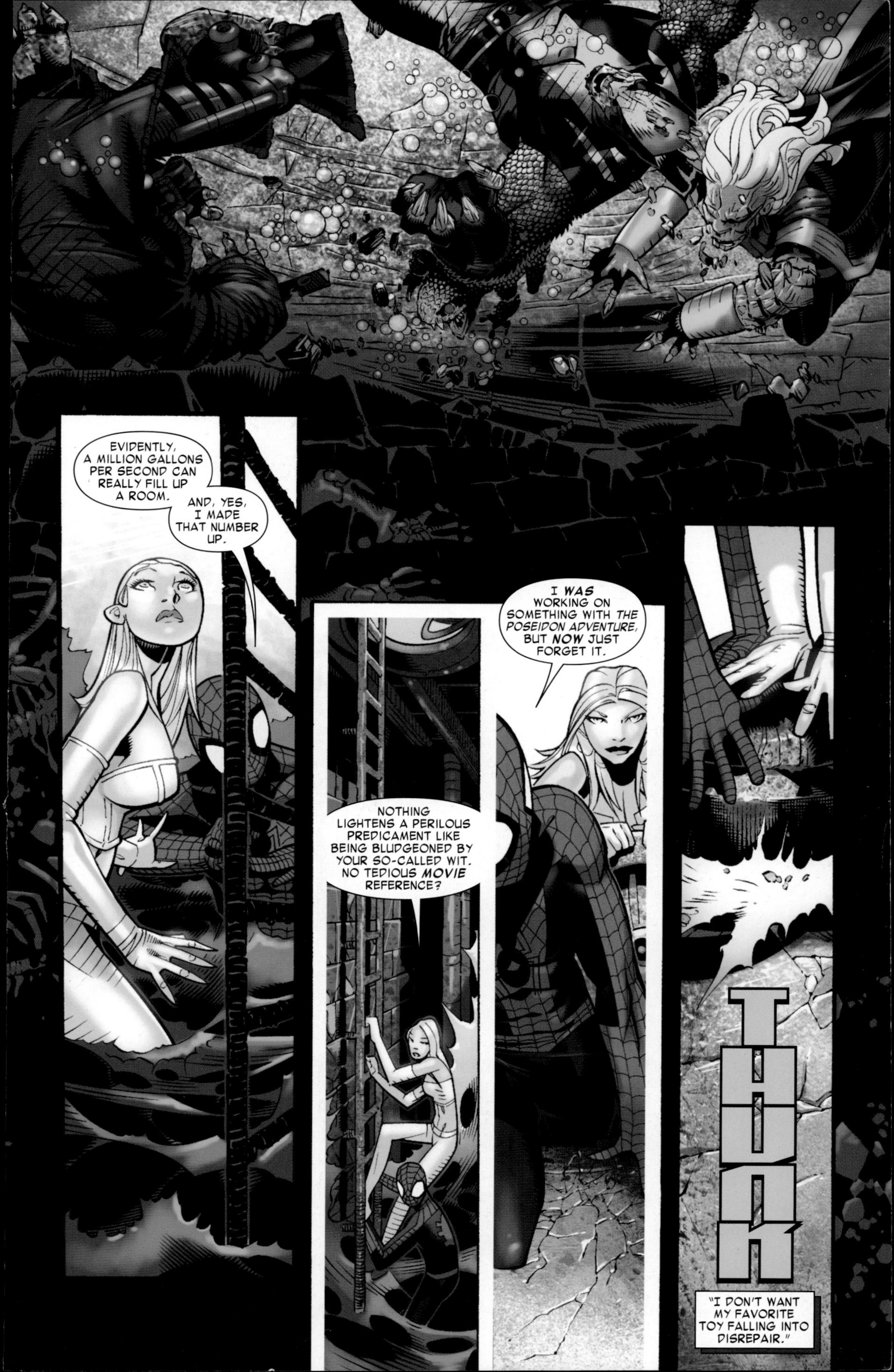
EVIDENTLY, A MILLION GALLONS PER SECOND CAN REALLY FILL UP A ROOM.
AND, YES, I MADE THAT NUMBER UP.
NOTHING LIGHTENS A PERILOUS PREDICAMENT LIKE BEING BLUDGEONED BY YOUR SO-CALLED WIT. NO TEDIOUS *MOVIE* REFERENCE?
I *WAS* WORKING ON SOMETHING WITH *THE POSEIDON ADVENTURE,* BUT *NOW* JUST FORGET IT.
THUNK
"I DON'T WANT MY FAVORITE TOY FALLING INTO DISREPAIR."

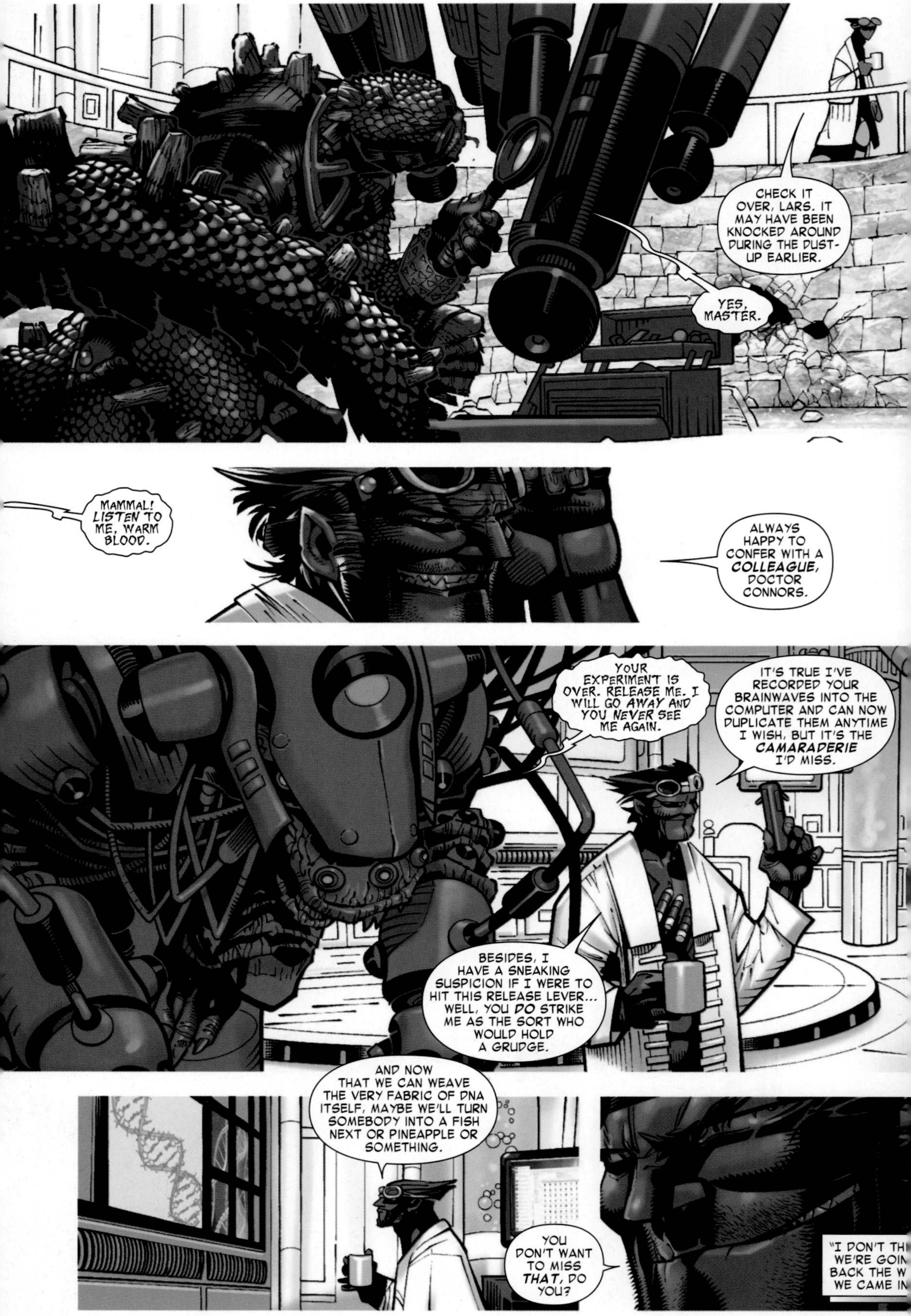
CHECK IT OVER, LARS. IT MAY HAVE BEEN KNOCKED AROUND DURING THE DUST-UP EARLIER.
YES, MASTER.
MAMMAL! LISTEN TO ME, WARM BLOOD.
ALWAYS HAPPY TO CONFER WITH A COLLEAGUE, DOCTOR CONNORS.
YOUR EXPERIMENT IS OVER. RELEASE ME. I WILL GO AWAY AND YOU NEVER SEE ME AGAIN.
IT'S TRUE I'VE RECORDED YOUR BRAINWAVES INTO THE COMPUTER AND CAN NOW DUPLICATE THEM ANYTIME I WISH, BUT IT'S THE CAMARADERIE I'D MISS.
BESIDES, I HAVE A SNEAKING SUSPICION IF I WERE TO HIT THIS RELEASE LEVER... WELL, YOU DO STRIKE ME AS THE SORT WHO WOULD HOLD A GRUDGE.
AND NOW THAT WE CAN WEAVE THE VERY FABRIC OF DNA ITSELF, MAYBE WE'LL TURN SOMEBODY INTO A FISH NEXT OR PINEAPPLE OR SOMETHING.
YOU DON'T WANT TO MISS THAT, DO YOU?

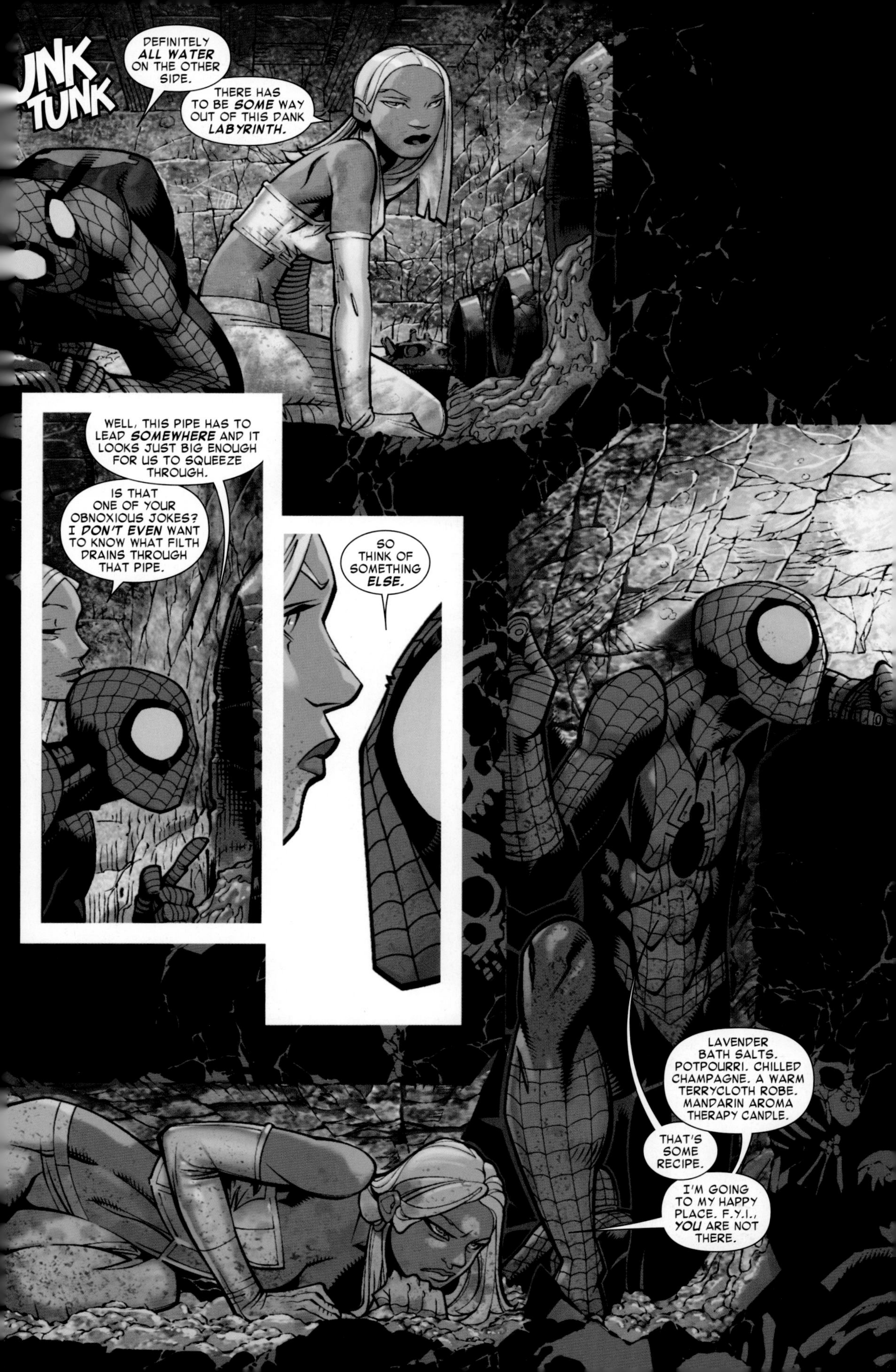
UNK TUNK
DEFINITELY ALL WATER ON THE OTHER SIDE.
THERE HAS TO BE SOME WAY OUT OF THIS DANK LABYRINTH.
WELL, THIS PIPE HAS TO LEAD SOMEWHERE AND IT LOOKS JUST BIG ENOUGH FOR US TO SQUEEZE THROUGH.
IS THAT ONE OF YOUR OBNOXIOUS JOKES? I DON'T EVEN WANT TO KNOW WHAT FILTH DRAINS THROUGH THAT PIPE.
SO THINK OF SOMETHING ELSE.
LAVENDER BATH SALTS. POTPOURRI. CHILLED CHAMPAGNE. A WARM TERRYCLOTH ROBE. MANDARIN AROMA THERAPY CANDLE.
THAT'S SOME RECIPE.
I'M GOING TO MY HAPPY PLACE. F.Y.I., YOU ARE NOT THERE.

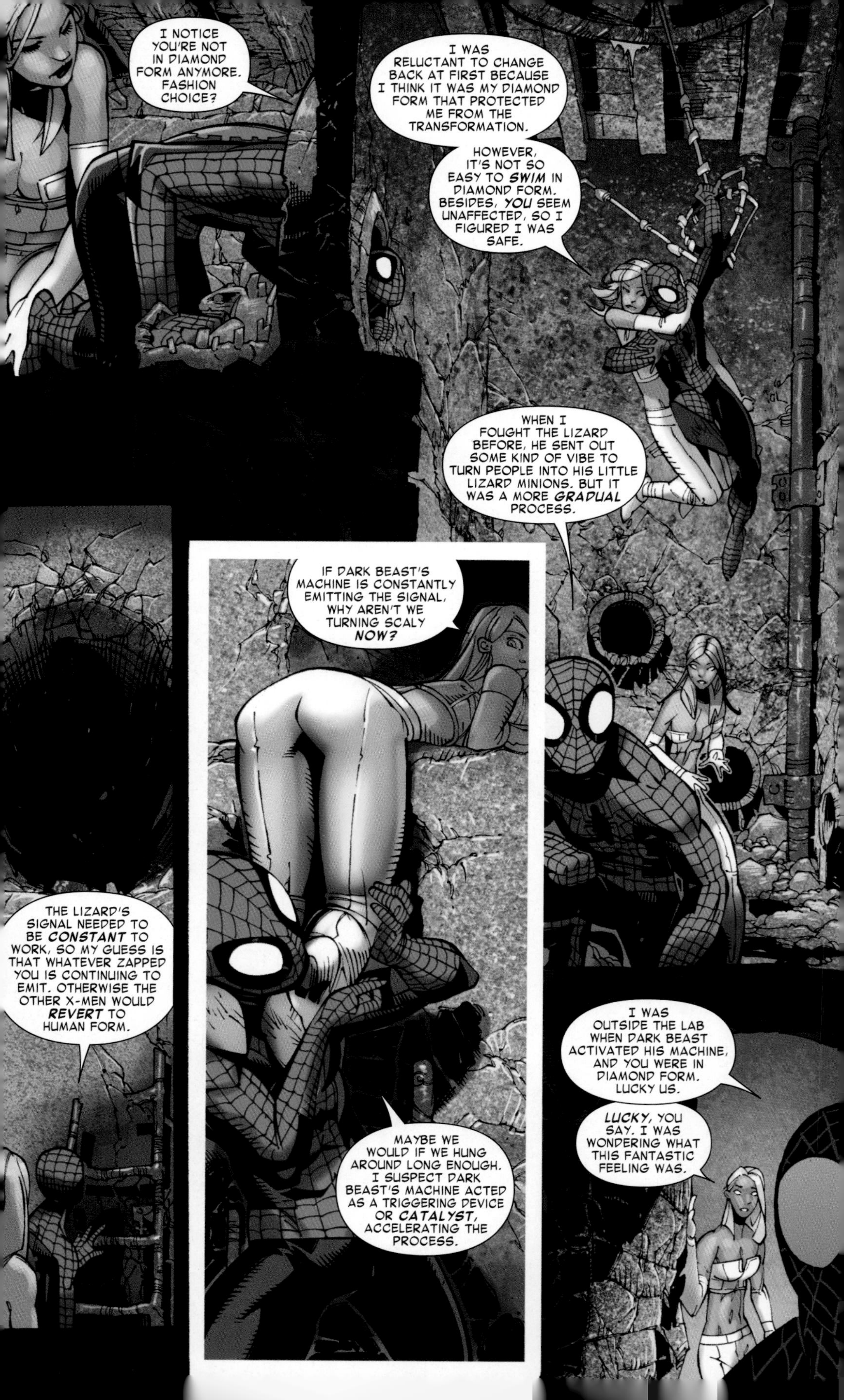

I NOTICE YOU'RE NOT IN DIAMOND FORM ANYMORE. FASHION CHOICE?
I WAS RELUCTANT TO CHANGE BACK AT FIRST BECAUSE I THINK IT WAS MY DIAMOND FORM THAT PROTECTED ME FROM THE TRANSFORMATION.
HOWEVER, IT'S NOT SO EASY TO SWIM IN DIAMOND FORM. BESIDES, YOU SEEM UNAFFECTED, SO I FIGURED I WAS SAFE.
WHEN I FOUGHT THE LIZARD BEFORE, HE SENT OUT SOME KIND OF VIBE TO TURN PEOPLE INTO HIS LITTLE LIZARD MINIONS. BUT IT WAS A MORE GRADUAL PROCESS.
IF DARK BEAST'S MACHINE IS CONSTANTLY EMITTING THE SIGNAL, WHY AREN'T WE TURNING SCALY NOW?
THE LIZARD'S SIGNAL NEEDED TO BE CONSTANT TO WORK, SO MY GUESS IS THAT WHATEVER ZAPPED YOU IS CONTINUING TO EMIT. OTHERWISE THE OTHER X-MEN WOULD REVERT TO HUMAN FORM.
MAYBE WE WOULD IF WE HUNG AROUND LONG ENOUGH. I SUSPECT DARK BEAST'S MACHINE ACTED AS A TRIGGERING DEVICE OR CATALYST, ACCELERATING THE PROCESS.
I WAS OUTSIDE THE LAB WHEN DARK BEAST ACTIVATED HIS MACHINE, AND YOU WERE IN DIAMOND FORM. LUCKY US.
LUCKY, YOU SAY. I WAS WONDERING WHAT THIS FANTASTIC FEELING WAS.

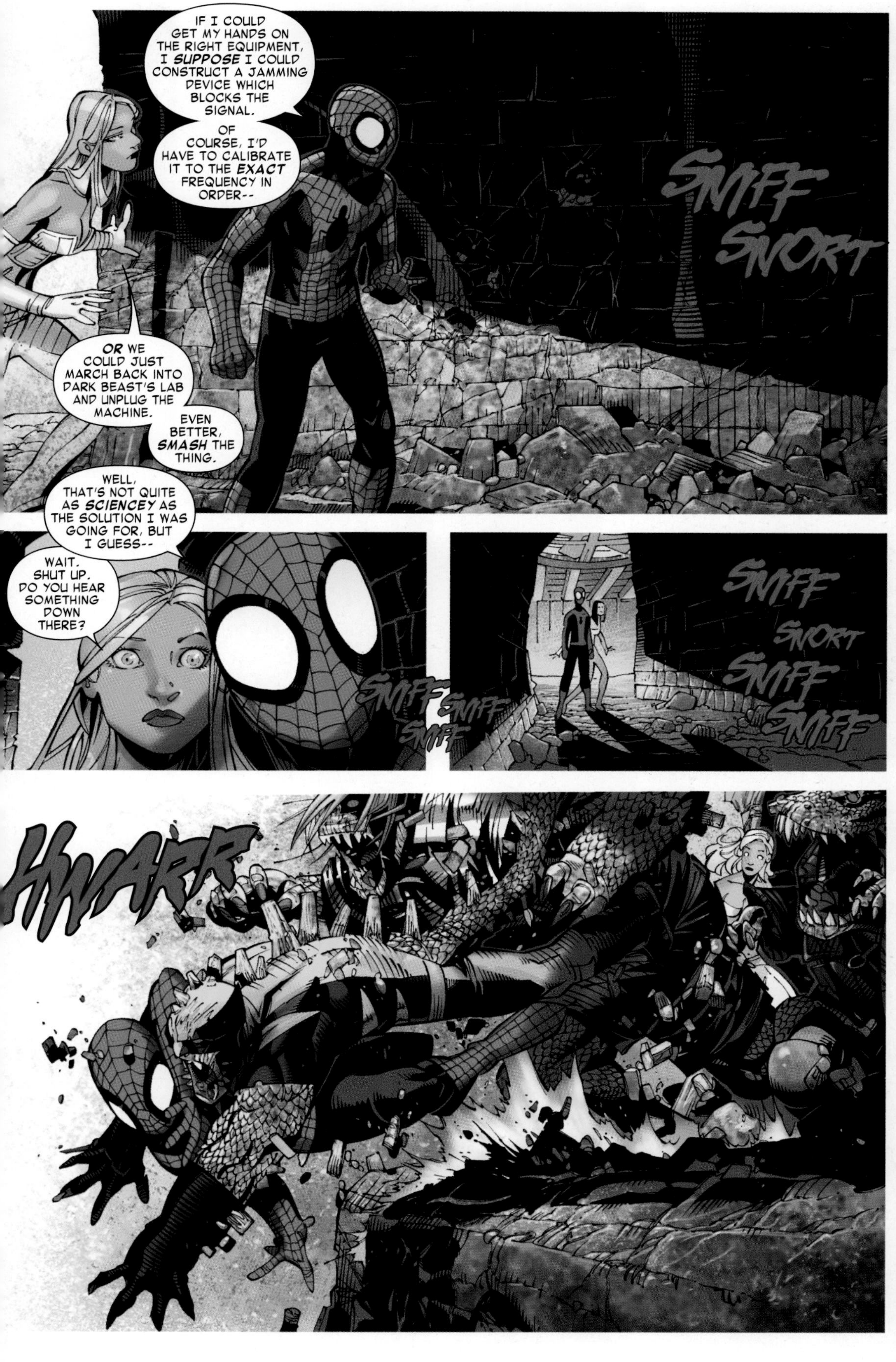
IF I COULD GET MY HANDS ON THE RIGHT EQUIPMENT, I SUPPOSE I COULD CONSTRUCT A JAMMING DEVICE WHICH BLOCKS THE SIGNAL.
OF COURSE, I'D HAVE TO CALIBRATE IT TO THE EXACT FREQUENCY IN ORDER--
SNIFF
SNORT
OR WE COULD JUST MARCH BACK INTO DARK BEAST'S LAB AND UNPLUG THE MACHINE.
EVEN BETTER, SMASH THE THING.
WELL, THAT'S NOT QUITE AS SCIENCEY AS THE SOLUTION I WAS GOING FOR, BUT I GUESS--
WAIT. SHUT UP. DO YOU HEAR SOMETHING DOWN THERE?
SNIFF SNIFF SNIFF
SNIFF
SNORT
SNIFF
SNIFF
HWARR

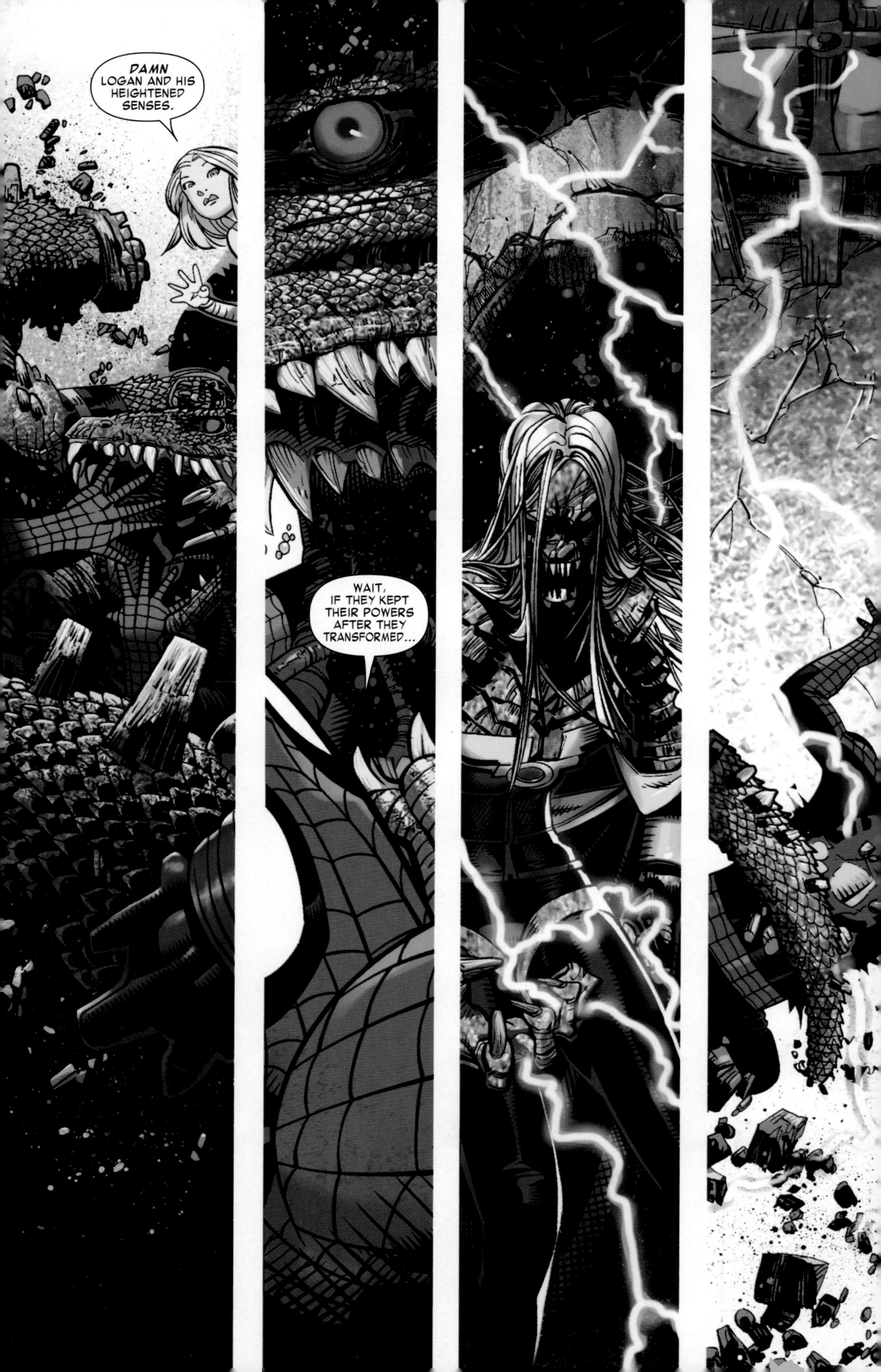
DAMN LOGAN AND HIS HEIGHTENED SENSES.
WAIT, IF THEY KEPT THEIR POWERS AFTER THEY TRANSFORMED...

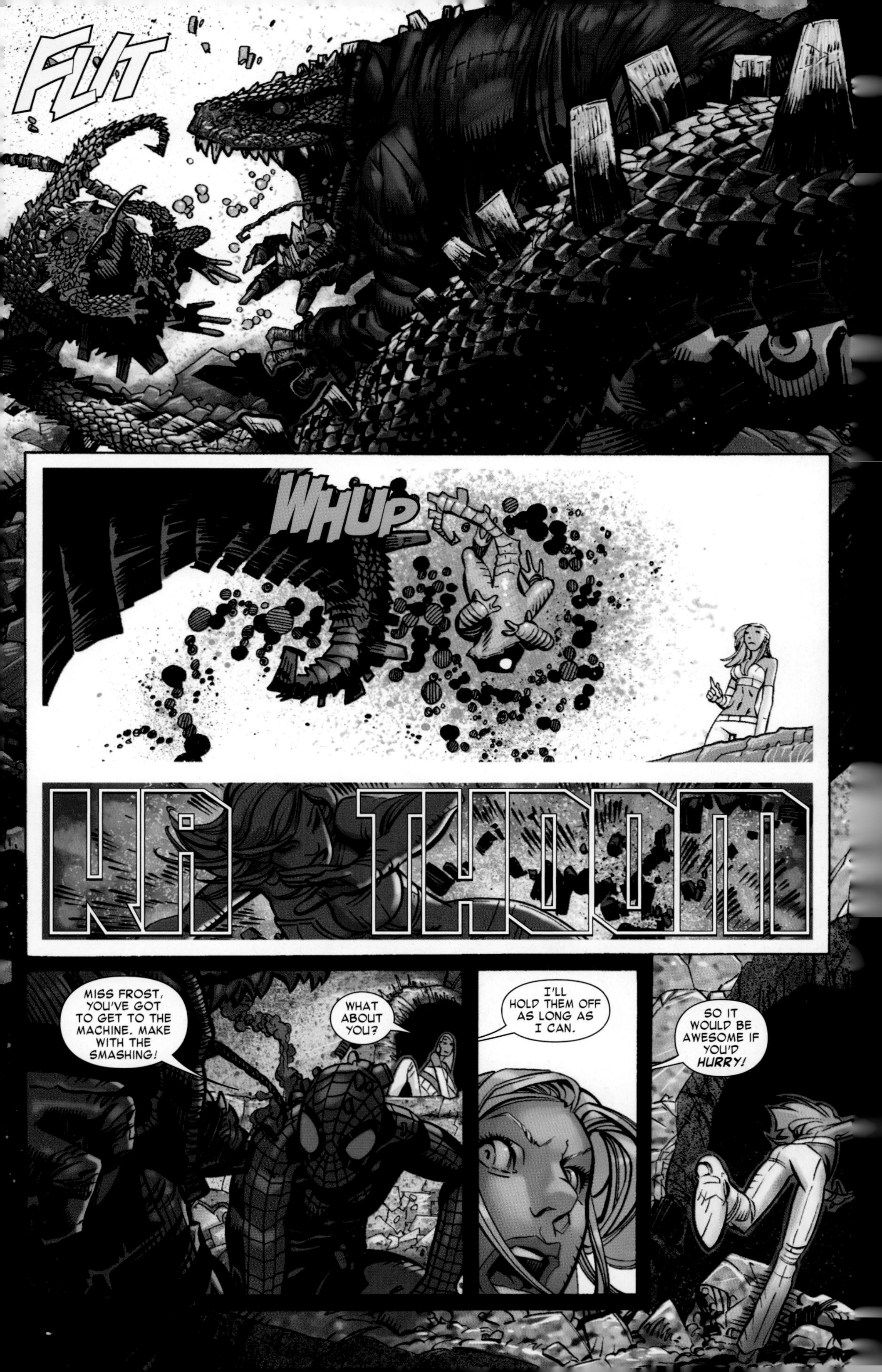
FLIT
WHUP
KRA THOOM
MISS FROST, YOU'VE GOT TO GET TO THE MACHINE. MAKE WITH THE SMASHING!
WHAT ABOUT YOU?
I'LL HOLD THEM OFF AS LONG AS I CAN.
SO IT WOULD BE AWESOME IF YOU'D *HURRY!*

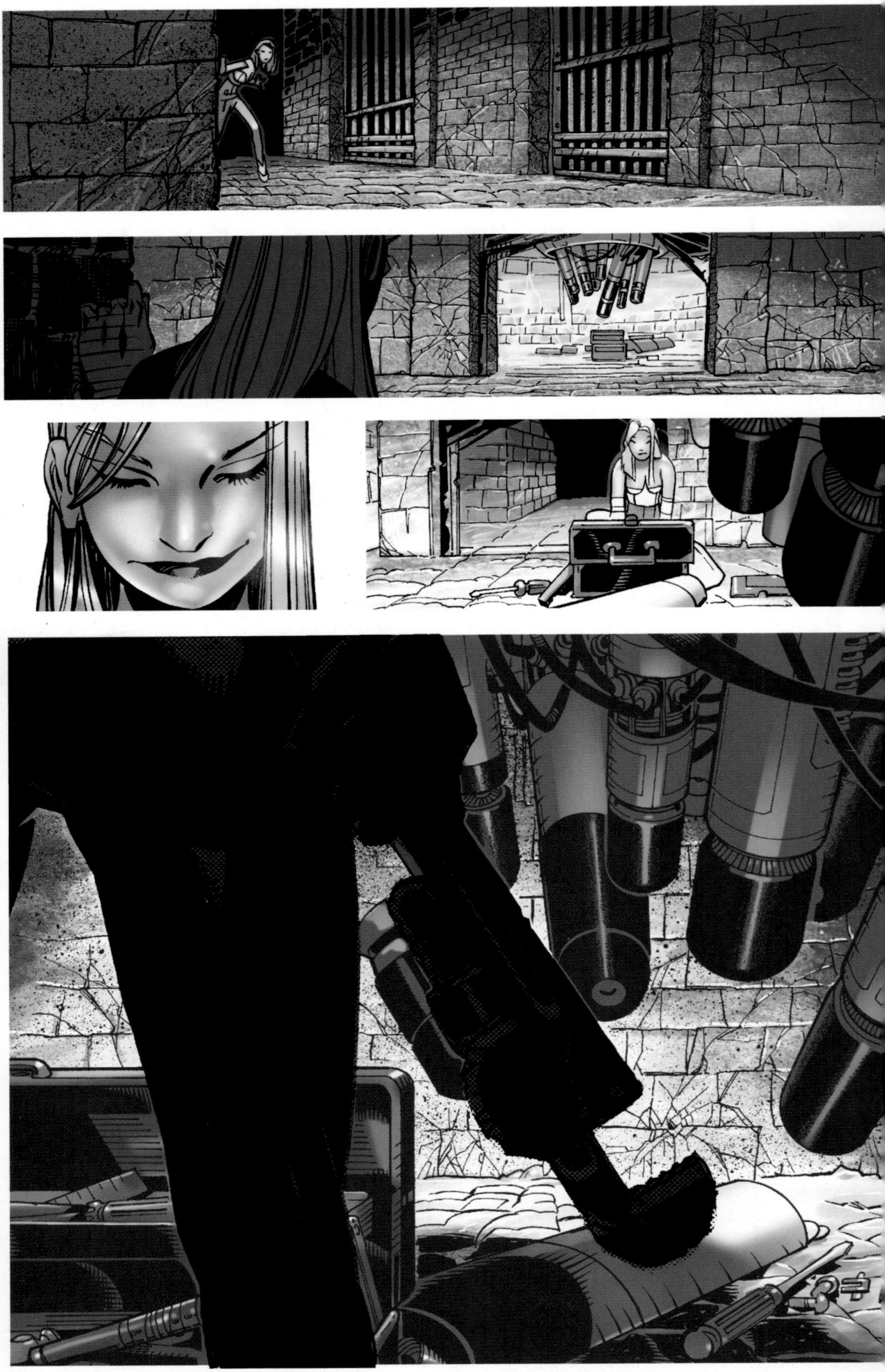

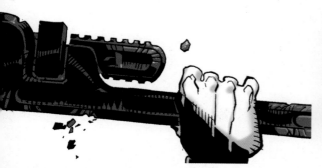

THUMP

THAPP

OOF

YOU'RE A RESILIENT LADY, MISS FROST. I'D THOUGHT MY PRETTIES WOULD HAVE *FINISHED* YOU BY NOW.

YOU DON'T REALLY THINK I'LL LET YOU WRECK WHAT WE'VE JUST SPENT SO MUCH TIME *REPAIRING*, DO YOU?

A PITY YOU CAN'T USE YOUR POWERS WHILE IN DIAMOND FORM. YOU COULD TAKE OVER MY MIND *EASILY.*

OR PERHAPS YOU'RE *FAST* ENOUGH. I WONDER IF YOU CAN DROP YOUR DIAMOND FORM AND USE YOUR POWERS BEFORE I PRESS THIS BUTTON. WOULD YOU LIKE TO JOIN YOUR MINDLESS FRIENDS?

YOUR RIDICULOUS MAD SCIENTIST PATTER *ALMOST* MAKES ME MISS SPIDER-MAN'S TERRIBLE JOKES.

KRAK

ALMOST.

FWHIP

KRKKK

YOU KNOW, I HAVE NOTHING BUT RESPECT FOR YOUR ABILITIES, EMMA. BUT AGAINST ME *AND* LARS, I DON'T REALLY THINK YOU HAVE MUCH OF A CHANCE.

MAY... I DO...

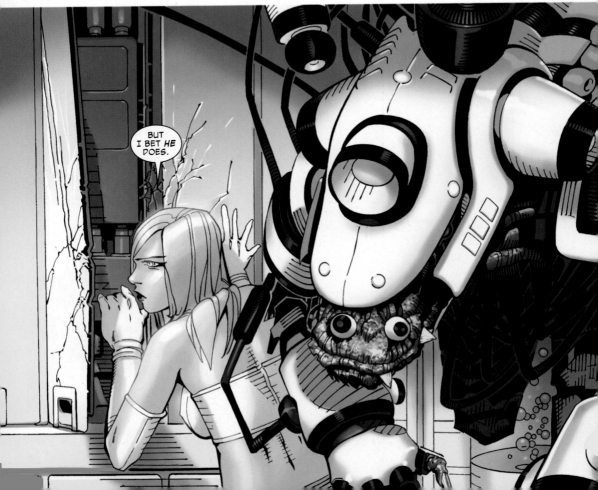

BUT I BET *HE* DOES.

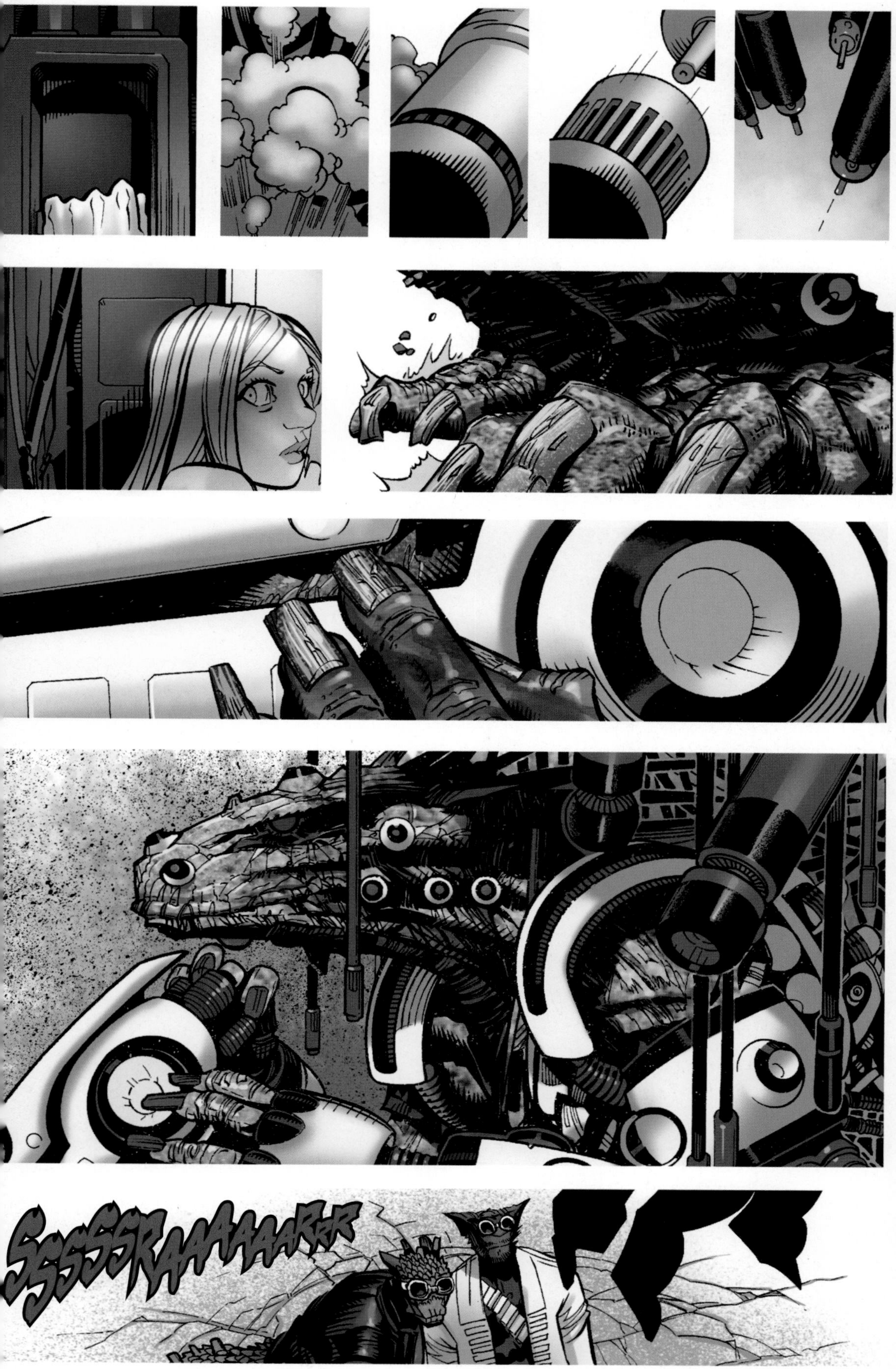
SSSSSRAAAAAARRR

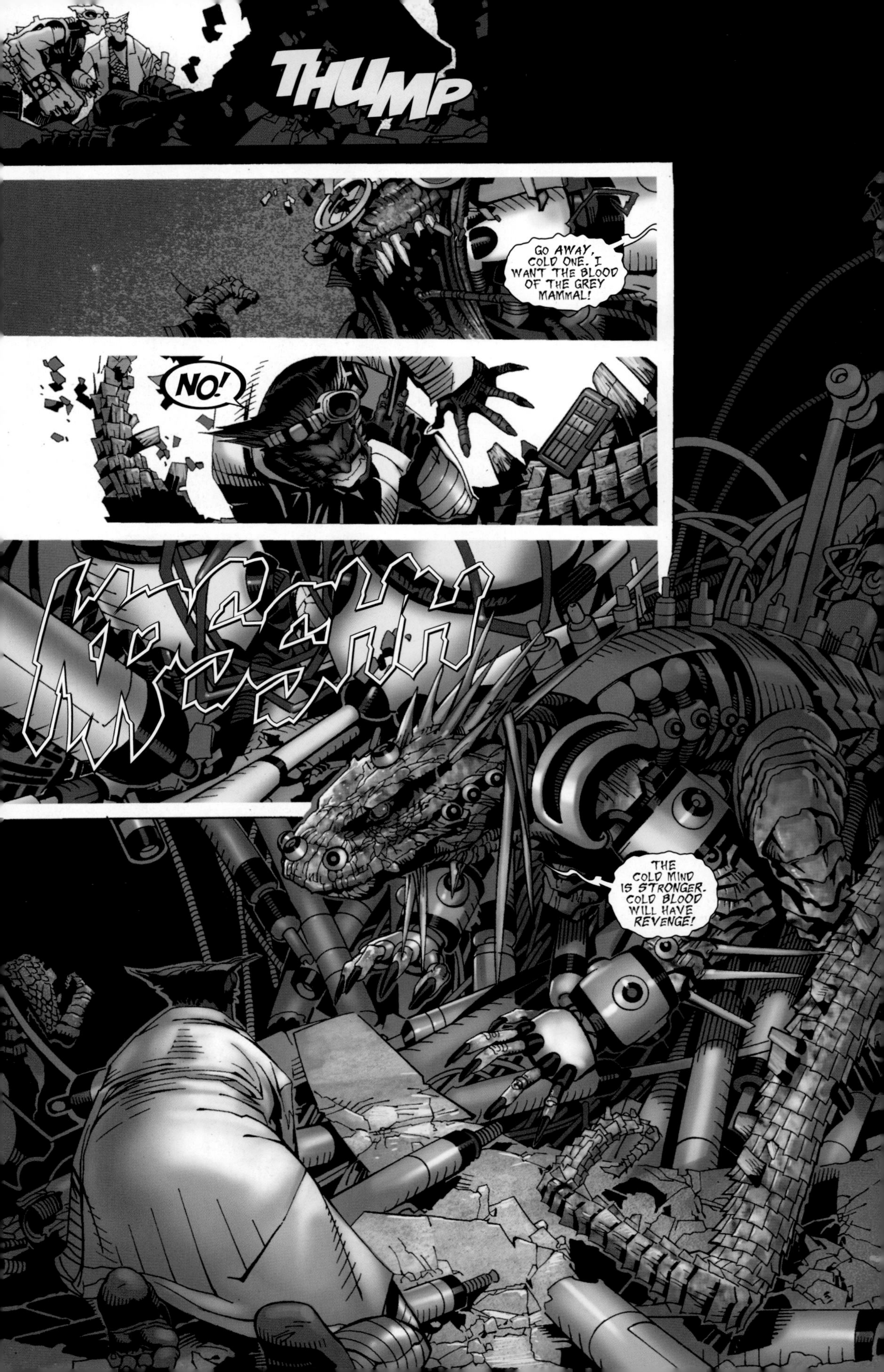
THUMP
GO AWAY, COLD ONE. I WANT THE BLOOD OF THE GREY MAMMAL!
NO!
KRESHH
THE COLD MIND IS STRONGER. COLD BLOOD WILL HAVE REVENGE!

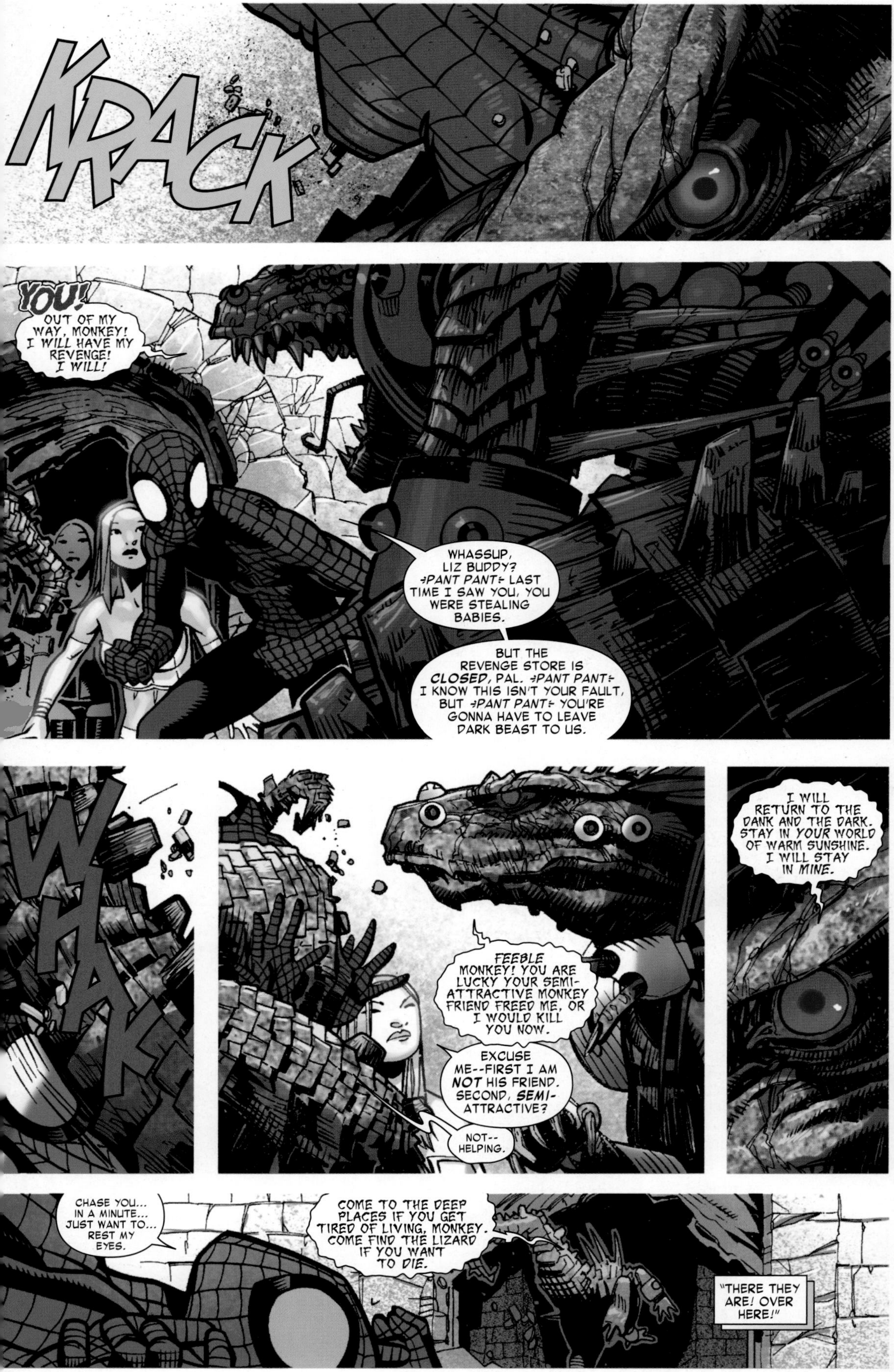
KRACK
YOU! OUT OF MY WAY, MONKEY! I WILL HAVE MY REVENGE! I WILL!
WHASSUP, LIZ BUDDY? =PANT PANT= LAST TIME I SAW YOU, YOU WERE STEALING BABIES.
BUT THE REVENGE STORE IS CLOSED, PAL. =PANT PANT= I KNOW THIS ISN'T YOUR FAULT, BUT =PANT PANT= YOU'RE GONNA HAVE TO LEAVE DARK BEAST TO US.
WHAK
FEEBLE MONKEY! YOU ARE LUCKY YOUR SEMI-ATTRACTIVE MONKEY FRIEND FREED ME, OR I WOULD KILL YOU NOW.
EXCUSE ME--FIRST I AM NOT HIS FRIEND. SECOND, SEMI-ATTRACTIVE?
NOT--HELPING.
I WILL RETURN TO THE DANK AND THE DARK. STAY IN YOUR WORLD OF WARM SUNSHINE. I WILL STAY IN MINE.
CHASE YOU... IN A MINUTE... JUST WANT TO... REST MY EYES.
COME TO THE DEEP PLACES IF YOU GET TIRED OF LIVING, MONKEY. COME FIND THE LIZARD IF YOU WANT TO DIE.
"THERE THEY ARE! OVER HERE!"

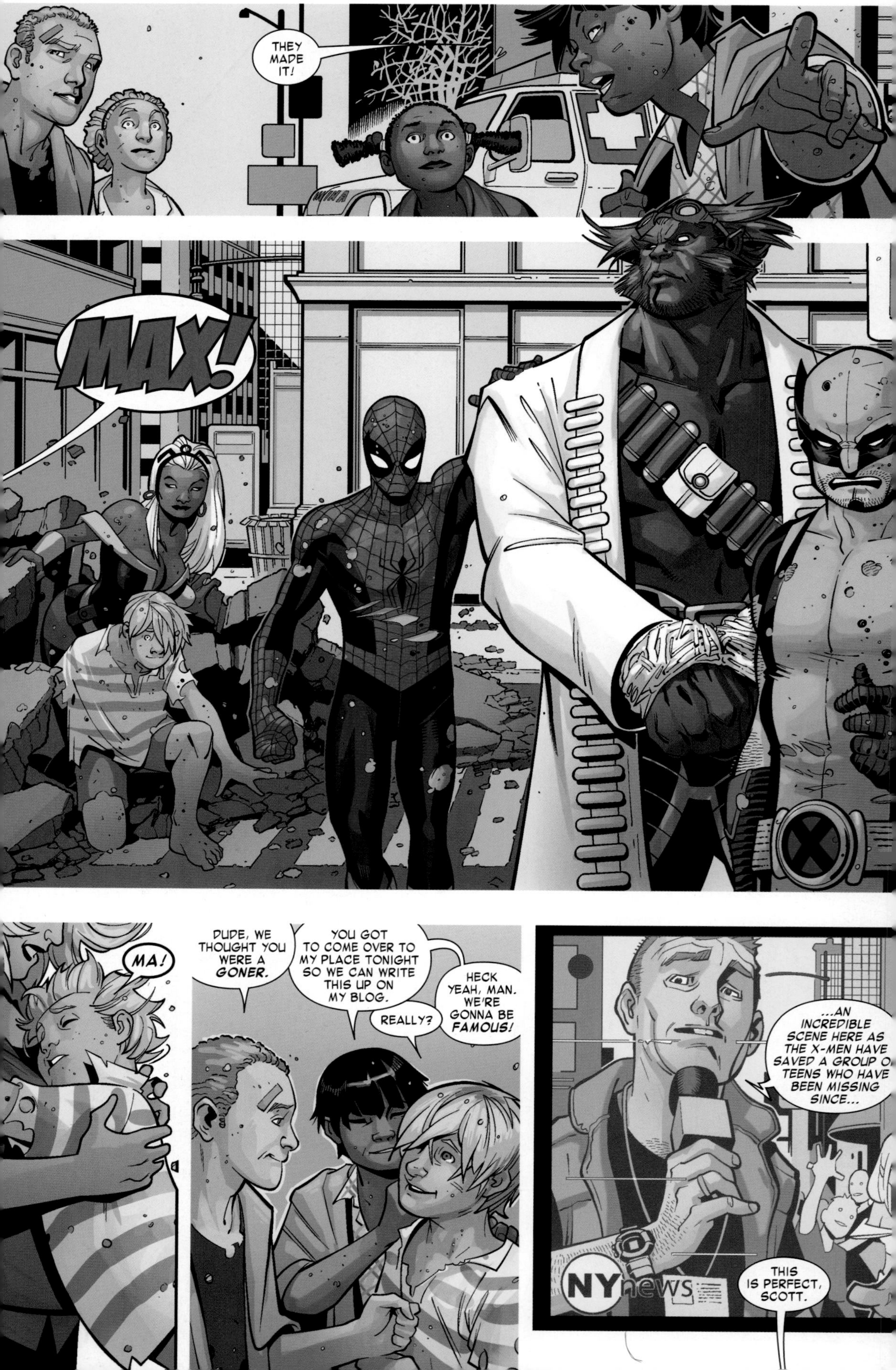
THEY MADE IT!
MAX!
MA!
DUDE, WE THOUGHT YOU WERE A GONER.
YOU GOT TO COME OVER TO MY PLACE TONIGHT SO WE CAN WRITE THIS UP ON MY BLOG.
REALLY?
HECK YEAH, MAN. WE'RE GONNA BE FAMOUS!
...AN INCREDIBLE SCENE HERE AS THE X-MEN HAVE SAVED A GROUP O TEENS WHO HAVE BEEN MISSING SINCE...
NY news
THIS IS PERFECT, SCOTT.

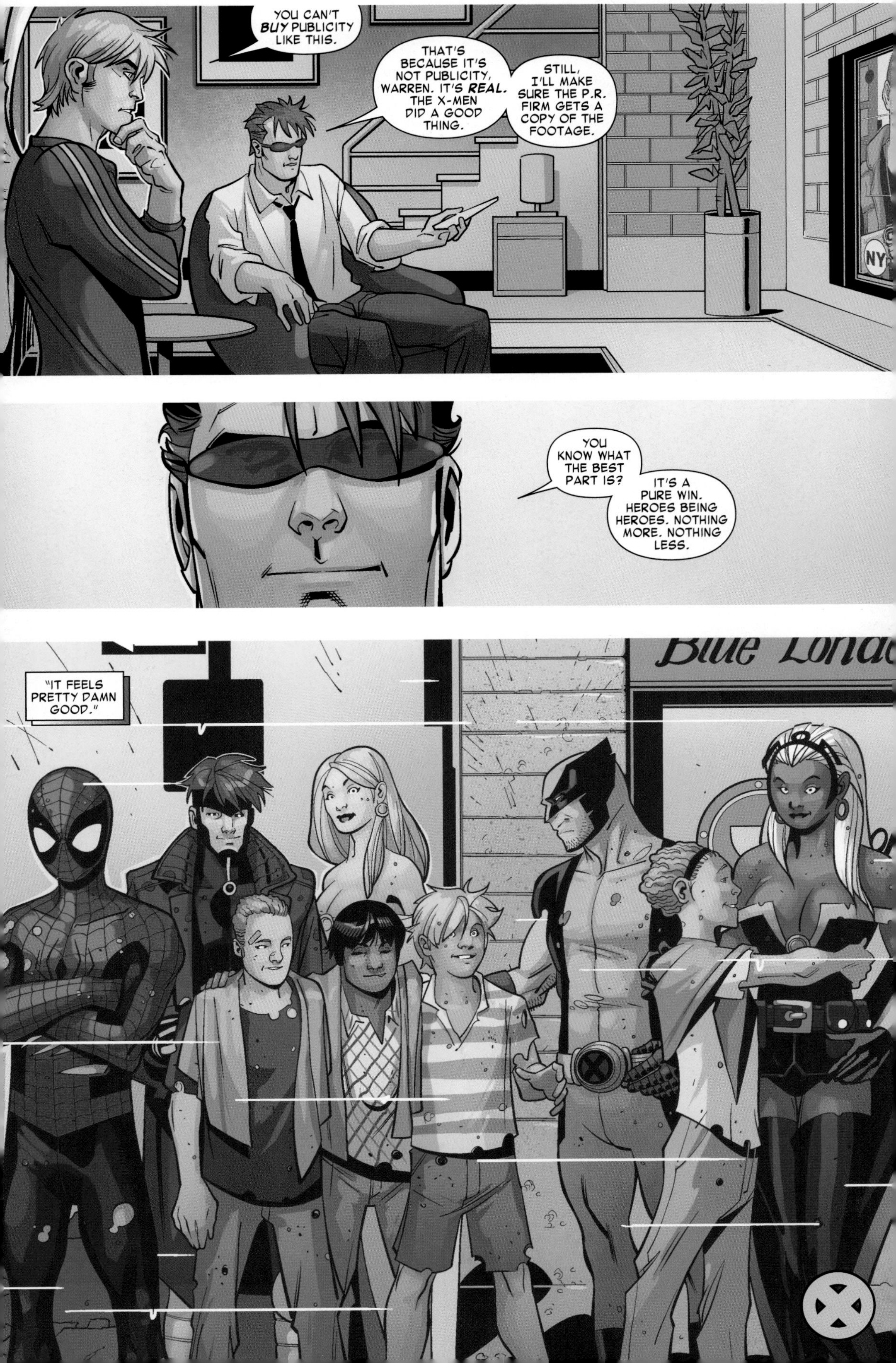
YOU CAN'T BUY PUBLICITY LIKE THIS.
THAT'S BECAUSE IT'S NOT PUBLICITY, WARREN. IT'S REAL. THE X-MEN DID A GOOD THING.
STILL, I'LL MAKE SURE THE P.R. FIRM GETS A COPY OF THE FOOTAGE.
NY
YOU KNOW WHAT THE BEST PART IS?
IT'S A PURE WIN. HEROES BEING HEROES. NOTHING MORE. NOTHING LESS.
Blue Londo
"IT FEELS PRETTY DAMN GOOD."

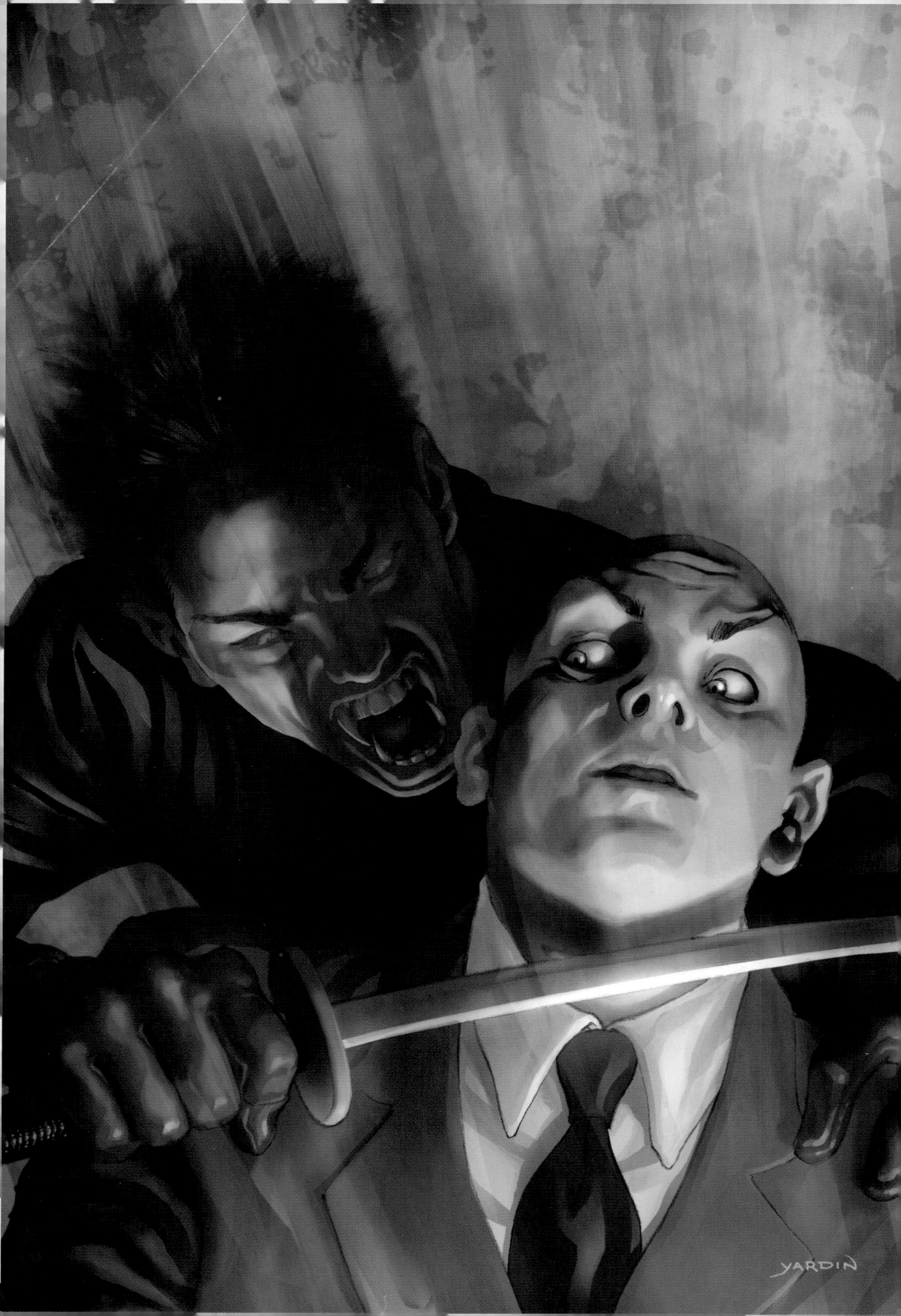
YARDIN

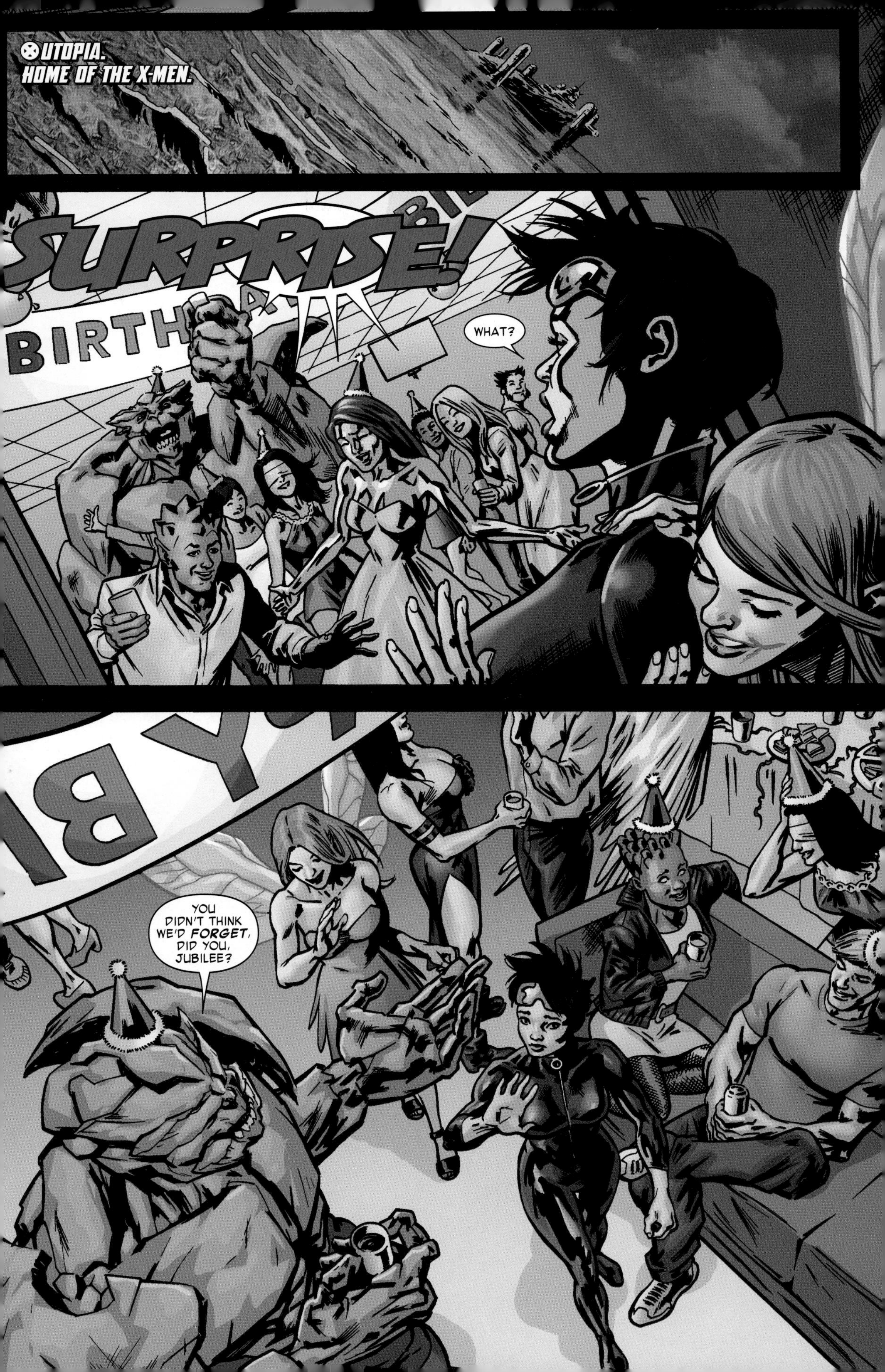
UTOPIA.
HOME OF THE X-MEN.
SURPRISE!
BIRTH
WHAT?
YOU DIDN'T THINK WE'D *FORGET*, DID YOU, JUBILEE?

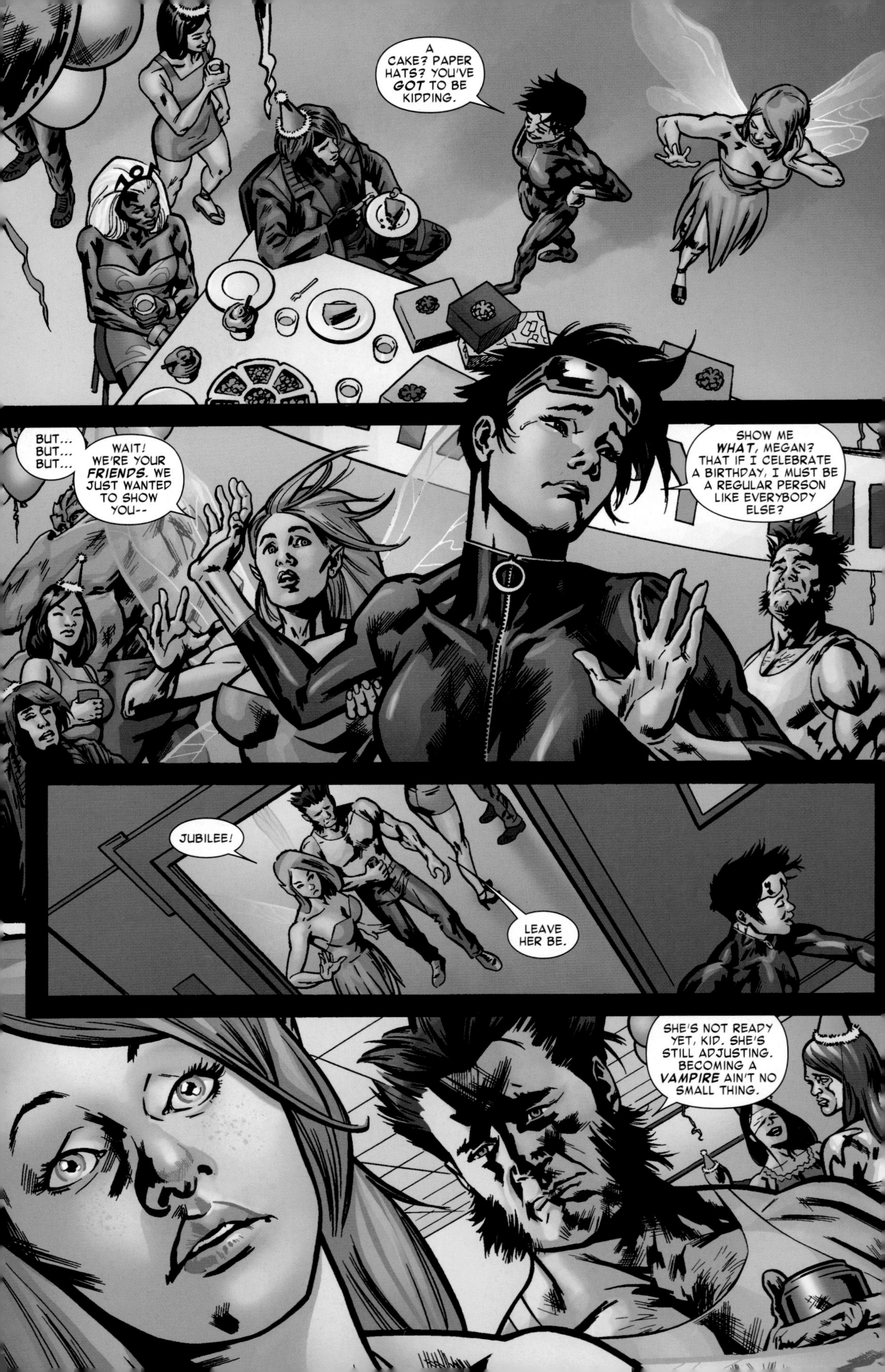
A CAKE? PAPER HATS? YOU'VE *GOT* TO BE KIDDING.
BUT... BUT... BUT...
WAIT! WE'RE YOUR *FRIENDS.* WE JUST WANTED TO SHOW YOU--
SHOW ME *WHAT,* MEGAN? THAT IF I CELEBRATE A BIRTHDAY, I MUST BE A REGULAR PERSON LIKE EVERYBODY ELSE?
JUBILEE!
LEAVE HER BE.
SHE'S NOT READY YET, KID. SHE'S STILL ADJUSTING. BECOMING A *VAMPIRE* AIN'T NO SMALL THING.

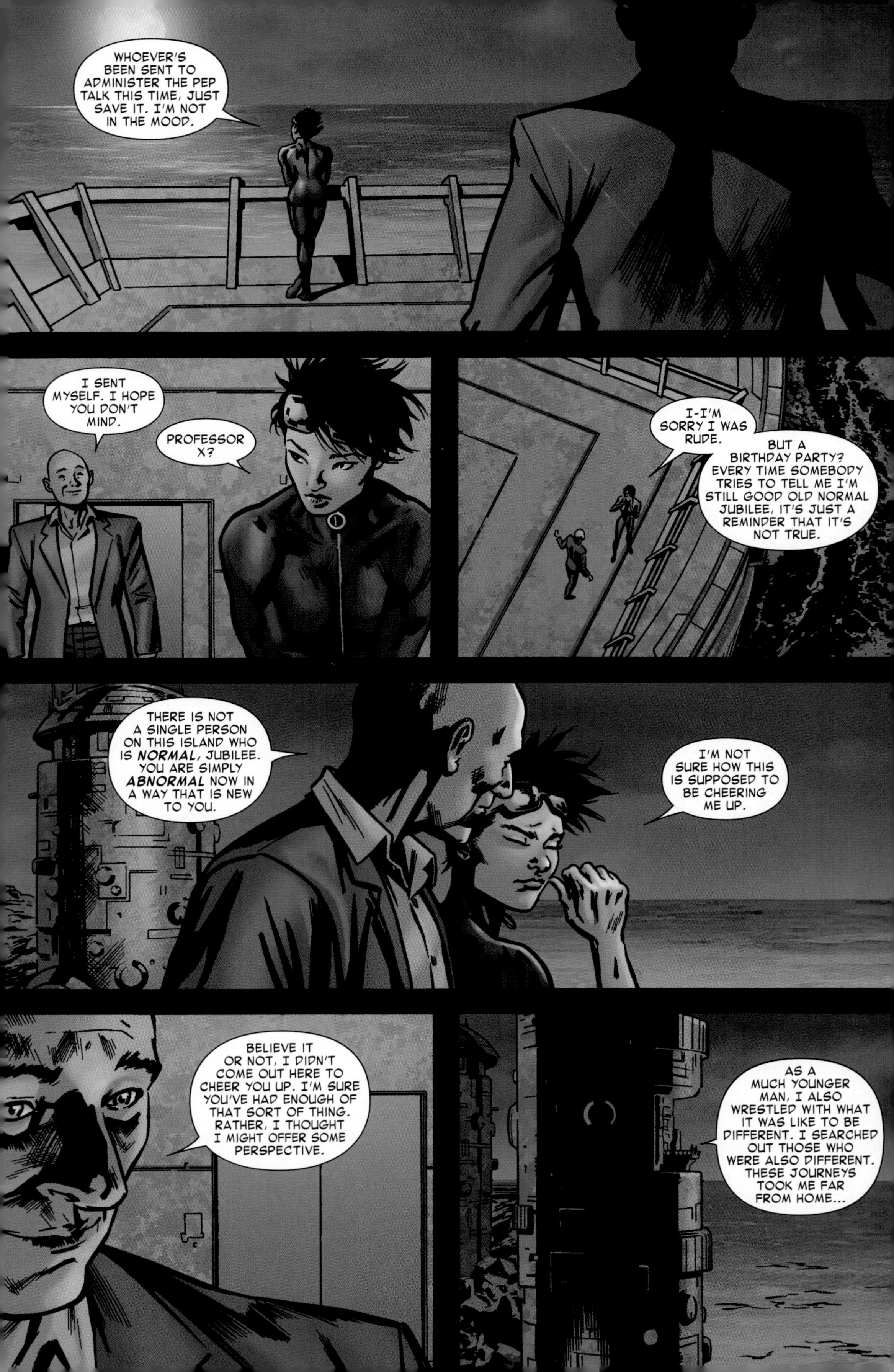
WHOEVER'S BEEN SENT TO ADMINISTER THE PEP TALK THIS TIME, JUST SAVE IT. I'M NOT IN THE MOOD.
I SENT MYSELF. I HOPE YOU DON'T MIND.
PROFESSOR X?
I-I'M SORRY I WAS RUDE.
BUT A BIRTHDAY PARTY? EVERY TIME SOMEBODY TRIES TO TELL ME I'M STILL GOOD OLD NORMAL JUBILEE, IT'S JUST A REMINDER THAT IT'S NOT TRUE.
THERE IS NOT A SINGLE PERSON ON THIS ISLAND WHO IS NORMAL, JUBILEE. YOU ARE SIMPLY ABNORMAL NOW IN A WAY THAT IS NEW TO YOU.
I'M NOT SURE HOW THIS IS SUPPOSED TO BE CHEERING ME UP.
BELIEVE IT OR NOT, I DIDN'T COME OUT HERE TO CHEER YOU UP. I'M SURE YOU'VE HAD ENOUGH OF THAT SORT OF THING. RATHER, I THOUGHT I MIGHT OFFER SOME PERSPECTIVE.
AS A MUCH YOUNGER MAN, I ALSO WRESTLED WITH WHAT IT WAS LIKE TO BE DIFFERENT. I SEARCHED OUT THOSE WHO WERE ALSO DIFFERENT. THESE JOURNEYS TOOK ME FAR FROM HOME...

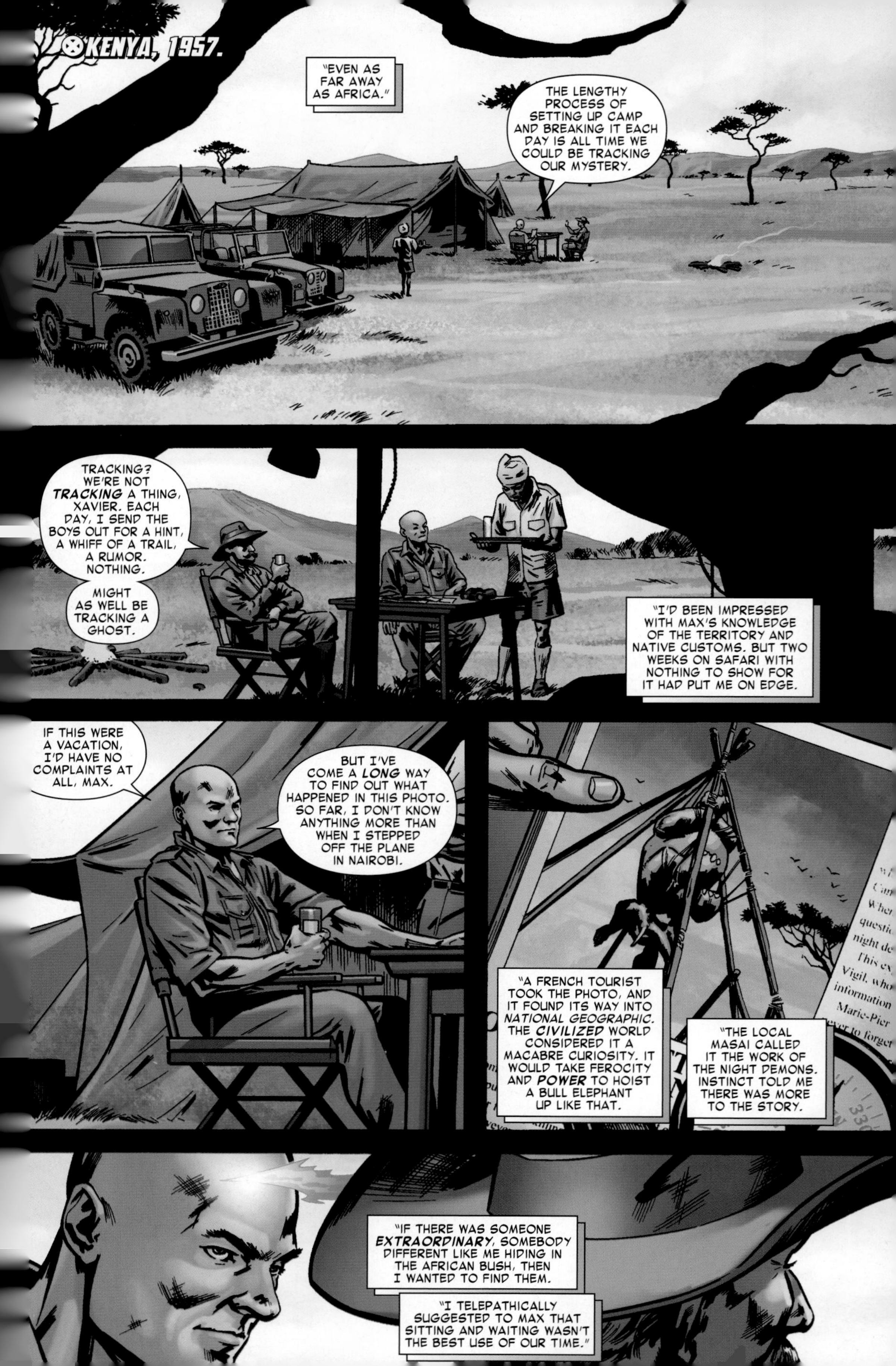
KENYA, 1957.
"EVEN AS FAR AWAY AS AFRICA."
THE LENGTHY PROCESS OF SETTING UP CAMP AND BREAKING IT EACH DAY IS ALL TIME WE COULD BE TRACKING OUR MYSTERY.
TRACKING? WE'RE NOT TRACKING A THING, XAVIER. EACH DAY, I SEND THE BOYS OUT FOR A HINT, A WHIFF OF A TRAIL, A RUMOR. NOTHING.
MIGHT AS WELL BE TRACKING A GHOST.
"I'D BEEN IMPRESSED WITH MAX'S KNOWLEDGE OF THE TERRITORY AND NATIVE CUSTOMS. BUT TWO WEEKS ON SAFARI WITH NOTHING TO SHOW FOR IT HAD PUT ME ON EDGE.
IF THIS WERE A VACATION, I'D HAVE NO COMPLAINTS AT ALL, MAX.
BUT I'VE COME A LONG WAY TO FIND OUT WHAT HAPPENED IN THIS PHOTO. SO FAR, I DON'T KNOW ANYTHING MORE THAN WHEN I STEPPED OFF THE PLANE IN NAIROBI.
"A FRENCH TOURIST TOOK THE PHOTO, AND IT FOUND ITS WAY INTO NATIONAL GEOGRAPHIC. THE CIVILIZED WORLD CONSIDERED IT A MACABRE CURIOSITY. IT WOULD TAKE FEROCITY AND POWER TO HOIST A BULL ELEPHANT UP LIKE THAT.
"THE LOCAL MASAI CALLED IT THE WORK OF THE NIGHT DEMONS. INSTINCT TOLD ME THERE WAS MORE TO THE STORY.
"IF THERE WAS SOMEONE EXTRAORDINARY, SOMEBODY DIFFERENT LIKE ME HIDING IN THE AFRICAN BUSH, THEN I WANTED TO FIND THEM.
"I TELEPATHICALLY SUGGESTED TO MAX THAT SITTING AND WAITING WASN'T THE BEST USE OF OUR TIME."

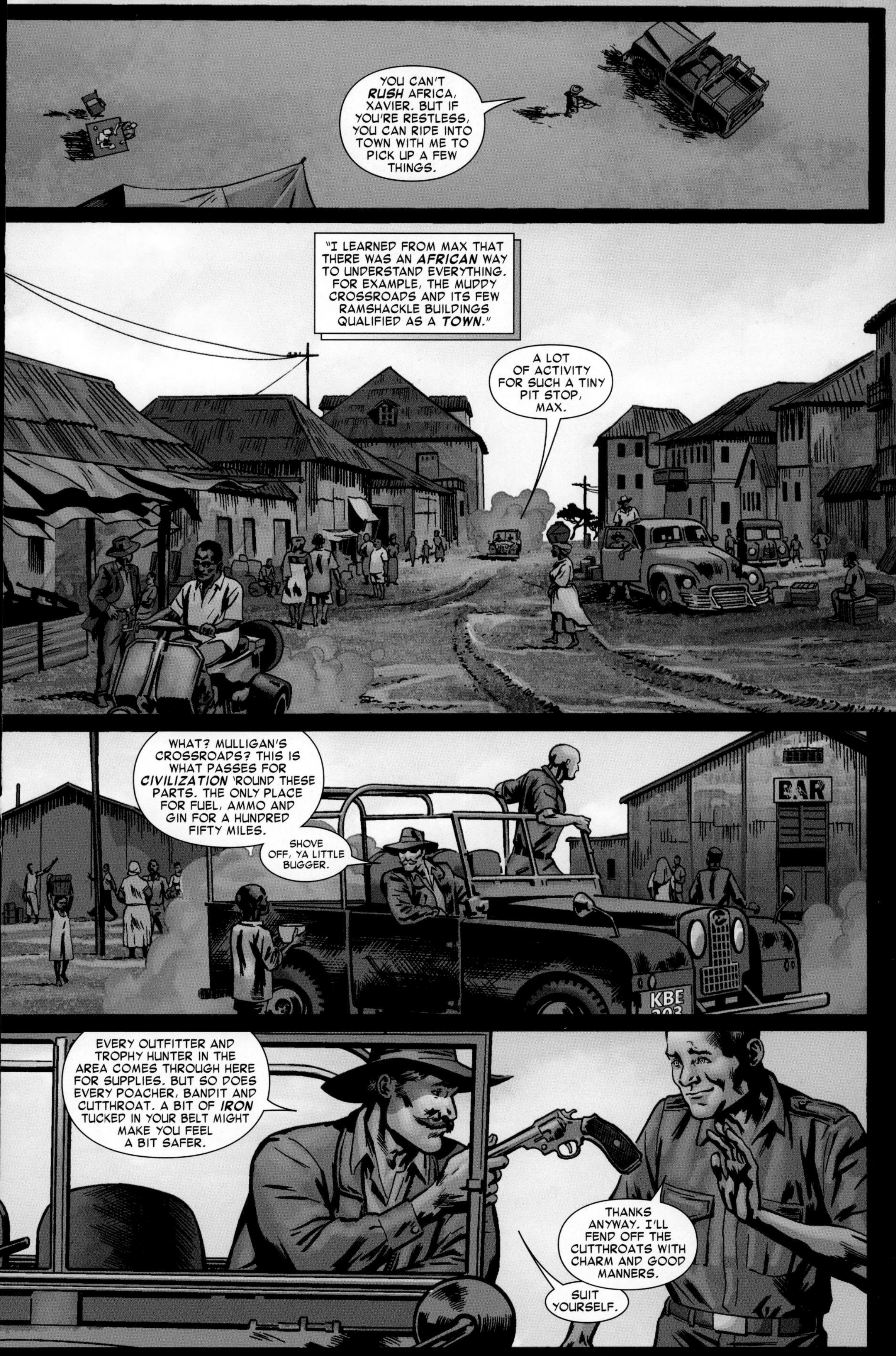
YOU CAN'T RUSH AFRICA, XAVIER. BUT IF YOU'RE RESTLESS, YOU CAN RIDE INTO TOWN WITH ME TO PICK UP A FEW THINGS.
"I LEARNED FROM MAX THAT THERE WAS AN AFRICAN WAY TO UNDERSTAND EVERYTHING. FOR EXAMPLE, THE MUDDY CROSSROADS AND ITS FEW RAMSHACKLE BUILDINGS QUALIFIED AS A TOWN."
A LOT OF ACTIVITY FOR SUCH A TINY PIT STOP, MAX.
WHAT? MULLIGAN'S CROSSROADS? THIS IS WHAT PASSES FOR CIVILIZATION 'ROUND THESE PARTS. THE ONLY PLACE FOR FUEL, AMMO AND GIN FOR A HUNDRED FIFTY MILES.
SHOVE OFF, YA LITTLE BUGGER.
BAR
KBE 303
EVERY OUTFITTER AND TROPHY HUNTER IN THE AREA COMES THROUGH HERE FOR SUPPLIES. BUT SO DOES EVERY POACHER, BANDIT AND CUTTHROAT. A BIT OF IRON TUCKED IN YOUR BELT MIGHT MAKE YOU FEEL A BIT SAFER.
THANKS ANYWAY. I'LL FEND OFF THE CUTTHROATS WITH CHARM AND GOOD MANNERS.
SUIT YOURSELF.

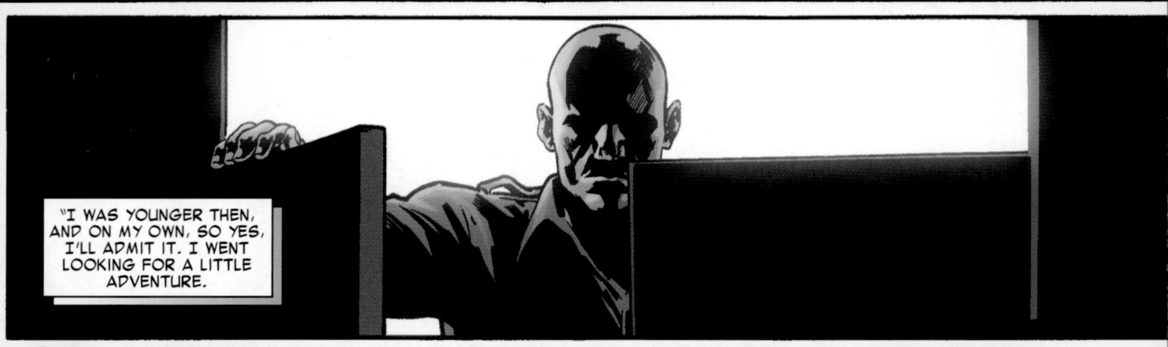
"I WAS YOUNGER THEN, AND ON MY OWN, SO YES, I'LL ADMIT IT. I WENT LOOKING FOR A LITTLE ADVENTURE.

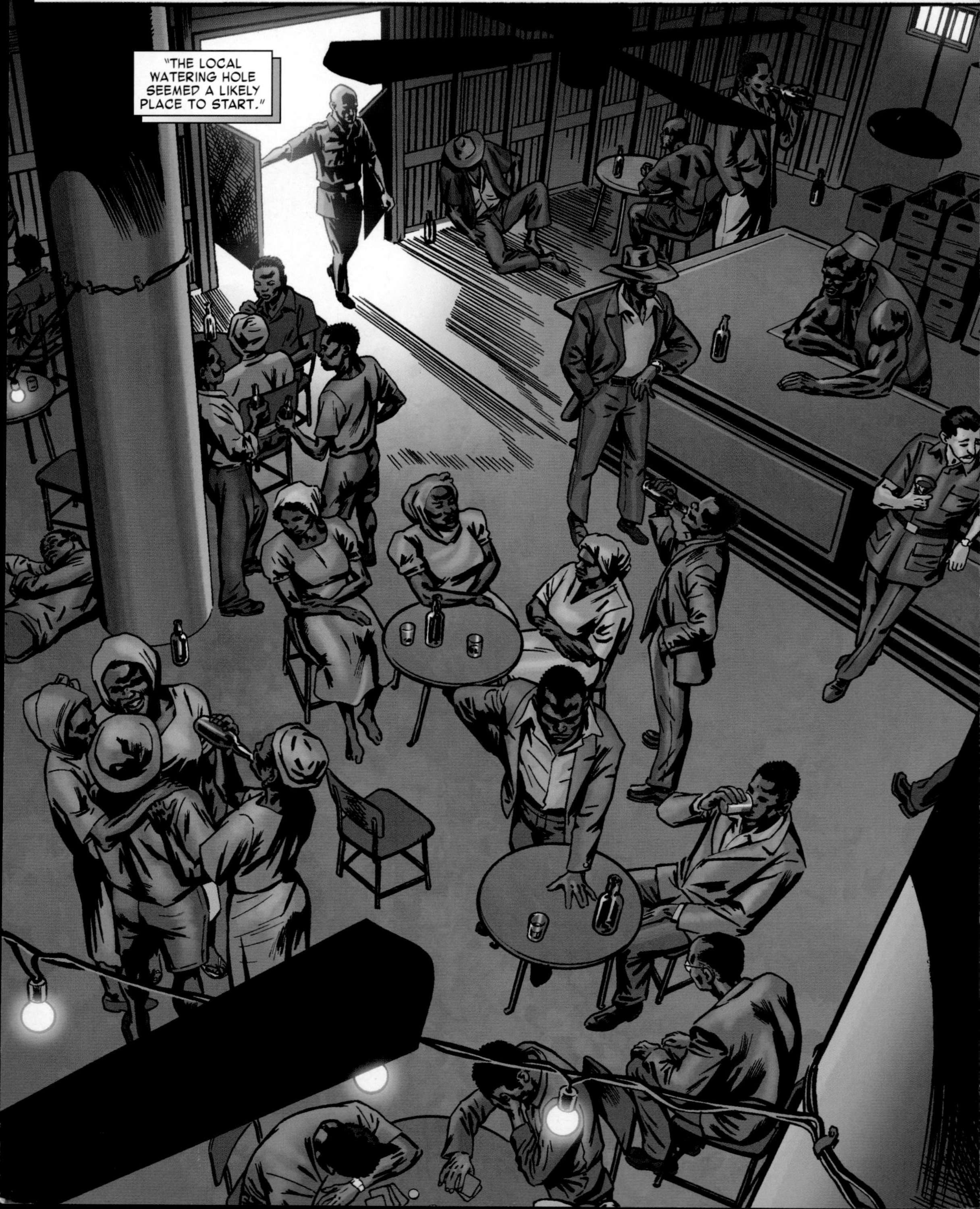
"THE LOCAL WATERING HOLE SEEMED A LIKELY PLACE TO START."

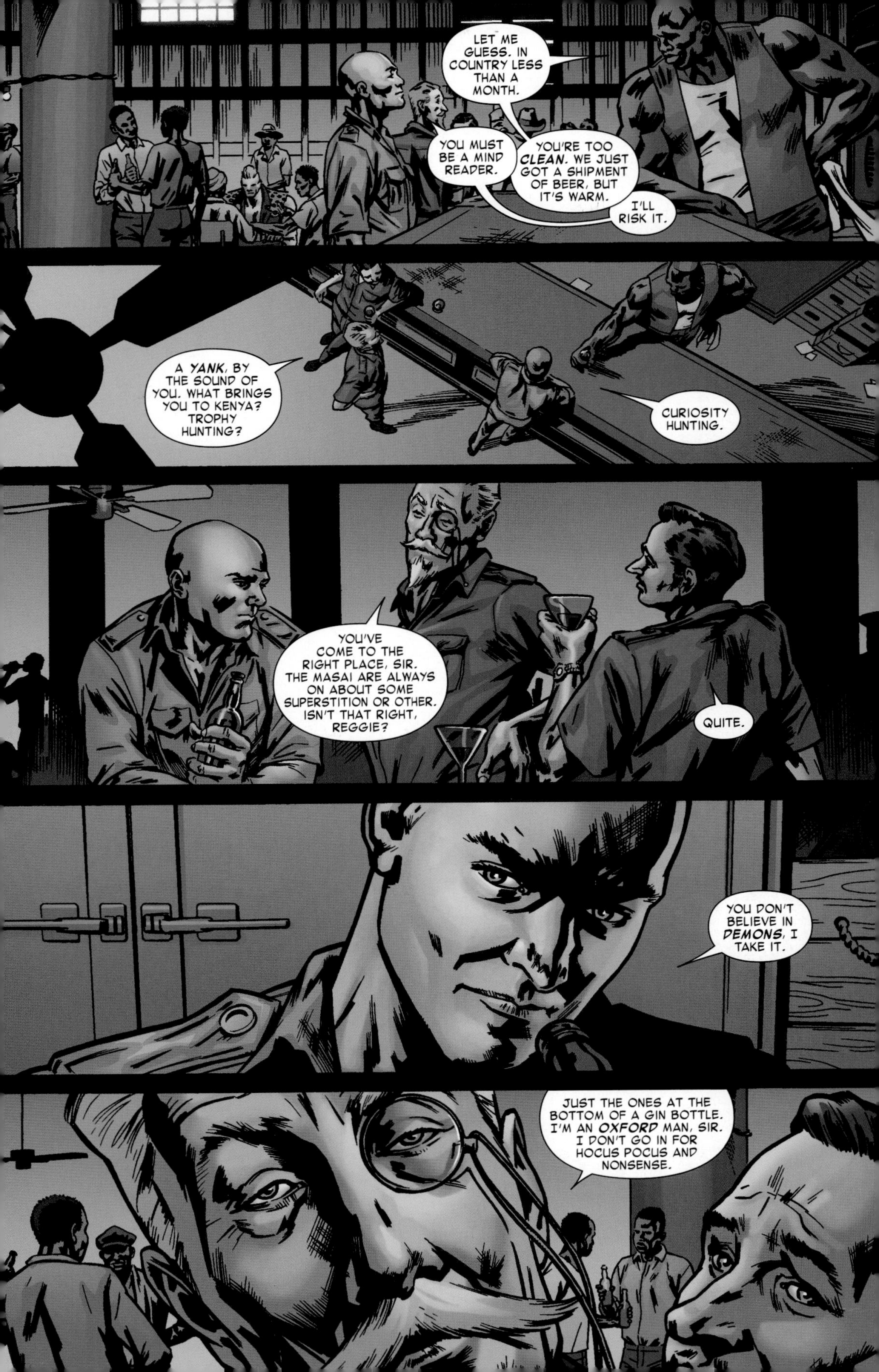
LET ME GUESS. IN COUNTRY LESS THAN A MONTH.
YOU MUST BE A MIND READER.
YOU'RE TOO CLEAN. WE JUST GOT A SHIPMENT OF BEER, BUT IT'S WARM.
I'LL RISK IT.
A YANK, BY THE SOUND OF YOU. WHAT BRINGS YOU TO KENYA? TROPHY HUNTING?
CURIOSITY HUNTING.
YOU'VE COME TO THE RIGHT PLACE, SIR. THE MASAI ARE ALWAYS ON ABOUT SOME SUPERSTITION OR OTHER. ISN'T THAT RIGHT, REGGIE?
QUITE.
YOU DON'T BELIEVE IN DEMONS, I TAKE IT.
JUST THE ONES AT THE BOTTOM OF A GIN BOTTLE. I'M AN OXFORD MAN, SIR. I DON'T GO IN FOR HOCUS POCUS AND NONSENSE.

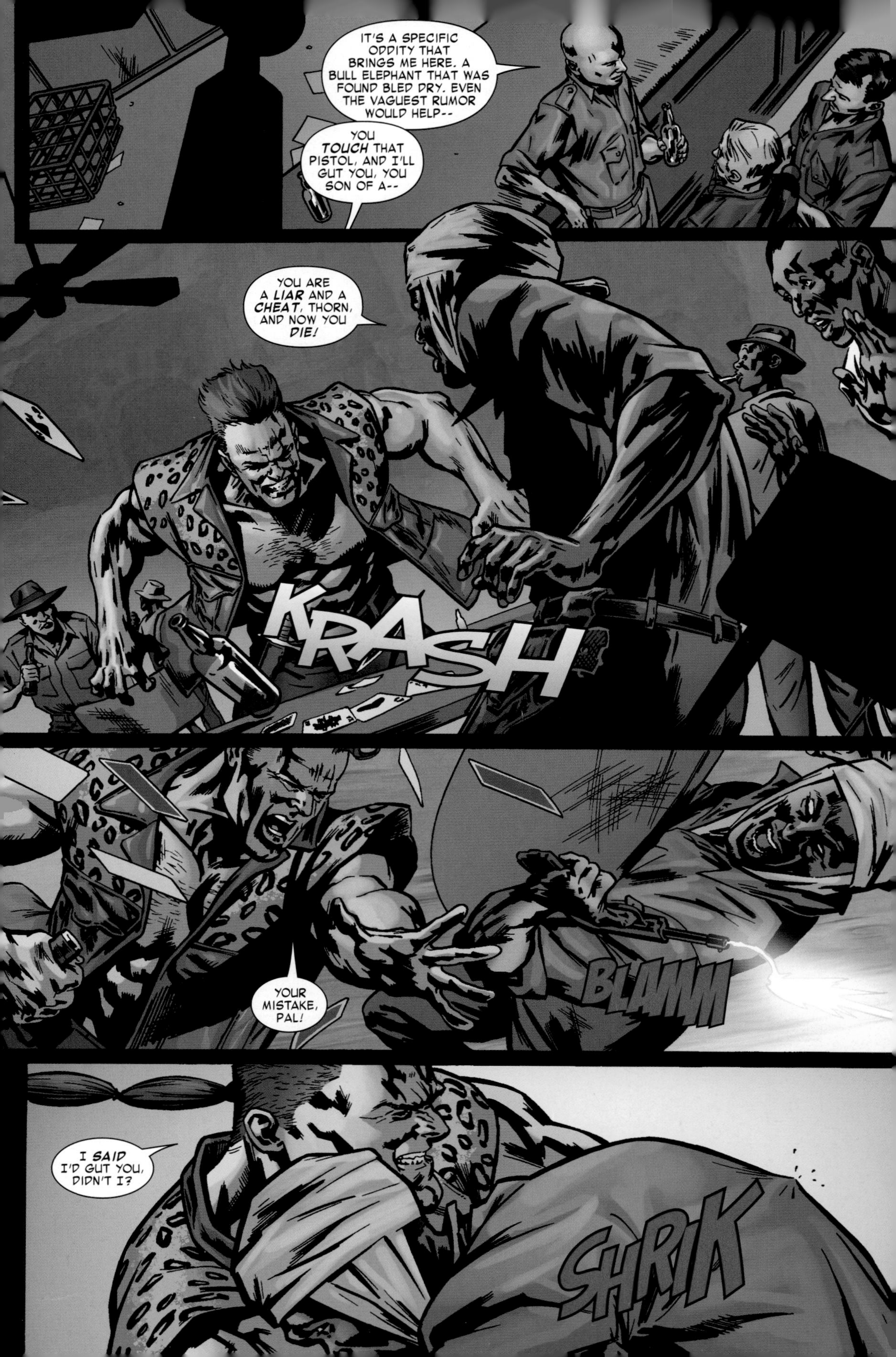
IT'S A SPECIFIC ODDITY THAT BRINGS ME HERE. A BULL ELEPHANT THAT WAS FOUND BLED DRY. EVEN THE VAGUEST RUMOR WOULD HELP--
YOU TOUCH THAT PISTOL, AND I'LL GUT YOU, YOU SON OF A--
YOU ARE A LIAR AND A CHEAT, THORN, AND NOW YOU DIE!
KRASH
YOUR MISTAKE, PAL!
BLAMM
I SAID I'D GUT YOU, DIDN'T I?
SHRIK

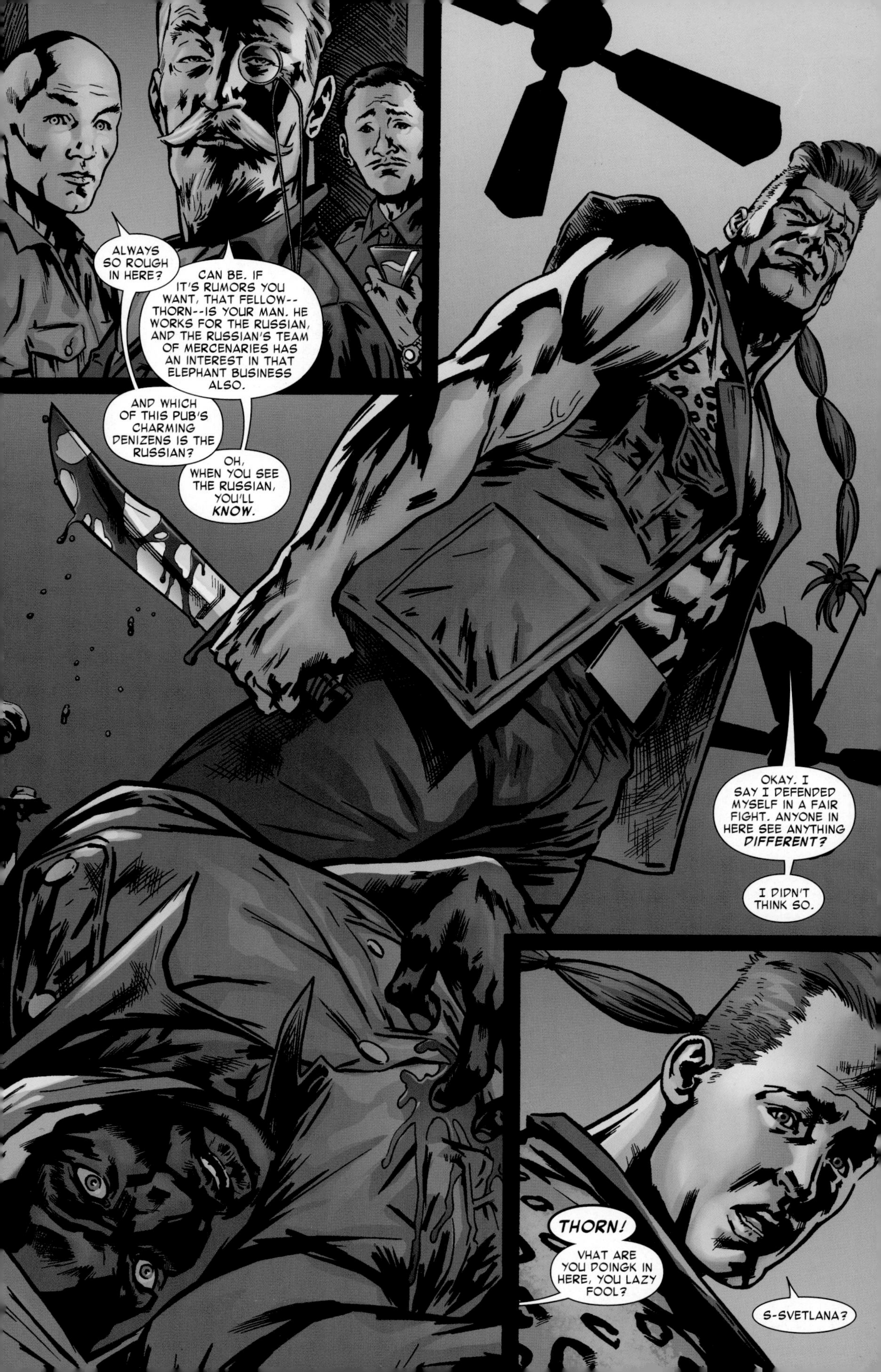
ALWAYS SO ROUGH IN HERE?
CAN BE. IF IT'S RUMORS YOU WANT, THAT FELLOW--THORN--IS YOUR MAN. HE WORKS FOR THE RUSSIAN, AND THE RUSSIAN'S TEAM OF MERCENARIES HAS AN INTEREST IN THAT ELEPHANT BUSINESS ALSO.
AND WHICH OF THIS PUB'S CHARMING DENIZENS IS THE RUSSIAN?
OH, WHEN YOU SEE THE RUSSIAN, YOU'LL KNOW.
OKAY. I SAY I DEFENDED MYSELF IN A FAIR FIGHT. ANYONE IN HERE SEE ANYTHING DIFFERENT?
I DIDN'T THINK SO.
THORN!
VHAT ARE YOU DOINGK IN HERE, YOU LAZY FOOL?
S-SVETLANA?

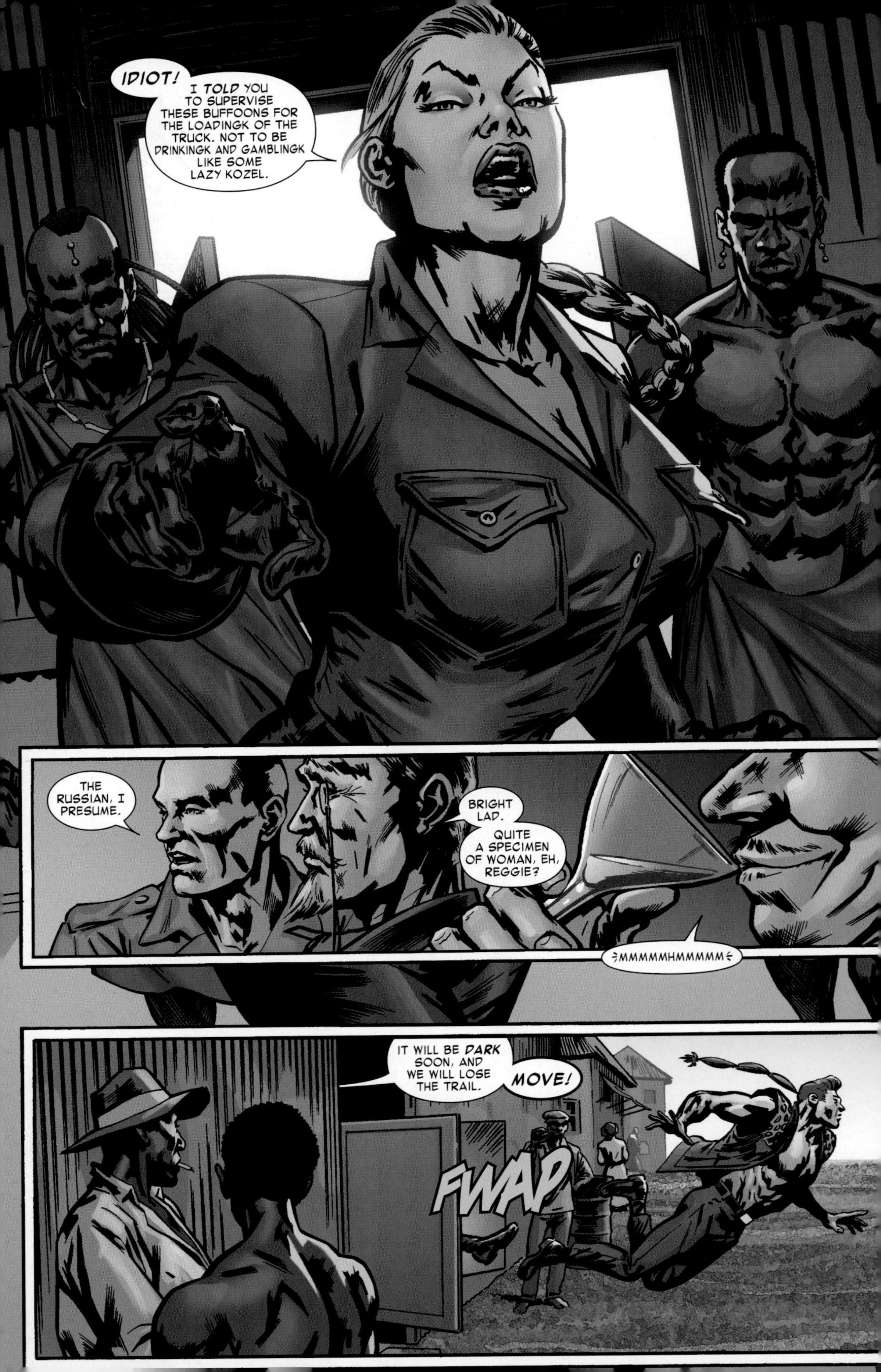
IDIOT!
I TOLD YOU TO SUPERVISE THESE BUFFOONS FOR THE LOADINGK OF THE TRUCK. NOT TO BE DRINKINGK AND GAMBLINGK LIKE SOME LAZY KOZEL.
THE RUSSIAN, I PRESUME.
BRIGHT LAD.
QUITE A SPECIMEN OF WOMAN, EH, REGGIE?
MMMMMHMMMMM
IT WILL BE DARK SOON, AND WE WILL LOSE THE TRAIL.
MOVE!
FWAP

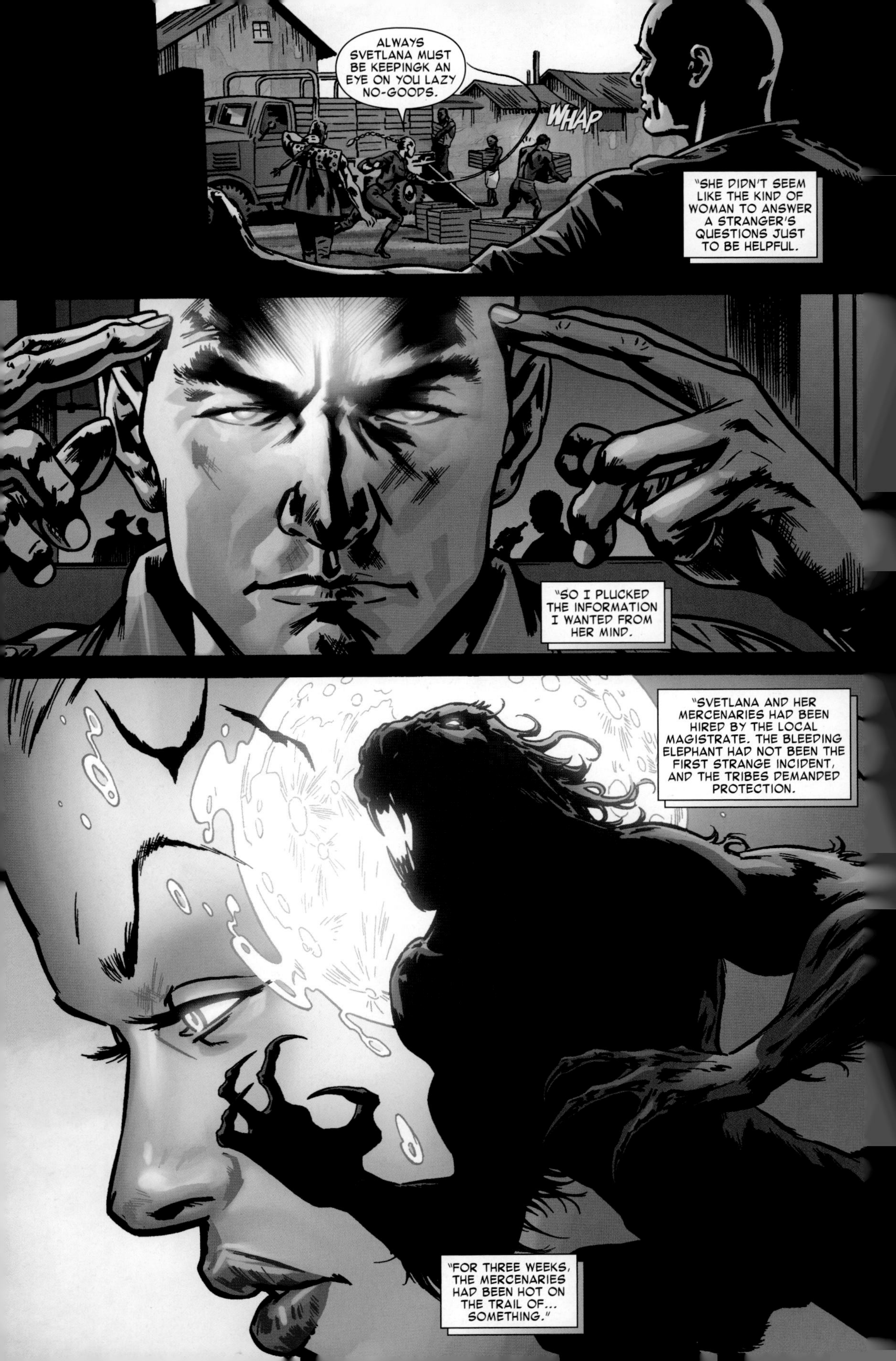
ALWAYS SVETLANA MUST BE KEEPINGK AN EYE ON YOU LAZY NO-GOODS.
WHAP
"SHE DIDN'T SEEM LIKE THE KIND OF WOMAN TO ANSWER A STRANGER'S QUESTIONS JUST TO BE HELPFUL.
"SO I PLUCKED THE INFORMATION I WANTED FROM HER MIND.
"SVETLANA AND HER MERCENARIES HAD BEEN HIRED BY THE LOCAL MAGISTRATE. THE BLEEDING ELEPHANT HAD NOT BEEN THE FIRST STRANGE INCIDENT, AND THE TRIBES DEMANDED PROTECTION.
"FOR THREE WEEKS, THE MERCENARIES HAD BEEN HOT ON THE TRAIL OF... SOMETHING."

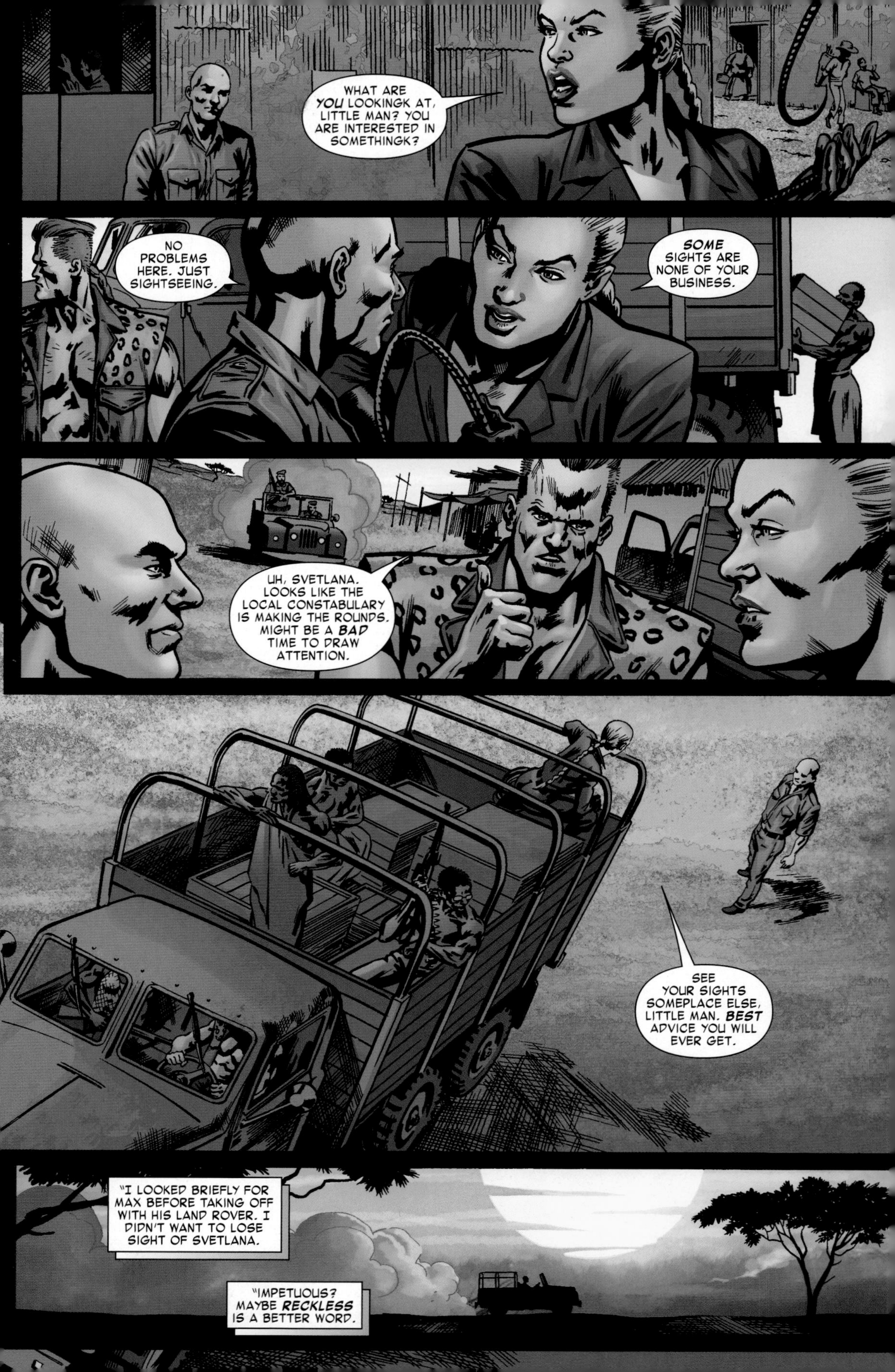

WHAT ARE YOU LOOKINGK AT, LITTLE MAN? YOU ARE INTERESTED IN SOMETHINGK?
NO PROBLEMS HERE. JUST SIGHTSEEING.
SOME SIGHTS ARE NONE OF YOUR BUSINESS.
UH, SVETLANA. LOOKS LIKE THE LOCAL CONSTABULARY IS MAKING THE ROUNDS. MIGHT BE A BAD TIME TO DRAW ATTENTION.
SEE YOUR SIGHTS SOMEPLACE ELSE, LITTLE MAN. BEST ADVICE YOU WILL EVER GET.
"I LOOKED BRIEFLY FOR MAX BEFORE TAKING OFF WITH HIS LAND ROVER. I DIDN'T WANT TO LOSE SIGHT OF SVETLANA.
"IMPETUOUS? MAYBE RECKLESS IS A BETTER WORD.

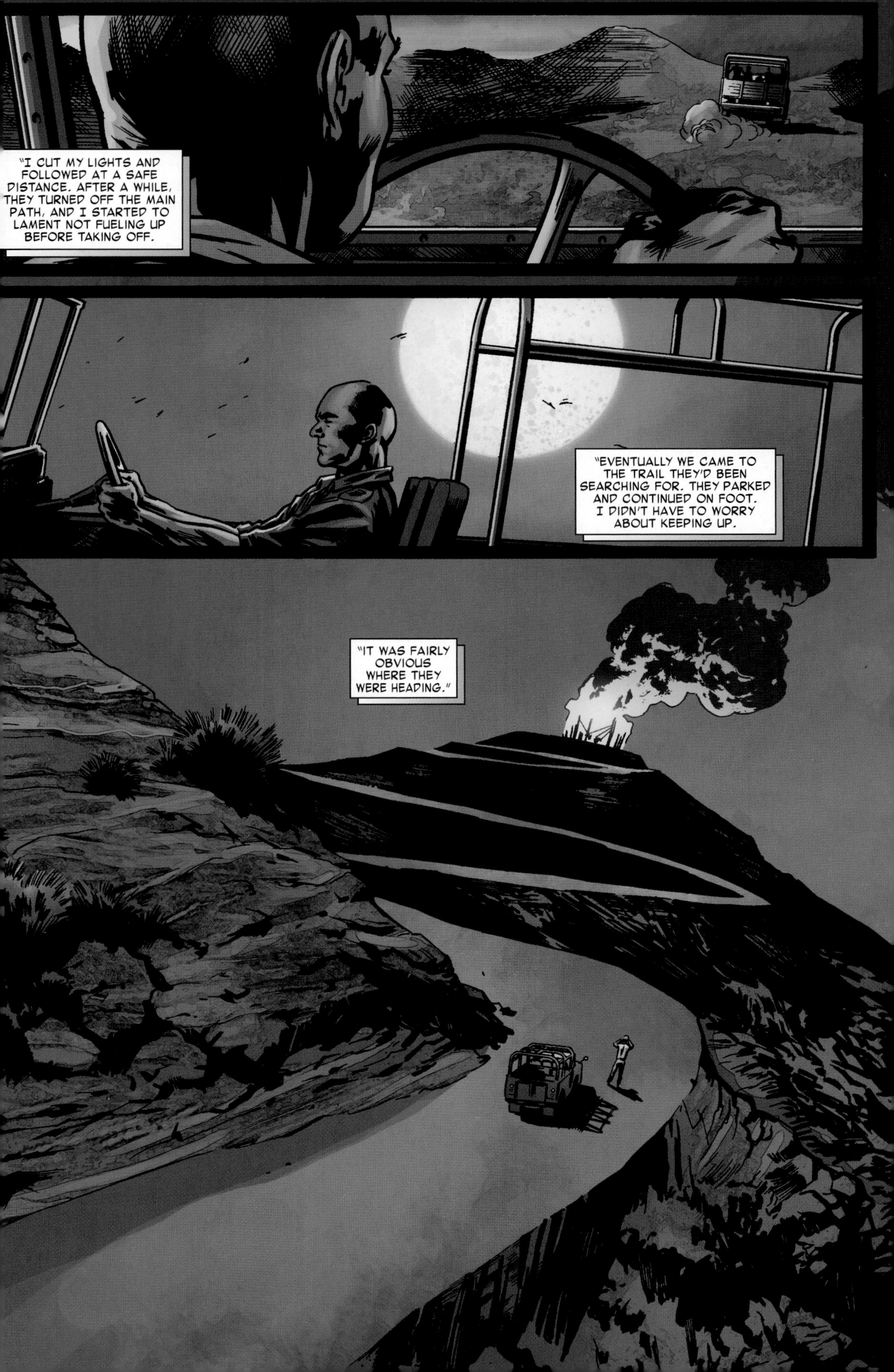
"I CUT MY LIGHTS AND FOLLOWED AT A SAFE DISTANCE. AFTER A WHILE, THEY TURNED OFF THE MAIN PATH, AND I STARTED TO LAMENT NOT FUELING UP BEFORE TAKING OFF.
"EVENTUALLY WE CAME TO THE TRAIL THEY'D BEEN SEARCHING FOR. THEY PARKED AND CONTINUED ON FOOT. I DIDN'T HAVE TO WORRY ABOUT KEEPING UP.
"IT WAS FAIRLY OBVIOUS WHERE THEY WERE HEADING."

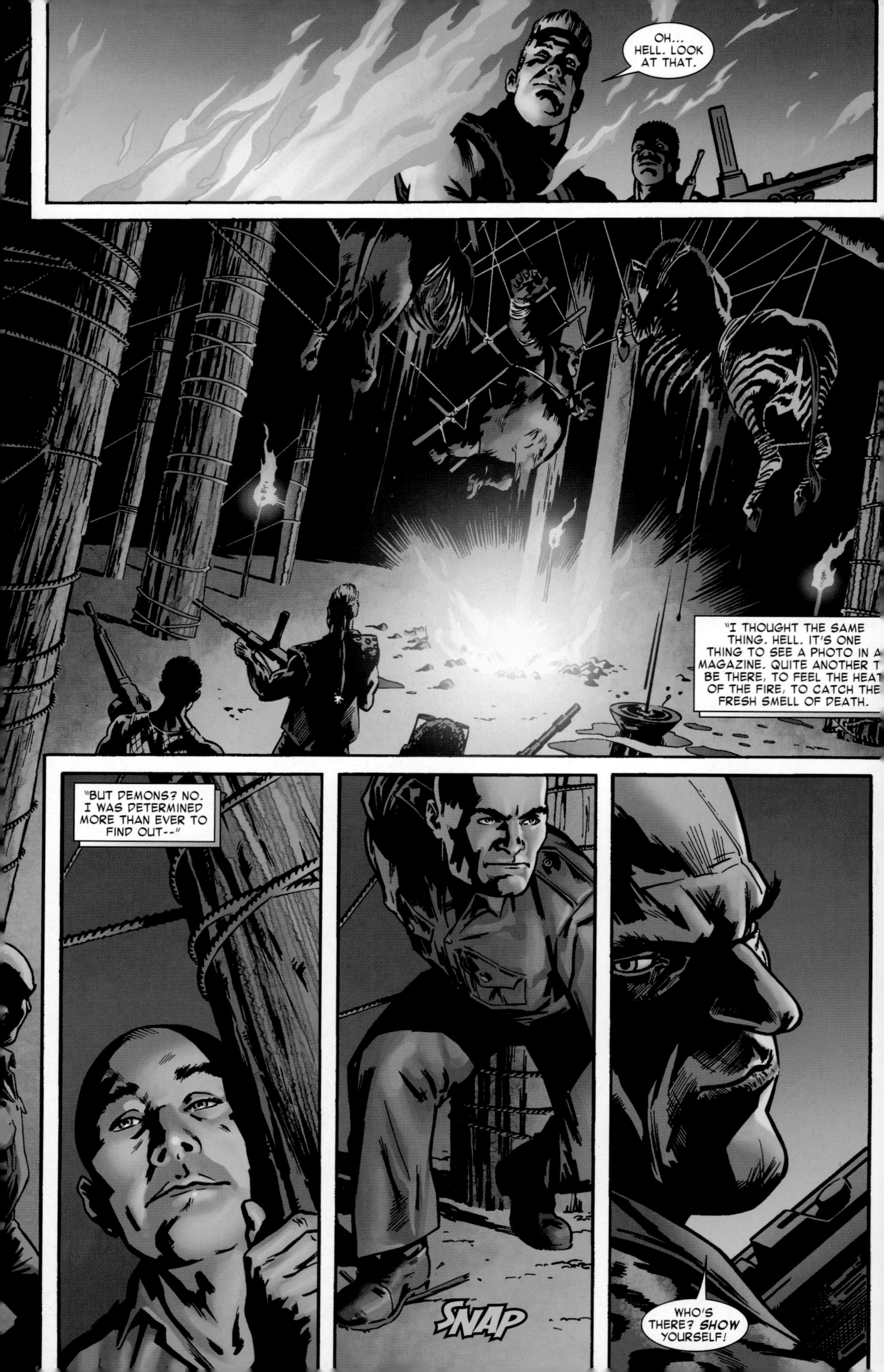
OH... HELL. LOOK AT THAT.
"I THOUGHT THE SAME THING. HELL. IT'S ONE THING TO SEE A PHOTO IN A MAGAZINE. QUITE ANOTHER T BE THERE, TO FEEL THE HEAT OF THE FIRE, TO CATCH THE FRESH SMELL OF DEATH.
"BUT DEMONS? NO. I WAS DETERMINED MORE THAN EVER TO FIND OUT--"
SNAP
WHO'S THERE? SHOW YOURSELF!

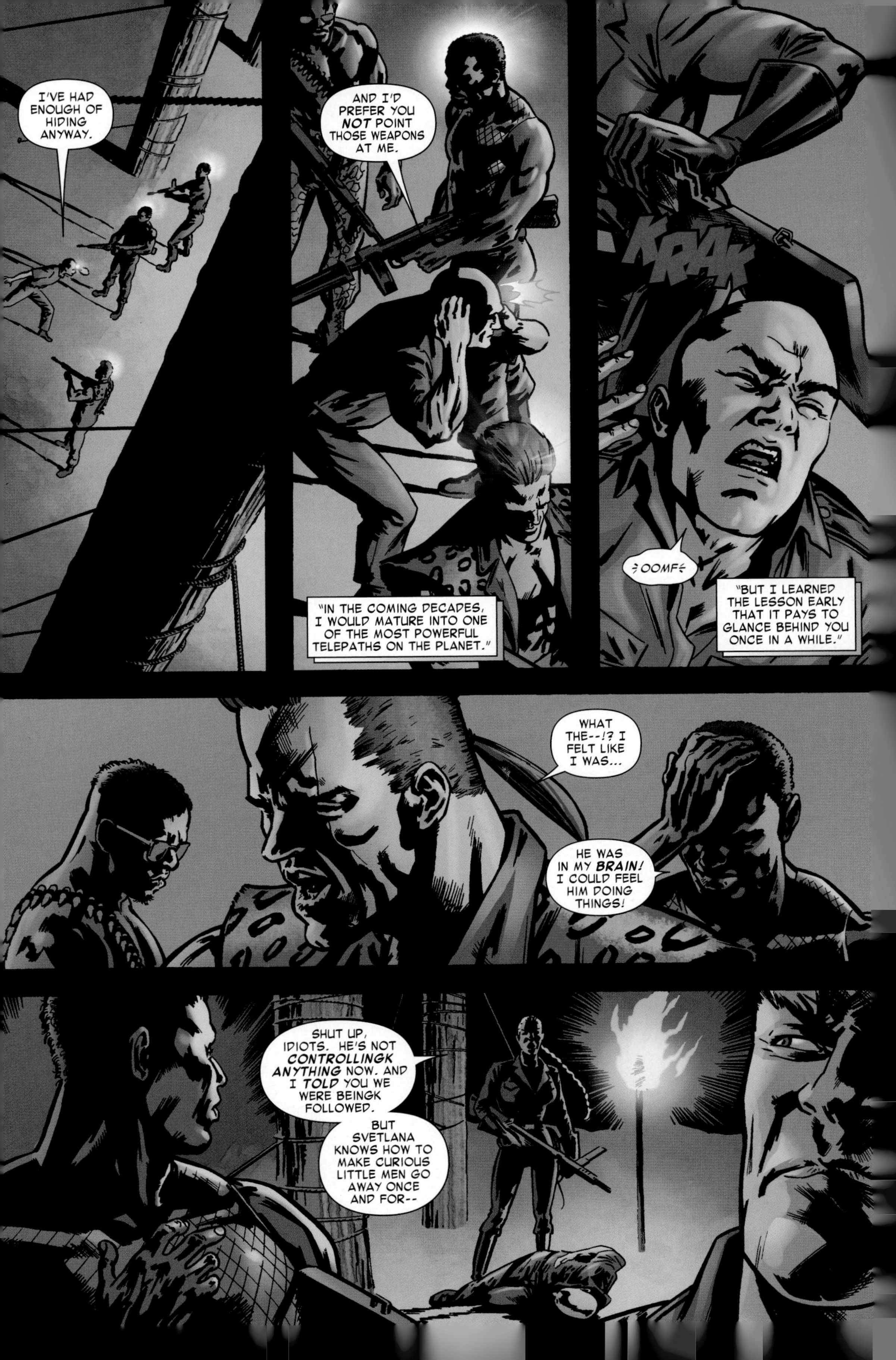
I'VE HAD ENOUGH OF HIDING ANYWAY.
AND I'D PREFER YOU NOT POINT THOSE WEAPONS AT ME.
"IN THE COMING DECADES, I WOULD MATURE INTO ONE OF THE MOST POWERFUL TELEPATHS ON THE PLANET."
KRAK
OOMF
"BUT I LEARNED THE LESSON EARLY THAT IT PAYS TO GLANCE BEHIND YOU ONCE IN A WHILE."
WHAT THE--!? I FELT LIKE I WAS...
HE WAS IN MY BRAIN! I COULD FEEL HIM DOING THINGS!
SHUT UP, IDIOTS. HE'S NOT CONTROLLINGK ANYTHING NOW. AND I TOLD YOU WE WERE BEINGK FOLLOWED.
BUT SVETLANA KNOWS HOW TO MAKE CURIOUS LITTLE MEN GO AWAY ONCE AND FOR--

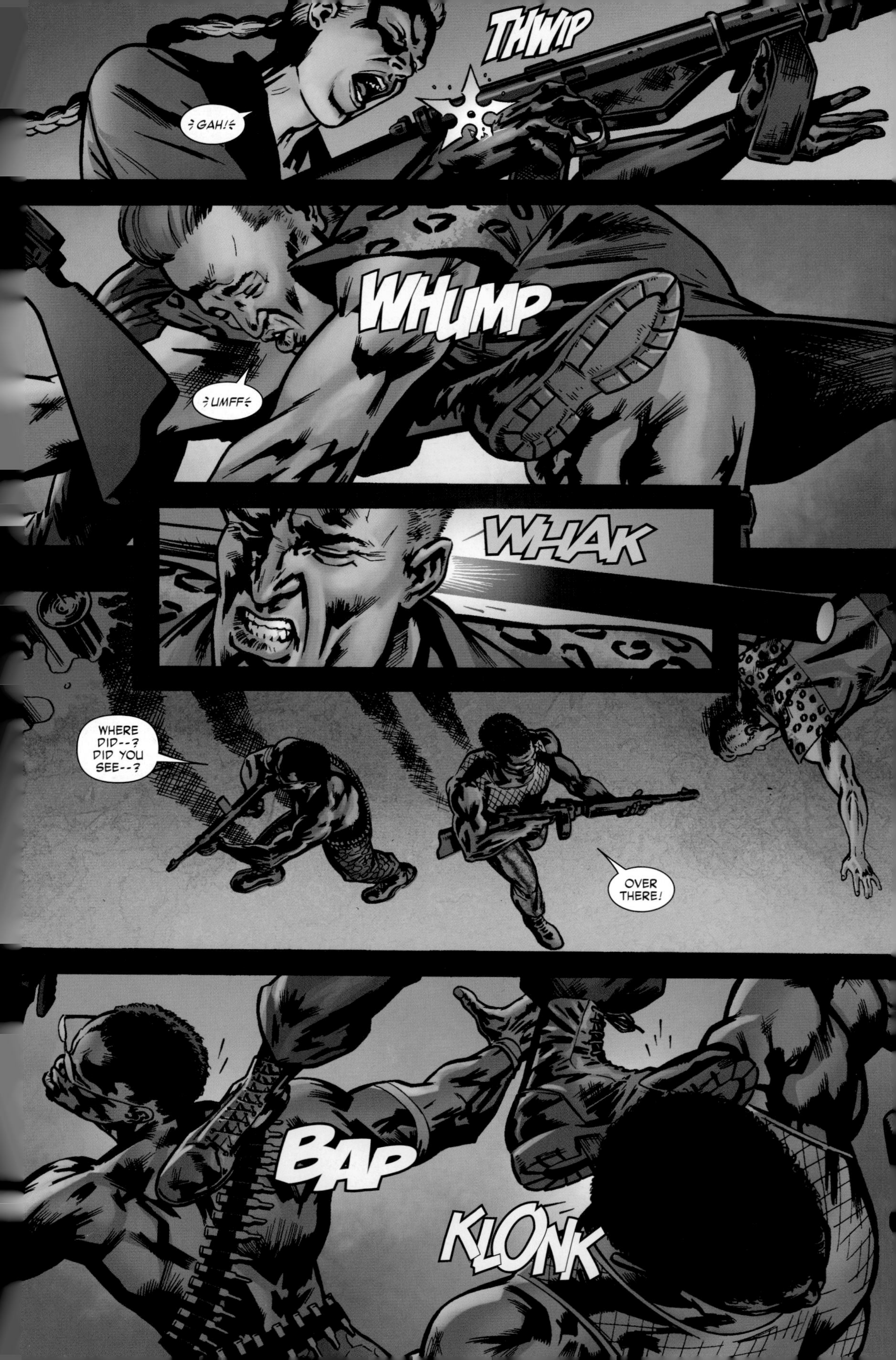
THWIP
GAH!
WHUMP
UMFF
WHAK
WHERE DID--? DID YOU SEE--?
OVER THERE!
BAP
KLONK

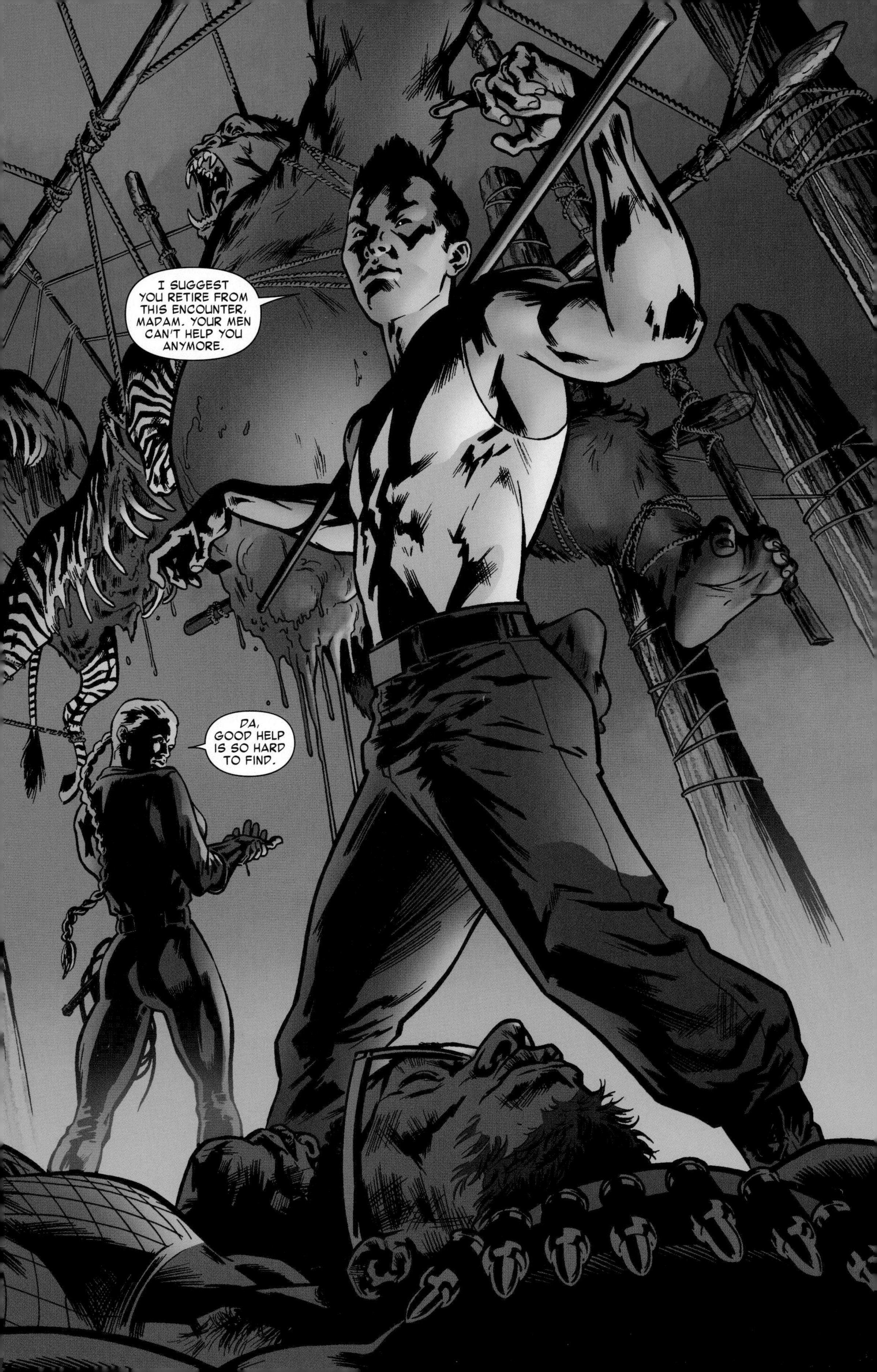
I SUGGEST YOU RETIRE FROM THIS ENCOUNTER, MADAM. YOUR MEN CAN'T HELP YOU ANYMORE.
DA, GOOD HELP IS SO HARD TO FIND.

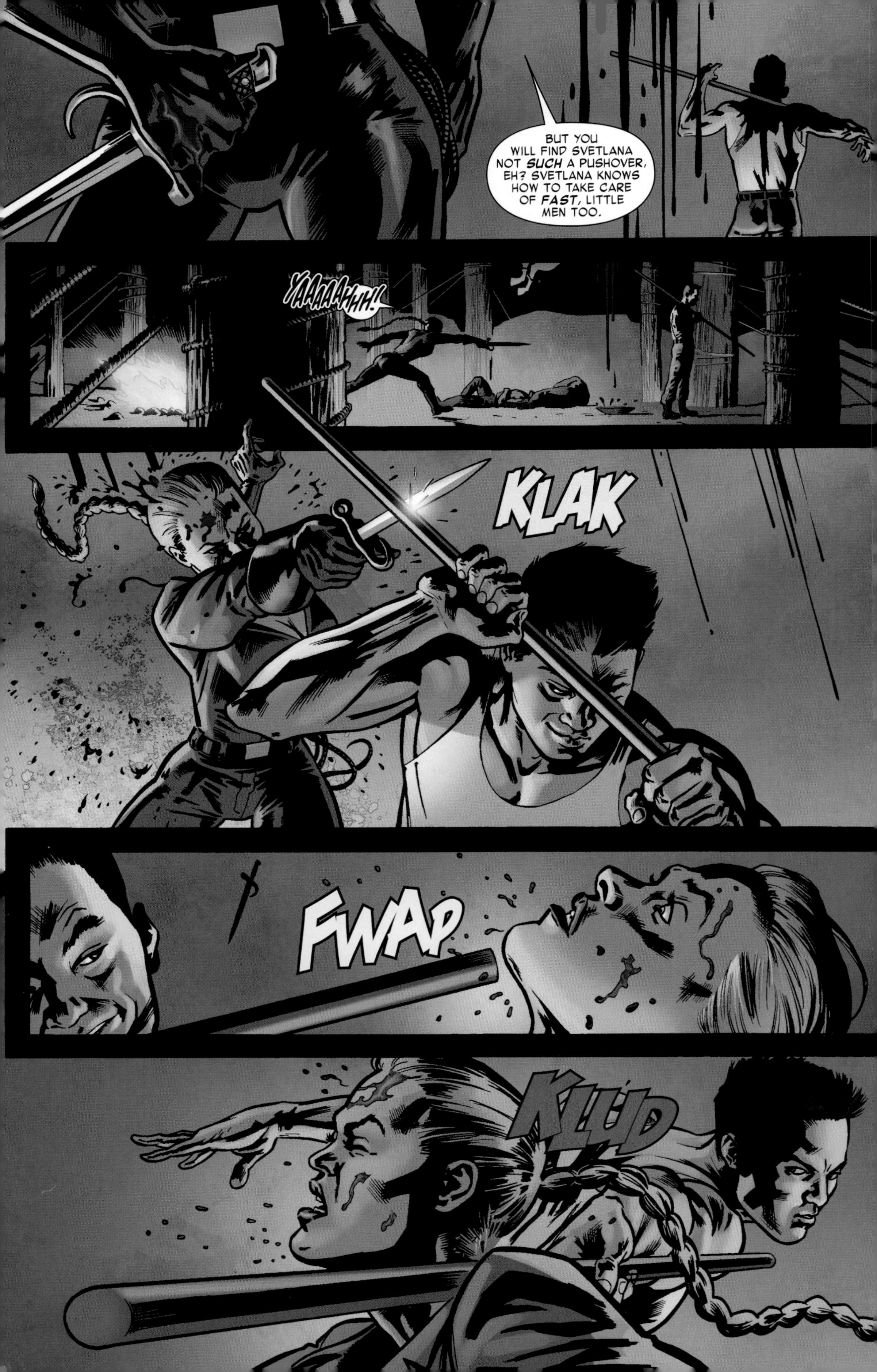
BUT YOU WILL FIND SVETLANA NOT SUCH A PUSHOVER, EH? SVETLANA KNOWS HOW TO TAKE CARE OF FAST, LITTLE MEN TOO.
YAAAAAHHH!
KLAK
FWAP
KLUD

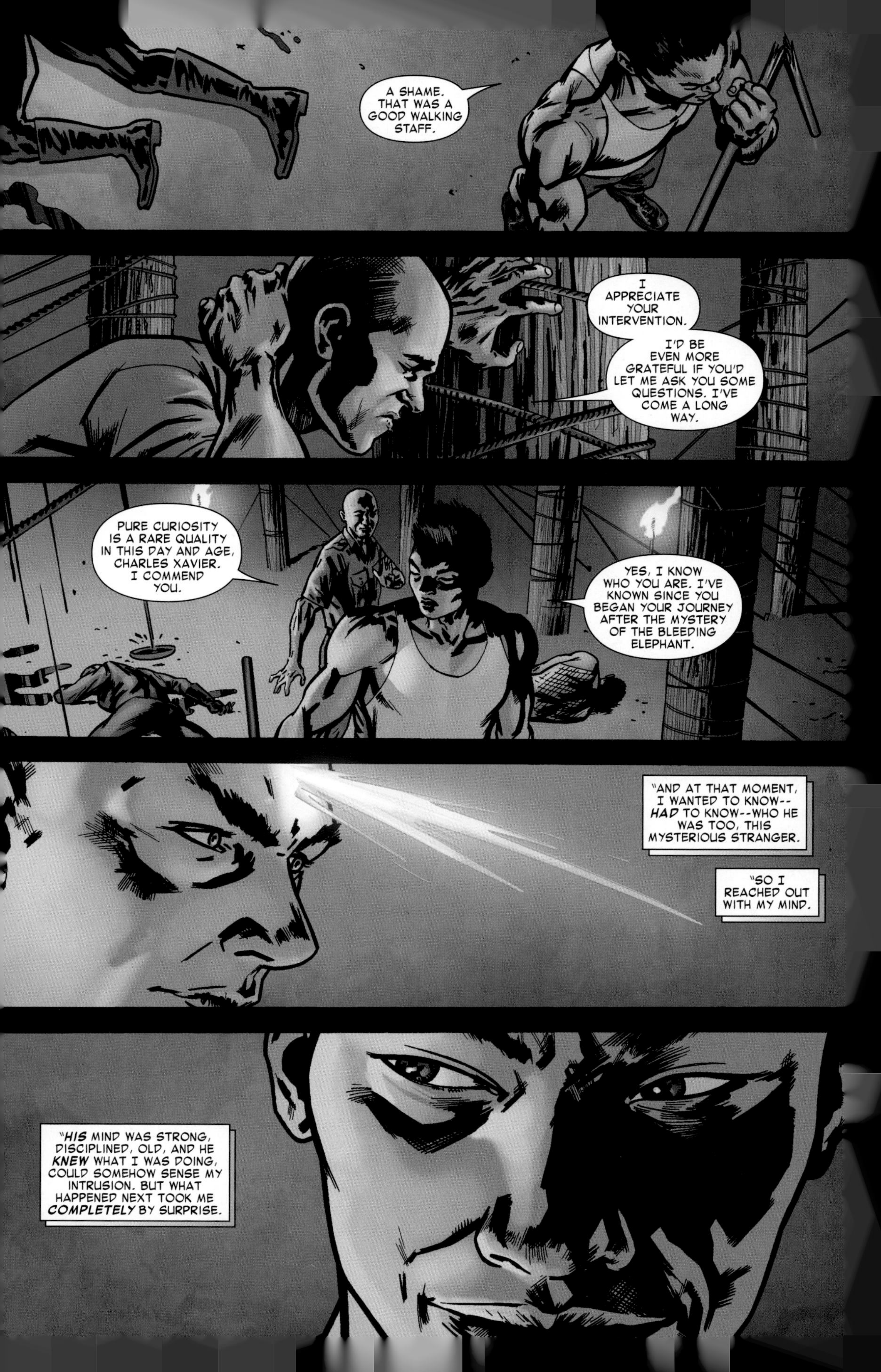
A SHAME. THAT WAS A GOOD WALKING STAFF.
I APPRECIATE YOUR INTERVENTION.
I'D BE EVEN MORE GRATEFUL IF YOU'D LET ME ASK YOU SOME QUESTIONS. I'VE COME A LONG WAY.
PURE CURIOSITY IS A RARE QUALITY IN THIS DAY AND AGE, CHARLES XAVIER. I COMMEND YOU.
YES, I KNOW WHO YOU ARE. I'VE KNOWN SINCE YOU BEGAN YOUR JOURNEY AFTER THE MYSTERY OF THE BLEEDING ELEPHANT.
"AND AT THAT MOMENT, I WANTED TO KNOW--*HAD* TO KNOW--WHO HE WAS TOO, THIS MYSTERIOUS STRANGER.
"SO I REACHED OUT WITH MY MIND.
"*HIS* MIND WAS STRONG, DISCIPLINED, OLD, AND HE *KNEW* WHAT I WAS DOING, COULD SOMEHOW SENSE MY INTRUSION. BUT WHAT HAPPENED NEXT TOOK ME *COMPLETELY* BY SURPRISE.

"HE LET ME IN.

"RAIZO KODA WAS CENTURIES OLD. HIS LIFE FLOODED INTO MY CONSCIOUSNESS AS A TORRENT OF INNER CONFLICT, A LIFE SPENT SEARCHING, WANTING TO KNOW. I COULD UNDERSTAND THAT. AND YET IT WAS ALL *TOO MUCH* TO UNDERSTAND AT ONCE."

YOU... YOU'RE A...

A VAMPIRE. YES.

THERE IS A GROUP OF MY PEOPLE WHO LIVE IN SECLUSION. THESE MERCENARIES, CLUMSY AS THEY ARE, MAY HAVE EXPOSED THEM.

I'VE BEEN LAYING THIS FALSE TRAIL, BUY TIME FOR THIS GROUP TO RELOCATE.

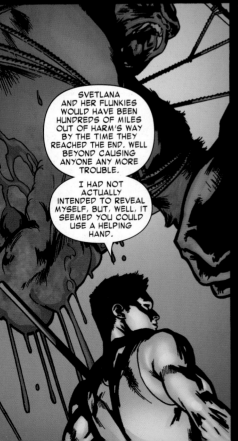

SVETLANA AND HER FLUNKIES WOULD HAVE BEEN HUNDREDS OF MILES OUT OF HARM'S WAY BY THE TIME THEY REACHED THE END. WELL BEYOND CAUSING ANYONE ANY MORE TROUBLE.

I HAD NOT ACTUALLY INTENDED TO REVEAL MYSELF, BUT, WELL, IT SEEMED YOU COULD USE A HELPING HAND.

I HAD HOPED TO LIMIT BLOODSHED, BUT THESE THUGS MUST BE SILENCED. I CAN THINK OF ONLY ONE WAY TO ASSURE A PERSON'S SILENCE *PERMANENTLY*.

UNLESS.

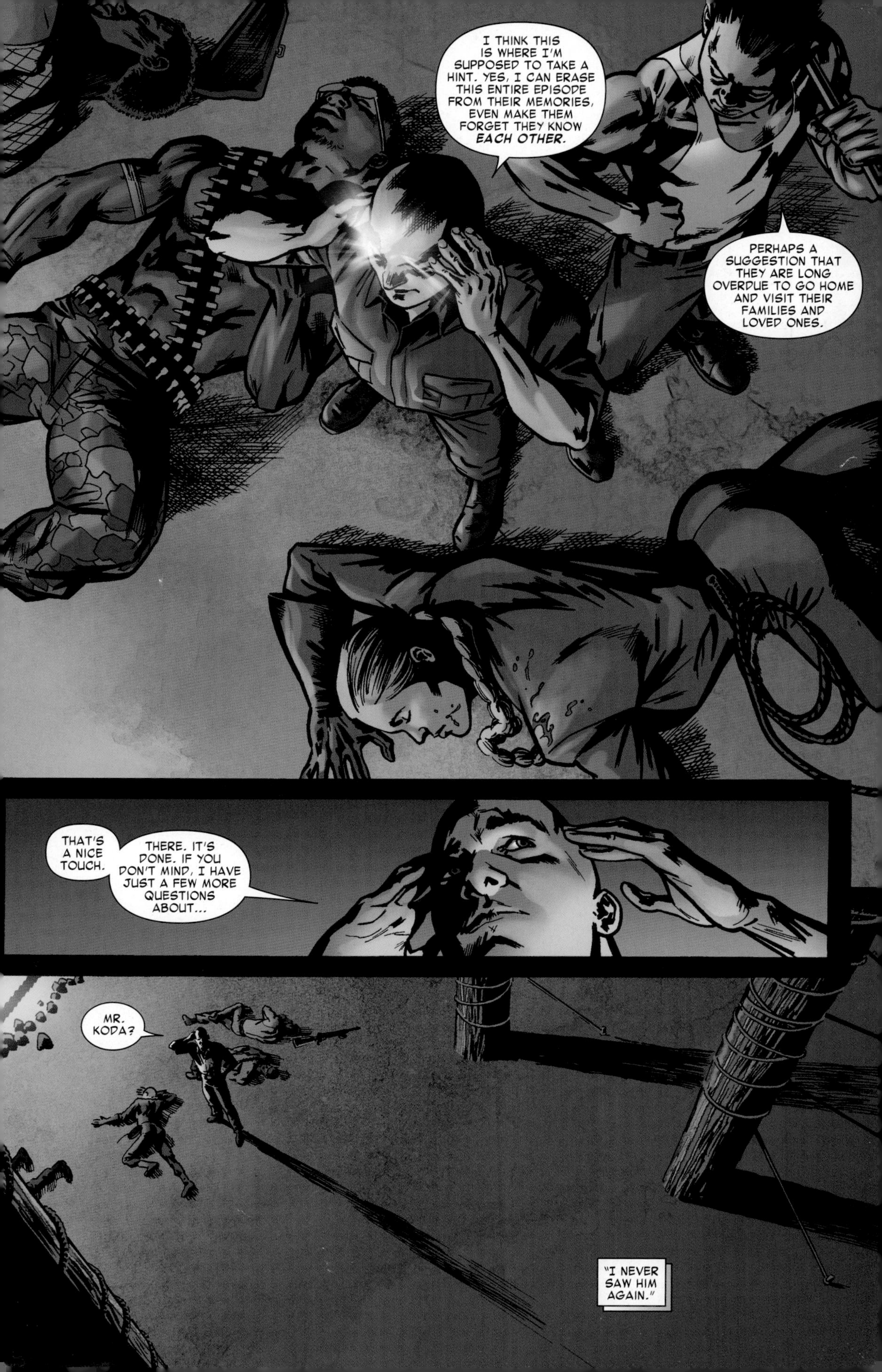
I THINK THIS IS WHERE I'M SUPPOSED TO TAKE A HINT. YES, I CAN ERASE THIS ENTIRE EPISODE FROM THEIR MEMORIES, EVEN MAKE THEM FORGET THEY KNOW *EACH OTHER*.
PERHAPS A SUGGESTION THAT THEY ARE LONG OVERDUE TO GO HOME AND VISIT THEIR FAMILIES AND LOVED ONES.
THAT'S A NICE TOUCH.
THERE. IT'S DONE. IF YOU DON'T MIND, I HAVE JUST A FEW MORE QUESTIONS ABOUT...
MR. KODA?
"I NEVER SAW HIM AGAIN."

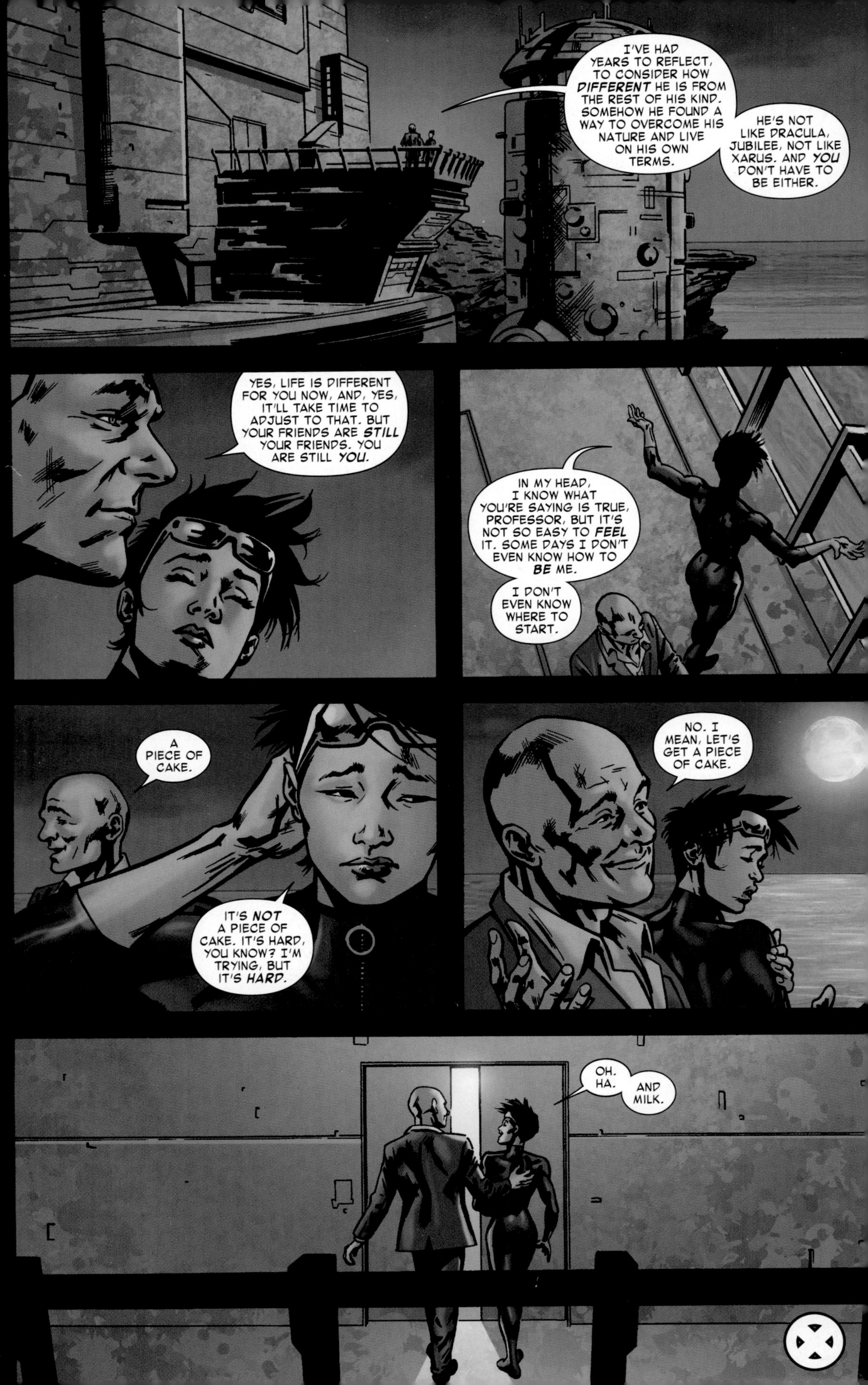
I'VE HAD YEARS TO REFLECT, TO CONSIDER HOW DIFFERENT HE IS FROM THE REST OF HIS KIND. SOMEHOW HE FOUND A WAY TO OVERCOME HIS NATURE AND LIVE ON HIS OWN TERMS.
HE'S NOT LIKE DRACULA, JUBILEE, NOT LIKE XARUS. AND YOU DON'T HAVE TO BE EITHER.
YES, LIFE IS DIFFERENT FOR YOU NOW, AND, YES, IT'LL TAKE TIME TO ADJUST TO THAT. BUT YOUR FRIENDS ARE STILL YOUR FRIENDS. YOU ARE STILL YOU.
IN MY HEAD, I KNOW WHAT YOU'RE SAYING IS TRUE, PROFESSOR, BUT IT'S NOT SO EASY TO FEEL IT. SOME DAYS I DON'T EVEN KNOW HOW TO BE ME.
I DON'T EVEN KNOW WHERE TO START.
A PIECE OF CAKE.
IT'S NOT A PIECE OF CAKE. IT'S HARD, YOU KNOW? I'M TRYING, BUT IT'S HARD.
NO. I MEAN, LET'S GET A PIECE OF CAKE.
OH. HA.
AND MILK.